$10.00

POLITICAL TERRORISM:

The Threat and the Response

Francis M. Watson

What is terrorism? The violence carried out by the Black September group at the 1972 Olympics? The actions of the SLA? The attempt on President Ford's life by Lynette Fromme? Is terrorism merely the result of the makeshift operations of isolated groups or is it something more sophisticated, frightening and insidious?

In this book Francis M. Watson examines how terrorism works through illustrations which include Black September, the Tupamaros, the Japanese Red Army, the Weather Underground, the SLA and the Manson family. Terrorist groups pay scrupulous attention to organization, supply and finance, and the design and execution of their plans. Particular care is taken to create propaganda and to maintain the discipline necessary to control their own members.

The focus shifts to reveal the kinds of organizations which commit terrorism. The groups are compared on the basis of their origins, goals, ideology and tactics. Relationships and cooperations often occur between terrorists of

e-
m
id
ns
is
n-
ny

ed
re
o-
en
of
ve
tw
es
his
gy
of
at
en

ity
ith
in
cal
an-
is a
s a
nor
ind
er-
ant
un-
ce-
ess
of
is

married, with two sons and two daughters.

Francis M. Watson

Political Terrorism:

The Threat and the Response

Robert B. Luce Co., Inc.
Washington—New York

Watson, Francis M 1921-
  Political terrorism.

  Includes index.
  1. Terrorism. 2. Violence. I. Title.
HV6431.W37   364.1'5   75-28548
ISBN 0-88331-078-3

Contents

To . . .

My wife, Virginia, for her constancy in the years I have been working in the areas which led to the writing of this book.

Our daughters and sons, Carol, Laura, Scott, and John, for their living encouragement and support—and to John for drawing some of the illustrations used.

Two special friends, Sidney and Mimi, for the real support they gave, and for introducing me to a whole family of people whose work and ideas are visible in the more positive aspects of the book.

And Susie, whose faith and energy went into the typing and retyping of page after page of manuscript.

Foreword

Terrorism is not new in world history. It has been one of the tactics of guerrilla warfare for hundreds of years. And guerrilla warfare itself has often been acquitted in history as the only means by which downtrodden masses could combat intolerable oppression. Even today it has its place where whole peoples have no voice in their own affairs. What *is* new in the current wave of terrorism is that its perpetrators are usually not downtrodden masses, but small groups of people who have adopted terrorist tactics in attempts to impose their particular ideology on the masses—whether the ideology be of the "left," the "right," or of some chaotic mixture in between.

Indeed, statistics show that today's terrorists do not strike where oppression is greatest. They demonstrate no belief in democracy. They show no inclination to exhaust the possibilities of legal methods. They hit societies that are already open to legal struggle. They seek to short-circuit legal processes, to compel oppressive measures out of governments not inclined toward them. They seek to erode the means of communication and trust between people and their governments—to promote internal conflict in the hope of toppling that which exists in favor of that which they propose, however vaguely formed it may be in their own minds.

In fact, there is no more apt expression for what these groups attempt to do than *brainwashing*—on a mass basis. The stereotype most of us seem to have of brainwashing causes us to miss this point. We tend to think of it happening only to a lone individual, locked away in a tiny cell, where his captors can do as they wish with his mind as well as his body. We are accustomed to thinking of tortures and deprivations which break the subject's will, and cause him to accept whatever is told him.

We miss the point that whatever devious or exotic procedures might be used to brainwash individuals, the essence of the idea is putting a subject under stress and providing him with only a single point of view of life and the world. This is exactly what terrorists try to do with the minds of millions of people. They produce stress by causing violence in public places. They literally force attention to what they have to say with attacks that will grab media time and space. Then, using the attention thus forced, they fill the public consciousness with their own side of whatever matters they are addressing, to the exclusion of all other sides. Their manufactured spectaculars are designed to be powerful. They steamroll over any possibilities for rational examination of issues. They blot out information as to what their own aims really are, or as to where they are trying to take a society. Their actions squeeze out everything but that which they seek to communicate.

Thus, in effect, the whole public mind is placed into a tiny cell where it is stressed and exposed to only a single point of view. This is the art and methodology of today's political terrorism, the biggest brainwash we have going.

The antidote for brainwashing of any sort has always been, and always will be, open discussion. It was with an aim in this direction that I have tried to lay out some information on terrorism in the following pages.

FMW

1. What is Terrorism?

The one means that wins easiest over reason: terror and force.
[Adolf Hitler, *Mein Kampf*]

Political terrorism can be defined as a strategy, a method by which an organized group or party tries to get attention for its aims, or force concessions toward its goals, through the systematic use of deliberate violence. Typical terrorists are individuals trained and disciplined to carry out the violence decided upon by their organizations. And, if caught, true terrorists can be expected to speak and act during their trials not primarily to win personal freedom, but to try to spread their organization's political ideas.*

In terms of human carnage, terrorism can be described as such acts as the setting of a bomb on a TWA 707, thus sending nearly a hundred citizens of a dozen countries plunging to their deaths in the Mediterranean Sea on August 8, 1974. The day after the explosion an Arab youth organization announced from Paris that it had downed this plane in furtherance of the "Liberation of Palestine."

It can be described as the May 1972 killing of 25 and wounding of over 70—most of them Puerto Rican pilgrims touring the Holy Land—when three members of the self-styled Japanese "United Red Army" opened fire into the crowded civilian air terminal at Lod in Israel. The surviving member of

---

*Not a new definition. It was based on a more detailed one in the *Encyclopedia of the Social Sciences* published in 1934.

1

the Japanese threesome sat stolidly at his trial and took full responsibility for the act in the name of the world "revolutionary struggle between the classes."

It was illustrated on December 17, 1973, when a small band of Arab terrorists sprayed the interior of the Rome airport with automatic weapons fire, then ran out onto the apron and threw two phosphorus grenades into a Pan American jetliner. Passengers and crew jumped out of every door, but 29 people, already trapped in their seats for take-off, died in the flaming mass of fuel and metal the airliner had become. The purpose of this attack was to wreck the then ongoing sessions of Mideast peace negotiations. In this case, though, the terrorists tacked on another mission in the course of their escape from Rome, and the killing continued. Leaving the Pan Am "Celestial Clipper" in flames they turned their attention to a nearby German Lufthansa jet, grabbed twelve hostages in and around the plane, and ordered its pilot to fly them to Greece. Once on the ground at Athens they shot one of their hostages and threw his body out of the plane. This was to try to force the release of two of their comrades Greek authorities were holding from a previous airport attack, in which four Americans and one Austrian were killed and 55 other passengers were wounded.

Defining terrorism in terms of the denial of personal freedom, it can be seen to include the hundreds of political kidnapings that have occurred in scattered parts of the world in the past seven years. In addition to being held captive for anywhere from a few days to months, about one out of ten of the businessmen, diplomats, government officials, and military officers seized were killed in the process of the kidnapings, or "executed" by the terrorists when their demands were not met. Latin America has been a hotbed of this variety of terrorism, there being a reported 190 kidnapings in a single country during one calendar year.

The ransom demands in these kidnapings in themselves offer some assistance in defining terrorism. By far the most common demand has been for the release of "political prisoners" — usually their own comrades jailed for previous terroristic acts.

2

However, the frequency, and size, of accompanying cash demands have increased as the incidents accumulated. For example, in 1970 the going cash demand was in the few hundreds of thousands of dollars. By 1973 it was usually over a million per kidnaping, but before that year was out had jumped to several times that figure. And when American Exxon executive Victor Samuelson was released in March of 1974 his company was reported to have paid in excess of $14,000,000 to his kidnapers. In June of 1975, $60,000,000 in cash and $1,000,000 in supplies distributed to villages in Argentina was exchanged for the release of the Born brothers —Argentine businessmen whose chauffeur and another company employee had been shot to death when members of the "Montoneros" organization, dressed as policemen and telephone repairmen, had dragged the two executives from their limousine on a city street.

Incidentally, the reason for release of prisoners being the most common demand is that all terrorist groups have members imprisoned at one time or another. They must try to get them released in order to continue operations. This is not simply because they need their services. Sometimes this is not the case at all. It is primarily because they must continually demonstrate that the group does not abandon its members, *and* that it is powerful enough to get them out of jail. Cash demands being less common is an entirely different matter. All terrorists need money, or the things that money will buy. None are in business to make a profit, but it takes money to operate. Some have to kidnap or rob banks for it, some are supported from other sources —private citizens, organizations, and governments in sympathy with the terrorists' cause.

Used against national leaders, diplomats, or business executives, though, terrorism is a means for obtaining more than the bare requirements for the organization's continued existence. It is a means for influencing political and economic decisions with far-reaching consequences. For example, in September 1973 two Arab terrorists crossed from Czechoslovakia into Austria and took four hostages which they threatened to kill unless Austria closed down the processing station through which Jews allowed out of Russia passed on their way to Israel. After extended negotiations the Chancellor of Austria gave in and agreed to close the station.

Thus, terrorists can sometimes achieve their objectives by merely intimidating people with the power to make decisions of high import. There is within the practice of terrorism, though, a seldom commented on paradox. Essentially all terrorists make a great deal of noise about being on the side of the common man, the weak and the powerless. Yet, they are generally hardest on people at the lower level of a power structure. Whereas they often force important concessions out of individuals with wealth or great influence they tend to let them off with their lives more often than they do people with lesser status. The minor official, or the mere citizen, who does not simply comply with their wishes is likely to be "punished," as an example to others of similar status. He does not make big decisions, or command great numbers of people. He has nothing to pay with but his life. And that is often exactly what is collected from him, the payment being exacted in a manner to have the most compelling impact on others who might be inclined to stand in the terrorists' way.

Thus, minor government officials may not be kidnaped, but simply killed as they go about their duties. At one period this was so prevalent in Uruguay that some police officers were literally afraid to do their jobs. In Ireland, a legislator answered his front door bell one night and was immediately shot to death by an Irish Republican Army squad. The terrorists then pulled his body into the living room for his wife to see, and proceded to set up a bomb which destroyed the house a few minutes later. In January 1973, a group from apparently the same organization shot a thirty-year-old steel erector to death as he and his children watched television. This man's offense: he was a part-time member of a local defense regiment.

As we have already seen, in the airport massacres especially, terrorism also comes down heavily sometimes on the mere bystander. Attitudes on this vary with the different terrorist groups. Some go to great pains in their efforts to see that innocent people are not hurt by their strikes. Others seem

4

not to care. Still others appear to look upon the innocent as mere pawns in the game they are playing. We will discuss some of the reasons for this a bit later. Whatever the intent might be, as the tempo of violence has increased and extended from government buildings to department stores, restaurants, bars, and private homes, and to the persons of ordinary citizens, no one appears exempt. The year 1975 kicked off with the bombing of the Fraunces Tavern in New York and the killing of four of its patrons. A tourist bureau was bombed in San Francisco. A bomb was thrown into the doorway of a bar in Belfast, killing three and wounding twenty. Again in Belfast, three members of a pop music group were shot to death and their minibus blown up. Two American enlisted men were kidnaped by terrorists in Ethiopia. A Dutch businessman was kidnaped in Dublin. At one point his IRA captors threatened to cut off his foot and send it to police to prove that they actually held him. Young Caroline Kennedy narrowly escaped death or injury when a bomb exploded at a private home in London —one person was killed and six others wounded in this blast. As 1975 was drawing toward its end an explosion in a restaurant in London killed a man and a woman and injured seventeen others. To the survivors of this incident terrorism was something crashing through a window and landing on a table in a room where they were eating supper. One young man said he remembered looking at that table and seeing the thing throw out red sparks as it momentarily sputtered. His girl friend said, "My God, it's a bomb!" Then it went off, the restaurant was dark and full of smoke, and people were running toward the street —some with blood streaming from their faces, some falling to the pavement outside, hurt or shocked to the stage of collapse.

One of the people killed in that restaurant was not even identified in time to get her name in the paper. As far as the strategy of the terrorists was concerned that did not matter. They were sending out a message that they could reach from Ireland right into London, and the media space the violence itself grabbed was spectacular enough to do that.

However, anyone trying to define terrorism in terms of

spectacular incidents, or media coverage, would have to give special attention to the sudden, violent attack at the Olympic games in Munich in 1972, or the kidnaping of Patricia Hearst in Berkeley in 1974. Both accounted for as much media time and space as some minor wars in the past. In the former, as TV watchers around the world will remember, Arab terrorists entered the Israeli quarters at Olympic Village where they killed one athlete and a coach and grabbed nine others as hostages.

Their stated demand was for the release of 200 of their comrades held in Israeli jails. Generally unstated, though always a part of their purpose, was the leveling of another psychological jab at world public opinion in the Arab-Israeli conflict. They planned to do enough physical damage to guarantee media attention, then somehow to shift the blame for it all onto the Israelis and their supporters in world politics. The damage done was enough. Two were dead almost immediately. And, in the midst of frantic transoceanic telephone calls and local negotiations the terrorists and their hostages were taken to the Munich airport by helicopter where a gun battle resulted in the deaths of all of the hostages, five terrorists, and one policeman. With the media personnel and equipment already massed in Munich to cover the inter-national games, it suddenly seemed to a world-wide audience that they were sitting within yards of the masked terrorists and uniformed law enforcement officials as the whole affair unfolded. The terrorists, members of "Black September," did not get their first demand —release of prisoners from Israeli jails. As to their basic purpose, international relations were strained, the Germans and Israelis criticized, and the three surviving terrorists were handed over to comrades who hijacked a Lufthansa jet two weeks later.

In the Hearst case, media audiences have been doused with details of the wildly changing saga of Patty and the so-called "SLA" (Symbionese Liberaton Army) for two years. In fact, there has been so much detail, and so much of that published has gravitated to an almost pro-SLA orientation, that the full meaning of terrorism may have been lost on many of us. Be that as it may, and the sometimes almost comic-opera behavior of the SLA notwithstanding, a living example of the definition of terrorism has been played out before the eyes of the public because it was this country's first political kidnaping.

Since about 1968, the kidnaping or killing of officials, executives, and private citizens, the bombing of buildings and industrial plants, and other acts of violence by political extremists had become almost daily occurrences somewhere in the world. The U.S. had a goodly share of most of these. Law enforcement officials have reported that there were 688 incidents of terrorist violence in the U.S. from January 1970 to mid 1975— 83 policemen and civilians were killed and 284 wounded. There had even been a bonafide terrorist assassination of a public official on a city street —by the SLA just weeks before it snatched Patricia out of her Berkeley apartment— but this was the first kidnaping that filled all of the requirements for an act of terrorism. With it, the procession of major types of terrorism was in full array right here at home.

Some of the impact of this signal event was lost, even in the beginning, because so much attention went to the understandable anguish of a prominent and traditionally colorful family suddenly the victims of a bizarre crime. Newspaper headlines blared such phrases as "PATRICIA HEARST KIDNAPED" and "HEARST PROMISES $2 MILLION IN FOOD." Beneath these headlines were long columns of the details of the kidnaping and Mr. Hearst's plans for the distribution of food to the needy in California in exchange for his daughter's release. The ink had hardly dried on these stories when additional headlines screamed Patricia's renunciation of her family —and the whole society— in favor of the revolutionary cause of the very people who had kidnaped her. Then her picture, holding an automatic rifle in the course of an SLA bank robbery, was flashed out around the world. Almost exactly a month later six members of the SLA were killed in an hour-long, televised shootout with police and other law enforcement officers in Los Angeles. The house from which the SLA members fought burned during the fight and their bodies were charred beyond recognition —for twenty-four hours no one knew but what Patricia's was one of those bodies. Finally, some 19½ months after she had been abducted by the SLA she was arrested as one of them —with a long list of state and federal offenses charged against her.

Hardly anyone could help but sympathize with the Hearsts and their almost unbelievable plight. A good deal of the not surprising friction between them and state and federal agencies had crept into the story as it had unfolded. Thus, the real unfolding, that is an actual, living display of the basic aim of terrorism, was beclouded to the point that much was lost that should have been of real significance to the public as to how it must react to future incidents of terrorism. With all of the bales of paper and hours of air time devoted to reporting the Hearst case, there were relatively few newscasts or paragraphs which analyzed the situation in such methodical terms as in the following Washington *Star* interview of Richard J. Gallagher, assistant director of the FBI who had overall direction of the search for Patricia Hearst:

> . . . Samuel Williams, commissioner of police in Los Angeles said the SLA was a small group of terrorists who couldn't possibly change anything by themselves. But if they could divert attention, if they could get a national audience and divert attention from themselves, and what they were doing, to law enforcement and the use of excessive force, in their minds they would have achieved their purpose . . .

The interviewer then asked Mr. Gallagher if, in effect, the SLA had not to some extent achieved that in Los Angeles during the shootout in which the six were killed. Mr. Gallagher said:

> This is what he [L.A. police commissioner Williams] was talking about. They had a national audience and the emphasis shifted from the SLA, and what they were doing, to the amount of force used by the Los Angeles Police Department. The whole point of this thing is that in situations like this, this is going to be one of the problems for law enforcement.
> [Washington *Star,* Oct. 2, 1975, p. A-1]

Using such observations as these to help us focus on the reality of the situation, it does not take much to put it back into a context that tells us a great deal about what terrorism is. The observations of these two law enforcement officials show they took some things from the SLA's revolutionary and hate-loaded propaganda that many of us, as newspaper readers, missed —even though much of their full-blown propaganda was published in our papers. From this propaganda it was obvious that although the demands of the SLA for food to be distributed to the needy were ballooned into front-page headlines, and lead sentences on evening newscasts, feeding the poor was not the primary aim of the organization. As early as August 21, 1973 they had written up a "Declaration of War and the Symbionese Program," in which they claimed "The Fascist United States of America" was "oppressive" and must be destroyed by "armed struggle" to "liberate" peoples of all races.

And even as the Hearsts were trying to gather the money for distribution of food, the SLA rather whimsically raised and lowered their demands for this food by various figures ranging from one or two million to tens of millions of dollars. Obviously, they had no well defined "needy" in mind. In fact, they showed little knowledge or interest in such matters. It was several weeks after they made the food distribution demand that they said anything realistic about what they did have in mind. In a taped communique they announced:

> Our strategy was to show by example what can be done . . . this goodwill gesture was intended to give some food to the people while at the same time point out our understanding that the people can never expect the enemy to feed them . . .
>
> [*Time* magazine, April 29, 1974, p. 14.]

There in the last third of the above, is what they were trying to get across. It is simply an extension of the theme of their "Declaration of War." They wanted to portray the present system as the evil and oppressive enemy. The SLA will fight for the people against this enemy, they were saying.

These are the basic themes running through all of the leaflets and communiques SLA put out. The themes were often woven into crude material, but were still recognizable as threads from the Latin American fabrics from which they came. In fact, they follow rather closely the philosophy of

Carlos Marighella, the slain Brazilian author of the *Minimanual of the Urban Guerrilla* —and two of his books were found in the SLA collection of the revolutionary handbooks and manuals. This philosophy insisted on "armed struggle" as the main means for advancing "the revolution," and specifically argued that the urban guerrilla must provoke authorities into repressive actions which will "reveal the true nature of their oppression of the people" and thus create a public clamor against the government.

SLA did it all. They played out the definition of terrorism quite precisely. They burst into the media in November 1973 by announcing they had killed Oakland school superintendent Dr. Marcus Foster with "cyanide tipped bullets" because he was running the school with "fascist American tactics of genocide," etc. From that point on, they tried to provoke the police at every turn.

The two SLA members eventually charged with this murder eluded capture until January 1974, then they were arrested only because they opened fire on a lone officer who stopped their van on a routine traffic check. The van was then found to contain one of the Foster murder weapons plus leaflets leading police to an SLA hideout that proved to be a veritable armory. It contained, among other items, an assortment of weapons, pipe bombs, explosives, several pounds of potassium cyanide, and bullets with the tips drilled and packed with cynaide.

The occupants of the house had fled, apparently leaving the things they could not load into the automobile in which they escaped. A week later the press received and published an SLA "Letter to the People," which rambled on and on about how "force of arms is now our only legal means" for "revolutionary justice." This letter tapered off with claims that all SLA personnel would from that time on be "heavily and offensively armed with cyanide bullets in all their weapons." The point of all the talk about cyanide bullets was an obvious effort to intimidate anyone who might be tempted to engage them in an exchange of gunfire. Although scientific evidence completely supporting it seems to be lacking, the implication was that even a flesh wound from an SLA weapon would be fatal because any of their bullets would take deadly cyanide into the victim's bloodstream. This threat was uttered two months after Doctor Foster had been murdered and just under a month before the Hearst kidnaping.

In February they took Miss Hearst from her apartment, beating her fiance and a neighbor, and spraying the outside area with gunfire in the process. In mid April they staged a bold, heavily armed bank robbery. A month later they popped up again when an automatic weapon was fired from a van onto the front of a sporting goods store as two SLA members were struggling with a store detective over a minor shoplifting offense.

The next day, May 17, 1974, six of their number fulfilled the final qualification in our definition of terrorism: *if caught, true terrorists will speak and act not primarily to win personal freedom, but to try to spread their organization's political message.* For, though cornered in a small, frame house, completely surrounded by obviously overwhelming forces, they replied with bursts of machine gun fire when police ordered them to throw out their weapons and surrender. As absolutely futile as such an action by only six people might seem, the SLA's words, in dozens of pieces they had written, leave no doubt as to the message it was intended to convey. In fact, one of their frequently used slogans was:

TO THOSE WHO WOULD BEAR THE HOPES AND FUTURE OF THE PEOPLE LET THE VOICE OF THEIR GUNS EXPRESS THE WORDS OF FREEDOM.

This often appeared over a signature block reading, "Gen. Field Marshall Cinque, S.L.A." the pitifully inflated title ex-convict Donald DeFreeze used as "commander-in-chief" of the "soldiers of the Symbionese Liberation Army."

The allusions to military forces comprising this army were so preposterous as to be almost humorous. The SLA may stand out from other groups as being most impressed with their own fiction and least aware of reality. The routes they took to the state of mind which prompted their deeds, however, were not atypical of their comrades in arms the world over. Terrorist

11

organizations are usually spawned from among people who are, for a variety of reasons, already disgruntled. The particles of satisfaction, faith, and trust in the society in which they are living are already at least partially dislodged from their minds. As individuals they have become literally obsessed with change. They find community with others similarly obsessed. This community gradully becomes a self-decreed imprisonment, as far as relations with the world outside are concerned. They share ideas only with each other, and these ideas gradually come to focus on a political goal. They seek only a strategy with which to implement it. Almost invariably that selected will be one of several strains of guerrilla theory readily available in literature that has all but inundated the young in the past decade or so. They saturate their brains with one or more of these theories, and then begin to train, equip, and discipline themselves to follow their adaptation of what they have studied and discussed. As a result of these group processes they acquire mental orientations and physical capabilities that will allow them to undertake actions most of them would not even have contemplated in their former situations. Also during these processes they begin to fit the rest of the world into the molds the revolutionary theories provide —"the people are enslaved and oppressed, only waiting for leadership in the struggle to deliver them to freedom." Thus, they come to see themselves not as a small group operating in isolation, but as a finely trained elite who will have masses of other people behind them as they engage the enemy. And, in their own minds, when they strike at that enemy —be it with the kidnaping or assassination of someone who represents it, or the exploding of a bomb in one of its buildings— they are doing so in the name of the people.

This is not to say that no cause espoused by terrorists is a worthy one, or that no one outside their ranks is interested in any of the changes they can be seen advocating. That is blatantly not a true picture of the situation, and we will try to explore this matter a bit further on. It is to say that terrorists habitually "psyche" themselves up to doing things that no sizeable element of the remainder of the population has chosen for them to do. Or, as one of our weekly newsmagazines has put it:

> One of the most dangerous trends in the current wave of political terrorism is the penchant of terrorists such as the Palestinians and the SLA to act as the self-apointed representatives of whole people and not just themselves . . .
>
> [*Newsweek,* February 25, 1974, p. 22]

It also seems to be typical that the more "altruistic" a terrorist group becomes, the more heedless is its plunge into non-negotiable confrontation. With the same self-hypnosis through which they become saviors of the world they come into a mental state of total and final dedication to such superfluous slogans as the one appearing over General Field Marshall Cinque's signature block. The SLA is by no means the only terrorist group to do that.

Yet, however weird such a group's rationale for having assumed it, the impressiveness of this level of dedication never seems to be completely lost on the rest of us as fellow human beings. However strange or wrong people's beliefs might seem, there is something about their willingness to die for them that tends to give whatever they say at least some bit of credibility. Six members of the SLA went down contending that their society was so insensitive and unjust that nothing was left but to try to destroy it. And, at one of their funerals the minister compared the dead terrorist with the crucified Christ in sacrificing life for a belief. Consciously or nonconsciously, a bit of this sort of thing was communicated in that May 17 shootout too. It is almost always a part of the terrorist's impact.

Still another bit of communication ricocheted off that affair. And though it is probably a little much to contend that it was by calculated design of the SLA-ers at the moment they opened fire, it was in strict compliance with one of the tenets of the guerrilla philosophy to which they subscribed: *provoke the authorities into the use of excessive force.* This was the point made by the FBI man in the interview we cited. He saw it as a problem law enforcement agencies will have to face in the future. But the simple facts of the matter are twofold. First, the

SLA had not only bragged about being heavily armed, cyanide bullets included, and sworn itself to a fight to the death, it had already shown its disposition to use weapons of all sorts, and had committed murder, kidnaping, and bank robbery. Secondly, hundreds of police officers fired thousands of rounds of ammunication into a small house containing only two young men and four young women. The weight of whatever provocation there might have been over the force used has not really been subjected to public debate.

For, only the visibility of the police firing into a building, which in a short time caught fire, was transmitted —live and in color— on network television. And, as another magazine put it shortly thereafter:

> The event, witnessed on the tube, blots out the viewer's never very clear perception of the issues. What he feels is horror, not understanding . . .

[*Nation*, June 1, 1974, p. 675.]

When such things happen, whatever brainwashing the terrorists are engaged in switches from the individual mind they may have indoctrinated to the minds of millions of people they could never otherwise reach.

In looking at terrorism in terms of media spectaculars we would certainly have to mention the attempts on President Ford's life occurring shortly before and after the SLA arrests in September 1975. We will come back to these because both cases do have significance in an understanding of terrorism. They are even significant in noting the degree to which terrorism has hit at the national level in this country over the past few years. Back in the later sixties and early seventies military installations, vehicles, and especially ROTC buildings, were bombed or burned all around the country. Since then, though, the Capitol itself has been bombed, as have the Pentagon and the State Department. In each of these last, terrorists publicly claimed "the credit."

The inflicting of physical damage, even to people and buildings at the very seat of national government, though, is not what terrorism finally is. As callous as it might seem to say so, it is not the injury, death, and destruction that has the real and final impact on the man in the street, or, if you will, on you and me and the country and world in which we live. Terrorism is, again, by definition, a strategy for forcing political concessions—ranging anywhere from relatively minor changes in how individuals will live, to major ones in how nations will conduct themselves.

People often wring their hands at the horror terrorism precipitates, including the reprisals it usually inspires, but the greatest threat it poses is that it drowns out rational discussion or negotiation, and forces decisions under pressure. Not only does it sway public opinion, but it forces policy, legislation, and the administration of public affairs. Thus, international agreements are altered, laws are made or changed, and regulations on people, institutions, and services are invoked virtually at the command of small numbers of individuals holding guns or bombs—even when it takes months or even a few years for the effect of the command to be felt. Terrorism is sometimes called "political blackmail." That is inaccurate. Gunpoint government of the many by the few is more properly called totalitarianism, and each of these incidents in which a bit or piece of government is engineered in this fashion is a microcosm of totalitarianism. The terrorist performs psychological magic to make it appear otherwise. That is, as he holds the gun to the public head he also runs a propaganda campaign to try to get *ex post facto* popular endorsement of his reasons for picking up the gun in the first place. As was suggested earlier, this bit of sleight of hand works because the violence distracts the public from what the terrorists are doing in the propaganda effort.

Therefore, terrorism must not be defined only in terms of violence, but also in terms of propaganda. The two are both in operation together.

The violence of terrorism is a *coercive* means for attempting to influence the thinking and actions of people. Propaganda is a *persuasive* means for doing the same thing. Especially at first blush, the two seem to be mutually exclusive. An act of violence tends to characterize its perpetrators as brutal, mindless and insensitive to such matters as politics or

15

public opinion. Propaganda, on the other hand, tends to credit its authors with mental faculties and sensitivities incompatible with mere brutality. Ordinary logic leads to the thinking that individuals with the capability and frame of mind for attempting the one would not use the other. Nothing could be further from the truth. The two are inseparable in the arsenals of political extremism.

The members of the SLA we have just been discussing offer excellent illustrations of this point. However any of us might feel about the way they died, it is hardly possible to argue that these people were not capable of brutal violence. Yet, most of them were educated and well equipped mentally to conduct propaganda. Of the twelve whose names figured in an out-and-out murder, a kidnaping, and in armed robbery, eight had college degrees or at least some college training. The majority of them came from middle class homes, and were rather high achievers as youngsters. Of the six who responded to the police surrender with bursts of gunfire, five had degrees or some college training. And in none of these statistics is the SLA unique. A survey of Latin American terrorists in 1970 reveals similar backgrounds. The Weatherman group, responsible for dozens of bombings in the U.S., including the national Capitol, is made up almost entirely of educated young people from middle class or well-to-do homes. They are enthusiastic and prolific propagandists as well as bomb throwers.

In fact, propaganda is the hallmark of political terrorism. It is the mark one should look for in deciding whether a particular act of violence is terrorism, the impulse of someone who is mentally disturbed, or the work of common criminals. The distinctions between these types of crime are important, of course, because society is required to react to them in different ways. Political terrorism suggests a completely different set of problems for a society than those posed by other forms of criminal behavior.

There is little need to confuse them, though. For an inevitable part of the political terrorists' attack, whatever its physical component, is a designed pyschological impact. The attack will be accompanied by political propaganda, or the physical act in itself will be so arranged as to make a propaganda point. A relatively brief consideration of any particular incident will tell us whether or not it was terrorism.

That is, an act of violence accompanied by genuine political propaganda can be considered to be the work of political extremists. Exactly the same act, committed with *no* propaganda objective, or merely cloaked with jargon in imitation of extremist propaganda, can be dismissed from the category of political terrorism. With the rarest of exceptions, terrorists simply do not do anything without trying to make their political point. And their propaganda, however laced with half-truths or unrealistic goals, has recognizable content and pattern that allow it to be distinguished from either the self-centered outpourings of a psychopath or the pseudo-political writings and utterances of the calculating hoaxer who seeks to throw suspicion for a personal-gain crime away from himself by imitating terrorists. Indeed, in the case of true terrorism, the whole operation will have been arranged to influence opinion —most usually opinion external to the organization committing the act, but sometimes internal, to build morale or inspire confidence.

As examples of some of the above, we might note that immediately following the Hearst kidnaping in early 1974 there was a rash of imitative incidents around the country. One, in particular, the kidnaping of the managing editor of the Atlanta *Constituion,* included a few sputterings of "propaganda" from a non-existent political group the kidnaper called "The American Revolutionary Army." Any newspaper reader could compare these sputterings with the more complex propaganda of the Hearst kidnapers and tell the difference. More recently, an apparently small group of men decided they could rake in a few million dollars by putting time bombs in gasoline storage tanks around the country and sending extortion letters to major oil companies. They did so in the name of the "Fighting American Indians." Two of them were arrested in September 1975, law enforcement officers have recovered the bombs, and nothing about the case so far suggests the men were terrorists or committed their crimes in the name of any real political organization —their plot made no propaganda point.

Again, such distinctions are important. To label these incidents of ordinary crime as terrorism, though they were imitative of it, would distort the picture of what the society is faced with. On the other hand, to consider acts of terrorism as having no significance beyond ordinary crime means subjecting the society to their propaganda manipulations without warning. It would suggest that no damage has been done beyond the physical act. That is not the case with terrorism.

Thus, an appraisal of the damage from a terrorist attack must look beyond the dead and wounded, and the rubble, for the destruction the propaganda of the incident inflicted. It will almost invariably have inflicted some, often more than the physical assault. This is another distinction between terrorism and other types of crime. Crime of the conventional sort tends to put the criminal in a bad light. A given crime, or the level of crime, may instill fear in the public mind, but the feelings are against the criminal not the victim. Even if the person committing a crime is obviously mentally ill, and thus judged not to be responsible, it is he that the public sees as the menace, to be removed from society, or to have his activities curbed in some fashion. Not so with a terrorist attack. Even when the initial public reaction seems to be unfavorable toward them, and their action repugnant, the propaganda arrangement the terrorists finally complete leaves the stigma on the target of the attack. Be it a person, a class of people, a company, or an institution, the victim is portrayed as the menace, and it is the victim's activities that are to be curbed in some way or another.

This is part of the psychological damage that can be expected from a terrorist attack. It may seem minor, at first, the sort of thing that will blow over. The terrorists have no intention, however, of letting any inroad they make, however minor, simply blow over. They will use it, build on it, and exploit it. For example, even a small propaganda victory against an industry may be turned into some form of public protest or legal action —a boycott, strike, law suit, or a movement toward government restriction, *against the victim, not the perpetrator* of the incident.

18

The other part of this psychological damage is more tangible. Any propaganda success terrorists have against a particular victim on one occasion tends to make that victim, or others like him, a more likely target for future attacks. Thus, the psychological damage from one attack can result in both physical and psychological damage in the future.

If the propaganda of the initial attack is not sufficient to do either of these, the subsequent propaganda maneuvers of the terrorists, in evading capture or prosecution, will be intensified to do the trick. And, if they are not successful in evading the law, and are actually taken to court, the trial will be used as a propaganda platform, and the assault on the victim continues until a damaging label of some kind is firmly affixed.

For example, a 500-foot tower, erected in connection with the construction of a nuclear power plant in Massachusetts, was destroyed. A young member of an anti-nuclear group surrendered himself to police, announcing that he had destroyed the tower in protest of the dangers the proposed plant would constitute to the community. He sought prosecution so his trial could be used as a "public forum on nuclear power." He eventually went free on a technicality, but his "moving testimony" on the evils of nuclear plants turned thousands of people in the local and surrounding areas against an industry they had earlier welcomed into their midst. It came close to inspiring legislation that would have completely denied the site to the plant builders and required dismantling of the construction already finished. The physical damage of this attack was assessed at $42,500 —the cost of the tower. The psychological damage could not even be assessed. It would have to include not only erosion of public support for nuclear power, both locally and nationally, but a very definite increase in the numbers and boldness of anti-nuclear activists, and a greater possibility that similar attacks could be justified in the future —there or elsewhere.

Further, in the course of such maneuvers as these, anyone, or any institution, taking the side of the victim becomes fair game —law enforcement agencies and the courts included.

The Hearst case offers examples of all of this —the

19

accumulative impact especially. Of course there is psychological damage in any kidnaping. If nothing else, the family and friends' fear for the victim's safety. In a political kidnaping, however, this damage is greater because, again, the accompanying propaganda is intended to portray the victim, and all he or she represents, as evil. The Hearst case took a bizarre turn when Patricia Hearst apparently became part of the terrorist force. She thus shed the role of victim and passed it on to her family, greatly increasing their pain and anguish in the process of doing so. They were destined to share in the psychological impact all along, because the propaganda accompanying the kidnaping was designed to depict evil in their wealth. As it turned out, they have been paraded before the public in an absolutely devastating way, including having themselves and everything they have stood for pilloried with propaganda from their own daughter's mouth —as she was photographed in the role of a guerrilla bank robber.

This psychological damage is astounding, but it is really only the beginning of the assessment that must be made. The propaganda operation continued long enough at the hands of the kidnap organization itself, but when they disappeared it was picked up wittingly, and unwittingly, by a seemingly unending stream of others. The damage has mounted accordingly. To cite just a fraction of it: the Los Angeles police department has received increasing accusations that it murdered the SLA terrorists in the shootout we have already discussed; and the FBI has been portrayed in the public press as everything from modern day Keystone cops to the Gestapo, as it has attempted to apprehend the surviving SLA members in the face of what appeared to be a growing tendency within the citizenry to shelter them. The tangible damage in this case, including not only the now mostly forgotten monies paid out by the Hearsts, but the mountainous sums law enforcement procedures have cost, has to run into the tens of millions. This is hardly comparable, though, to the psychological damage — not only in the amount of public faith lost in agencies trying to deal with the case, but in the number of other attacks it may have encouraged —to say nothing of the number of would-be revolutionaries it probably nudged over the brink.

We may begin to see the political terrorist in his own environment by noting some generalizations that can be made about how he operates. By definition, the terrorist does not commit his acts for personal gain, nor does he operate alone. Even if he moves in by himself to commit a particular act, he is functioning as part of a group, seeking to accomplish a mission decided by that group as beneficial to its cause. He and his fellows are insurrectionists of one kind or another. That is, they have risen up against civil or political authority.

They may call themselves revolutionaries, with the goal of overthrowing an entire political system. In this category are such groups as: The National Liberation Movement of Uruguay, better known as the Tupamaros, whose thefts, kidnapings, and attacks on police have been romanticized into a movie, "State of Seige;" the People's Revolutionary Army, or ERP, of Argentina, the well-organized and highly-disciplined group responsible for several dozen acts of violence and extortion since 1970, including the kidnapping of the Exxon executive for whose release they collected the reported $14,000,000; and the Weather Underground, or Weatherman faction of the splintered Students for a Democratic Society in the U.S., which since its formation in 1969 has attacked numerous buildings and installations in the U.S., including the Capitol, the Pentagon, and most recently, the State Department.

Other groups, using the same tactics, may claim more limited objectives, such as the discontinuance of some national or international political policy, or the rejection of some economic or industrial plan. These would include Black September, which, in its drive for the creation of a Palestinian state and the elimination of Israel, has been responsible for the injury and killing of scores of people, including the athletes at Munich; the Liberation Front of Quebec, or FLQ, which has conducted a campaign of kidnaping, killing, and attacking police in its attempts to sever political ties between the province of Quebec and the rest of Canada; and a number of smaller, less well-known groups such as the one that toppled the tower in

Massachusetts in protest against nuclear power.

Still other groups, although usually small and certainly comprising the minority of terrorist organizations, may be fighting for the restoration of some policy, practice, or condition in a society. These would include groups, mostly on the extreme right whose objectives are racial or militantly nationalistic. Among the boldest examples from this category perhaps was the unsuccessful attempt of the Argentine nationalist movement, MANO, to kidnap a Soviet diplomat in early 1970.

Whatever the circumstances, and whatever the country, terrorists function from a group base, not as individuals. They have gathered themselves together to seek political change which they believe cannot be effected through totally legal or ethical methods as accepted in the existing authority system. They have come together around a political objective for which they are willing to sacrifice all else. They will have devised a strategy for attaining this objective. They will have selected and trained themselves in tactics with which to follow this strategy. And, at every step of the way, they will have had occasion to rationalize, even among themselves, the objective they are pursuing and the means they have chosen for doing so. Thus, they will have produced a body of interrelated arguments which they believe will support their activities. It is from these that they will conduct propaganda. And, however unrealistic their political objectives may at times seem, or however bizarre their actions, the thrasing-out processes through which their propaganda has passed will produce a recognizable pattern and order.

It is the pattern, the order, and the invariable primacy of political over personal objectives that distinguish the propaganda of the terrorist from the ravings of the psychopath or the imitative utterances of the criminal out for material gain. Of course, as most law enforcement agencies in modern times realize, to make this distinction quickly and accurately is important because, again, these three separate categories of criminals require different—sometimes completely contradictory—responses.

For example, the political terrorist cannot be understood or dealt with in terms of perceived personality disorders. He may or may not have them, but as a member of a terrorist group these are not the determinants of his behavior —group directions are. The concentration on the personal history or characteristics of the members of a terrorist group will usually not only fail to provide explanations for acts already committed, but will cause us to miss clues as to what they will do next.. In fact, it is not uncommon at all for individuals to make a complete about face in personal behavior after joining a terrorist group. One need only look at Patricia Hearst as such a case. This reversal in personality has been commented on, even with before and after pictures, in the public news. It is simply that the terrorist recruit submerges his or her personality and submits to group discipline. We need to look at the patterns of the group's behavior, not the individual's, in order to understand terrorism.

By the same token, it cannot be understood, or even negotiated with, on the basis of material gain. The terrorist organization may use money obtained from theft or extortion on one occasion to help finance future actions, but the primary purpose of an act of terror, even when a cash demand is part of it, is not money. The purpose is to guarantee that people will read, or listen to, the propaganda message involved. Unlike the kidnap-for-profit criminal, for example, terrorists do not carefully calculate a ransom demand according to what they believe they can quickly and anonymously collect and escape. They calculate the whole affair according to the amount of public attention they can get for their political ideas. While a victim's family or associates are trying to negotiate over ransom payment the terrorists are actually negotiating for media space. As recent experience has repeatedly shown, they may have no intention of collecting the money themselves, even from the beginning. They may demand that it be distributed in food or medical supplies among some element of the population, thus playing Robin Hood in something of a remote control fashion. In those instances where the terrorists do receive money, they are not so anxious to convert it to personal use that they get themselves caught trying to pass it. They may actually share it with others. Money is just not what motivates the political terrorist, the opportunity to make a propaganda point is.

Beyond the probability that failure to recognize an act of political terror for what it is will disarm the public in the face of its propaganda assault, attempts to explain the act in terms of the personal histories and traits of the individual terrorists usually dovetails quite nicely with their propaganda. That is, one of the prime objectives of their propaganda campaign is to create public sympathy for their cause. Details on the true nature of the group, its aggregate ruthlessness, its discipline, its training, or its eventual goals for the society, might well do the opposite. But focusing on the individuals' lives before they adopted the strategy and goals of the group, and submitted to its discipline, will almost invariably paint them in a sympathetic light. As this view of them is pumped into the public consciousness through long press accounts of the gentle man or woman driven to violence by evils he or she could no longer ignore, the propaganda victories drop bit by bit into the hands of the terrorists. This is such an important part of the propaganda operation that we will return to it later. We need, first, though, to explore further the general purposes of this propaganda.

The overall purpose of the terrorists' propaganda is to accumulate political power. They have taken up terror in the first place because they seek to make changes in the institutions, the society, or in international conditions that are beyond the reach of the power already available to them. Terror tactics provide power where there is none, or magnify it where there is little. These tactics are a means by which a relatively small number of people, with small resources, can fight far superior strength. In its broadest sense, terror hinges on the idea of boldly breaking the public peace, the law, a cherished tradition, or a deeply held taboo, as a device for grabbing enough attention to dramatize a cause. It may involve destruction, kidnaping, or murder, but it may also involve acts of less actual violence such as telephone threats, spray painting

24

political slogans on monuments, or setting fire to a flag in a public place. The basic idea is to commit an act of sufficient audacity not only to compel attention but to demonstrate beyond doubt the inability of existing authority to prevent its commission or apprehend its perpetrators. If they are caught, the thesis is then extended to using the apprehension, investigation, and trial in similar fashion —behaving in such a bizzare manner as to gain additional media attention with which to flaunt disdain for the laws or traditions of the society.

Thus, another purpose of terrorists' propaganda is to call attention to their ability to strike when and where they choose, and the inability of any government agency to prevent them from doing so.

This is a tricky proposition, though. If an act is not sufficiently threatening it may be disregarded, looked upon merely as a nuisance, or even laughed at. If it is too threatening, it may bring on public cries for the terrorists' skins, not sympathy for their cause. As suggested earlier, some of the theories terrorists follow are designed to provoke repressive action from the government, but never public support for a campaign against them. Therefore, the idea is to conduct an act of terror with careful attention to the propaganda of the deed, to stage it in such a way that the act itself, at least to some degree, will tend to justify itself. The victim, or object, chosen for an act will thus usually be one already in some public disfavor or distrust, or one that can easily be made so. This is simply an extension of the psychology of an attack on the town bully, or stealing from the local Shylock, containing its own self-justification.

Experience from rural areas in Asia and Latin America, particularly, is abundant in examples where the already despised local official or hated landlord was murdered in the night. Radical literature in this country has repeatedly advocated attacking banks —"everyone hates the banks already." On the other hand, when misjudgments occur and the object of violence is not sufficiently known or disliked the terrorists can lose what public support they have already gained. The murder of the American AID official, Daniel

Mitrione, was probably the undoing of the Tupamaros in Uruguay. They had counted on stories about Mitrione teaching torture methods to Uruguayan police as justification for his kidnaping and subsequent execution, but the stories carried little weight. Uruguayans were instead shocked at the killing of the father of nine children. Essentially the same public reaction in Canada followed the murder of Pierre LaPorte, Quebec Labor Minister, by FLQ terrorists in 1970. La Porte, a respected former journalist and effective member of the new Provincial cabinet was found dead in the trunk of an automobile, strangled with a chain he wore about his neck to hold a religious medal. Canadians were shocked from coast to coast and the government easily won backing for a massive manhunt which resulted in the apprehension and conviction of two FLQ members charged with the murder. The FLQ itself lost much of its appeal as the self-appointed champion of French-Canadians.

Again, it is a tricky proposition. The propaganda objective being sought in these cases was the portrayal of the terrorists as the defenders of the people against their enemies. Our point in citing how it sometimes has backfired is not to suggest that it always does so. It certainly does not. Acts of both terror and counter-terror in the Mideast have repeatedly received overwhelming public approval within whichever country considered itself to be avenged by a particular incident. The terrorists come out on top when their actions make the correct discrimination between the people and their enemies —whether the individuals killed or wounded can be assigned any real blame for the grievances over which an act was committed or not.

Indeed, the whole body of terrorist theory is actually somewhat ambivalent on the matter of killing innocent people. Some groups make a big point of their never intentionally hurting innocent people. For example, terrorist groups of the Weatherman variety in the United States frequently point out that they set off their bombs at times when buildings are empty, to avoid harming the innocent. And when a graduate student, who happened to be working late, was killed in the New Year's

Gang's bombing at the Army math lab on the University of Wisconsin campus in 1970, a footnote of regret was appended to the propaganda letter claiming credit for the act.

Some other terrorist groups say little on such matters, but liberally demonstrate their willingness to kill anyone who happens to be in their way. Black September's Munich operation and their firing into the crowd at Lod airport are examples. Perhaps one of the more enigmatic statements on the subject, though, was that said to come from five young Moluccans who hijacked a Dutch train with over thirty passenger-hostages in late 1975. After one hostage had been shot, and his body thrown from the train, the statement explained:

> We want to show the world and the Dutch government that we will fight for our country even if innocent people are hurt.
> [The Washington *Post,* Dec. 10, 1975, p. A19]

"Our country" was not The Netherlands, in which they were operating, but the South Moluccan islands in the Pacific, which were given independence, as the South Moluccan Republic, by the Dutch in 1949 but later forceably annexed by Indonesia under the Sukarno regime. The hijacking of the train was an attempt to regain their independence from Indonesia.

Of course, the particular body of guerrilla theory upon which so many of the North and South American terrorists base so much of their thinking does discourage the killing of the innocent —for tactical reasons. As we shall discuss at some length later, under this theory the terrorists should be highly selective in the targets they hit lest they frighten away support their cause must have from among the common people. There is little question but that many of the followers of this doctrine believe very deeply in it. There is also little question but that even they tend to let this sort of caution slide away as the frequency and intensity of their operations increases.

On balance, the killing of innocents seems to hinge more on whether a terrorist group is operating within the boundaries of its native country or outside them. Within these boundaries the guerrilla theory mentioned above seems generally to be

27

observed. Outside them, the theory does not apply. Practically speaking, operations outside their own country are more risky, and must be conducted with more haste and bravado than will allow for careful picking and choosing of victims. From a propaganda standpoint, even the innocent in an enemy country are representative or symbolic of that which must be struck down, so they can be sacrificed for the larger cause to which the terrorists are dedicated.

Usually, by the time their process of rationalization has run its course, the innocent were not so innocent anyway. For example, though the three diplomats, two Americans and one Belgian, Black Septembrists killed in Khartoum in March 1973 were thought of in the international community as good and honorable men, the killers explained it all in these words:

> Those who ostensibly weep today over the executing of three enemies of the Arab nation, for which the United States has been directly responsible, realize that thousands of the sons of this people, have been atrociously slaughtered and that thousands of others are suffering all kinds of torture in Jordanian and Israeli jails.

> [*Black September*, by Christopher Dobson, p. 117]

The demands at the time these three men —the American Ambassador to the Sudan, his charge d'affaires, and the Belgian charge d'affaires— were shot to death, were for the release of Palestinians from a Jordanian prison and Sirhan Sirhan from an American one.* But, as seen here, after-the-fact propaganda often tries to justify the deed in terms of the larger cause of thousands and thousands of people.

Thus, another purpose of terrorist propaganda is the justification of the acts committed on the basis of the worthiness of a larger cause.

As illustrated above, part of this justification is always the contention of the inherent evil of the object of the attack. And, indeed, in its early stages a terrorist movement tends to restrict

---

*Sirhan, of course, is the convicted killer of Robert F. Kennedy. In 1973 his brother was convicted of mailing a letter, signed "Palestinian Liberation Front," threatening the U.S. secretary of state and the Israeli prime minister then visiting the U.S.

itself to attacking individuals and institutions it believes are already sufficiently unpopular to make attacks on them self-justifying.

If the leverage aspects of the theory of terrorism are to work, that is, if a few people with small resources are going to fight superior strength, they must get the absolute most from their limited numbers and resources. One of the ways in which they do this is surprise. They can tie up security forces many, many times their own numbers because it is so difficult to tell when and where they are going to strike next. Even so, actual physical attacks are risky and use up hard-to-replace resources. If the terrorists are going to get the most out of what they have they must extend their assault beyond their capabilities to deliver physical attacks. In other words, they must damn more than they bomb. They must mount a psychological assault which seeks to portray all elements of the other side as evil beyond redemption.

If the terrorist movement is trying to overthrow an entire system of government, these psychological attacks will take aim at every institution and every aspect of that system — social, economic, educational, and religious, as well as political. And these psychological attacks will be so severe that they do real damage. Protracted campaigns on the inhumanity of the social order, the exploitation of the consumer by business, or the brutality of the police, as examples, can hurt these institutions in ways that physical attacks could never do.

Thus, another purpose of terrorist propaganda is pervasive and continuous condemnation of the other side.

Herein, incidentally, lies the previously mentioned danger of handing the terrorist cause a propaganda bonus when anyone tries to explain their actions in terms of the personal histories of individual members rather than in terms of the nature and history of the group itself. As often as not these accounts simply melt into sad reminiscences of the backgrounds of nice, ordinary people who have "turned to violence because there is no other way to obtain justice," etc. Usually various specific grievances are listed as having driven this or that person to the extremes to which he or she has gone.

In short, these individual history expositions finally just plug into the propaganda the group itself is trying to pump out. There is absolutely no question but that many promising young people have become terrorists because they were frustrated in ideals to which they were deeply dedicated. One hears Charlie Brown saying, "How could I be wrong when I am so sincere." The point is that the change they undergo, spoken of among themselves as having been radicalized, is so complete that their behavior no longer stems from their personal backgrounds, but from the teaching and discipline of the particular group of which they have literally become a part. It is this teaching, and this discipline, that must be examined to explain what they are doing, and what they are likely to do next. Reiterating the brainwashing they went through to become members of the group serves only to mislead the public in general, and to prepare the way for other individuals in the reading audience to follow in their footsteps.

There have been numerous examples of this over the past few years. Individuals within the Weatherman group have been described as the typical boy or girl next door, a little brighter than most, perhaps, and people like those you've known all your life. One was a quiet Greek classics major who loved dogs. Another was a rabid football fan. Another liked to help his mother in her garden. But all were so nauseated by some evil in the society they found around them that they had to set out to change it with violence.

Perhaps no more thoroughgoing examples exist than within the Hearst case. The SLA lacks much as far as having a well-worked out strategy for conducting the revolution its literature hawks. Indeed, the organization has been severely criticized in radical and revolutionary publications for its alleged poor understanding of what revolutionary strategy is all about, especially for its poor timing in the use of violence. Whether or not the SLA was correct in these matters, its propaganda was easily recognizable as that of a group of genuine terrorists. Thus the action of its members must be explained in terms of the group's teaching, not in terms of the tragedies of their individual lives. As these stories rolled out, particularly after the shootout in May 1974, they simply complied with the propaganda sketch the SLA itself had devised. This was unmistakable in the well-publicized transcript of the SLA tape in which Patricia "explains" her decision to join her kidnapers in "their fight." In the early days of March 1974 the Associated Press ticked out the whole tape, coming to some 35 column inches as it was printed in newspapers across the country. All of it was heavily laden with the organization's propaganda. The following excerpts are illustrative:

> Mom, Dad, I would like to comment on your efforts to supposedly secure my safety. The PIN [People In Need] give-away was a sham. You attempted to deceive the people, the SLA and me with statements about your concern for myself and the people. You were playing games —stalling for time— which the FBI was using in their attempts to assassinate me and the SLA elements which guarded me . . .
> I have been given the choice of 1, being released in a safe area, or 2, joining the forces of the Symbionese Liberation Army and fighting for my freedom and the freedom of all oppressed people. I have chosen to stay and fight.
> One thing I learned is that the corporate ruling class will do anything in their power in order to maintain their position of control over the masses . . .
> I should have known that if you and the rest of the corporate state were willing to do this to millions of people to maintain your power and to serve your needs you would also kill me if necessary to serve these same needs . . .
> I have been given the name of Tania after a comrade who fought alongside Che [Guevara] in Bolivia for the people of Bolivia. I embrace the name with the determination to continue fighting with her spirit . . .
> I have learned how vicious the pig really is, and our comrades are teaching me to attack with even greater viciousness, in the knowledge that the people will win . . .

The whole tape illustrates almost every point we have been discussing as the purposes of terrorist propaganda, but most of all it illustrates the intent to condemn society as a whole.

And it really says nothing of Patty Hearst's predicament.

It speaks with the voice of the "Tania" she says she has become, and it only parrots the propaganda line of the organization she says she has joined.

Of course, condemnation propaganda works on the faith and trust the public has in its institutions. To the extent it is successful, people tend to support these institutions less than in the past. Often some people who are normally solidly behind them will unwittingly join in the fray and encourage, or even demand, government actions to restrict these institutions — thus reducing some of the very power they need to react to the situations in which they find themselves. This is basic to the strategy being used. One of the ways by which a few people with small resources can take on superior forces is to erode as much of the superior forces' strength as possible. Some of this eroded strength will accrue to the attackers, but even if it does not the weakening process operates in their favor.

Businesses, educational institutions, churches, and traditional labor organizations, for example, will be hit in this fashion. One of the main targets will be law enforcement agencies. Since the police are usually the first line of defense against internal attacks, they will be hit first. The military will be next, because it can be used to back up the police. The intelligence gathering capabilities of both will be put under attack as soon as possible because of the great importance of intelligence in the power struggle underway.

Attacks against security forces will eventually manifest themselves in attempts to intimidate their personnel. The aim will be to put operational personnel in fear of their lives and to put management and control elements in fear of their charters and budgets.

There is no question but what extremist organizations have campaigned for several years against U.S. security forces. Underground newspapers were laced with agitation against the police, the military, the CIA, and the FBI beginning in the late 1960's. These papers were rife with claims of police brutality, the inhumanity of the military, and invasion of privacy by intelligence agencies. Hard on the heel of the purely psychological assault came exhortations toward physical attacks. The Black Panthers publicly announced their intent to kill policemen. Numerous extremist organizations circulated literature in the U.S. and in Vietnam urging soldiers to turn their guns on their own leaders. The number of police officers and military leaders who died as a result of such propaganda campaigns will probably never be finally determined, but it was large enough to force attention to the threat. In the same way, the degree to which the psychological attacks have affected law enforcement operations will probably never be deermined, but they have undoubtedly cut into the efficiency of the agencies under fire.

In Asia, Latin America, and the Middle East security forces have at times been intimidated to the point of acquiescing to terrorist activities, if not at times providing actual assistance to them. The impact of the terror the Viet Cong in Asia, and the Tupamaros in Latin America, rained on local officials are excellent examples.

The classic model for this whole process of the weakening of security forces probably is the combination of coercion and persuasion used against the police and military in Russia before the Bolshevik takeover in 1917. A detailed examination of how it worked in Petrograd, where the revolutionaries made their first move, is contained in Robert V. Daniels' book *Red October,* listed in the bibliography. It is recommended for close study by those who seek a fuller understanding of such tactics.

Thus, another purpose of terrorist propaganda—always—is to cripple law enforcement and security forces available to the society.

The final purpose of terrorist propaganda we should examine is that of proposing alternatives to the situation or system they have under attack. By all logic this should be the most important message the terrorists have to get across. Yet it is usually the most illusive part of their propaganda campaign. In other words, the most sympathetic and understanding view the public could take toward a group's use of violence or shock tactics to get attention is to assume that the group is seeking a dialogue—that it has alternatives to the conditions it is attacking, that if brought out in the open can be the subject of negotiation. Indeed, such a view has been repeatedly taken. Almost invariably, though, the terrorists' response is anything but clear and straightforward. Even if it appears to be so at first, it shortly turns out to be just the opposite. It slips off into vagueness, or it is suddenly clouded with rhetoric, or it escalates into terms so broad they are impossible to meet.

There are some tactical reasons for this, and we will discuss them as we look at how terrorism works, in chapter five. Most of these reasons, however, boil down to the generalization that terrorists deliberately fuzz up that part of their propaganda which deals with the alternatives they propose because they are simply not in the business to negotiate. People who lay out a clearly stated proposition—"you do this and we will do that"— are leaving themselves open to someone accepting the terms. The terrorists' game would thus be over, and it would be time for them to produce. That is not the way the strategy works. Terrorists operate on a non-negotiating basis. And they do so quite purposely. As has been suggested all along, people take up the tactics of terrorism in order to accumulate power, not to trade it away. That, finally, is what terrorism is.

2. How Does it Work?

Political power grows out of the barrel of a gun.
. [Mao Tse-tung, 1938]

The accumulation of political power through terrorism does not lead to the immediate agricultural miracle Mao's famous remark might suggest. Of course, he did not mean that it would. When he made that remark he had been working some eighteen years at the cultivation of this power, and was still about eleven years from the big harvest that put him at the head of the People's Republic of China.

And as simple as such things as bombing a building, or taking a few hostages, and forcing some political concessions might appear, they take some doing. Terrorism is a complex business, requiring a great deal of detailed preliminary work even to pull off a minor operation.

True, anyone who can heave the weight of a couple of bricks can throw a bomb through a window. But, to explode one with any assurance of its having a useful political effect requires intricate preparations —both in the pure mechanics of procuring, assembling, and installing the device for causing the physical destruction, and in recruiting, training, and organizing the people to perform the propaganda job the action is intended to do.

Of course, since terrorism inherently makes its practitioners outlaws, terrorists have all of the problems of living and working without falling into the hands of the police that

35

any band of criminals does. They need such things as supplies —for day-to-day living as well as for carrying out attacks— information, escape routes, hideouts, medical attention, false identities, transportation, and means of communication. They have to recruit people to their ranks, including some with special skills, and they must develop dependable contacts with people and organizations they can call on for special or emergency help.

The big difference, and the thing that complicates their task immeasurably, is in the basic motivation that sustains them and that must be used as the incentive for others helping them. Their motive is some political cause, often expressible in only the most nebulous and futuristic terms. They cannot hope for immediate, tangible gain for themselves, nor can they offer it to most of the people from whom they have to have cooperation or help. Of course, as part of their mode of operation they will also sometimes obtain money, supplies, and cooperation or assistance from people outside their ranks at gunpoint —terrorism is in itself a system of intimidation. They cannot furnish any appreciable fraction of their total needs, however, with mere force. Initially, they usually can't furnish any of them in this manner. They don't even have the means for exerting enough force to get anyone to do anything!

For example, many people do not realize it, but the two men who founded the Black Panthers obtained the money to buy their first gun by buying copies of the *Little Red Book of Quotations from Chairman Mao* at a Chinese bookstore for fifty cents and selling them to students at Berkeley for a dollar.

The run of the mill criminal can see his reward in dollars and cents, to come from the till of the store to be held up, or the vault of the bank to be robbed. People join him in his efforts because they believe he has a chance for success and they see an opportunity for personal gain, now or in the immediate future. Even the psychopathic criminal destroys something or kills someone because he sees his reward —his personal gain— in the obedience to twisted forces within himself or in the satisfaction of crazed desires which drive him. The terrorist organization cannot promise its members any of these things.

The initiation into its ranks includes the sacrifice of all that the recruit had or can hope to have, as an individual. He or she is to do whatever the organization decides—lie, steal, destroy, kidnap, or murder, in the name of the cause—"for the people," usually. And the organization can offer little or nothing to outsiders in terms of dollars and cents, or however grotesque the attempt at levity might sound, little to most of us even in terms of sense.

Thus, terrorists have a propaganda job from the very beginning. Instead of walking straight up to someone and saying "follow us and we will make you rich," they must lead people, including their own members, to discard beliefs, traditions, and loyalties they have held all of their lives for some sort of bag of ideas that, at best, can first appear as no more than a dream. That takes some doing. It continuously involves remaking people. As noted earlier, terrorists tend to recruit from among people who are already inclined to be seriously disgruntled with things as they are. Even so they have to funnel and discipline this disgruntlement so that it will serve the organization's purposes. Terrorists can, and do, use some people with somewhat disordered minds, some people whose previous paths are strewn with drugs, and some whose main accomplishments are purely criminal. As we have pointed out before, and will discuss more in a later chapter, their ranks and the preponderance of their supporters are not comprised of hardened criminals, drug addicts, or psychopaths.

Many people in these latter categories would be "security risks" for the organization and thus must be rejected. All that are accepted must be remade. The druggie must be converted to an addiction to the group's politics and cause, rather than drugs. The criminal, whose experience and basic skills may be highly useful to the group, must be convinced to forego the prospects of personal gain as the reason for practicing his trade, in favor of doing it for the cause. The intellectual, the iconoclast, or the gentle reformer, must be schooled to accept violence as a justifiable means for accomplishing ends compatible with his or her previous thinking, and trained in the use of weapons and explosives. Again, all of this takes some doing —laborious, time-consuming planning and organizing.

Perhaps the clearest way to see how all of this comes about, and to get some understanding of the complexities and vulnerabilities involved, is to trace the activities of some actual organizations, as they have originated, been built into viable forces, and have put themselves into operation. At least two models of organizational and operational activity can be seen in most of the terrorism occurring in the world today. The differences in the two are not finally basic —both function within the definition of terrorism we discussed in the previous chapter— but there are differences in how they organize and support themselves, and in their patterns of activity. Of course, there are incidents of unmistakable terrorist activity that do not follow precisely either of these models. However, we can see similarities in what goes on, either with the numerous and well-publicized incidents coming out of the Mideast, or with the also numerous, but less well-publicized, incidents coming out of Latin America. Incidents in Europe and Africa may be seen coinciding with either model. Those in North America and the Pacific are more likely to be found in the Latin American mode.

In fact, there are two groups in Latin America which exemplify the pattern of terrorism used by the small group of extremists who made up the SLA we have looked at previously. These two are the People's Revolutionary army (ERP) of Argentina and the National Liberation Movement (Tupamaros) of Uruguay.

Both the ERP and the Tupamaros provide a great deal of organizational and operational activity to copy. Within a three-year period beginning in the spring of 1971 ERP figured in dozens of major incidents of terror. Among their kidnap victims were close to twenty foreign or domestic diplomats, businessmen, and military offiicals, five of which they killed or gravely wounded. All in all, they collected some twenty-five or thirty million dollars. One single ransom they picked up was the more than $14,000,000 paid for the U.S. business executive

*Although this was a record at the time, it has since been surpassed by a collection of $60 million, by the Montoneros, a group formed by the merger of five of Argentina's largest guerrilla organizations.

we mentioned in the prevous chapter.* This they shared with Bolivian, Chilean, and Uruguayan [Tupamaros] terrorists to finance what they spoke of as "a new stage of military development."

In the course of their kidnapings, bombings, and threats of assorted violence the ERP extorted or attempted to extort not simply from individuals or families mere money, but from corporations, and even governments, money and economic or political concessions. They destroyed or took over buildings and industrial installations. One occasion they seized an airfield temporarily in order to force its aircraft to drop propaganda leaflets for them. They stole weapons and explosives from commercial and government stocks, and made an attempt to take over the entire military arsenal for the weapons and ammunition it contained. They hit a newspaper office with a force of fifty armed men and women, sprayed it with machinegun fire, wounded several of its employees, and left the premises in flames.

In neighboring Uruguay, the Tupamaros have probably more such escapades in their column of the ledger than the ERP —some with twists quite their own. They have been noted for their kidnaping of foreign nationals—some of whom they have killed— and they have engaged in the usual arson and bombing, against both domestic and foreign-owned properties. But, they have helped to finance their operations with an amazing number of bank robberies, taking anywhere from the equivalent of a few hundred dollars at a time to more than a million. They have been spectacular in the timing and coordination of their attacks —setting off as many as seven bombs at different locations within a few minutes on a single morning. They have hit both police and fire departments, cut communications lines, set fires, and then proceeded to rob several banks simultaneously. They have been quite brazen, stealing commercial explosives by the case, and looting an armory within fifty yards of a police station. They have been discovered operating their own crude munitions factories — complete with power driven equipment— and have not only taken over radio stations for propaganda purposes, but provided themselves with a clandestine station powerful enough to override commercial stations on their own frequencies.

There is no question about either of these groups being terroristic, and an examination of the activities of either of them could serve our present purposes of illustrating how such groups come to be —how they work, what they started with, and how it was possible for them to grow into forces with capabilities for striking essentially where and when they wished. There are two primary reasons for choosing the Tupamaros. First, their history and methods have been more extensively chronicled —both in print and on film— in the United States and in Europe. Second, although it is still too early to say the Tupamaros have been defeated, there is a complete cycle of terrorism, from beginning to at least temporary defeat, visible to us in the history of the Tupamaros. We can see in their history both great successes and great failures of a terrorist group.

Much of the Tupamaros' early history is either vague, because other people considered their very first activities were too benign or politically inconsequential to bother to record them, or shrouded in secrecy, because they themselves knew otherwise. For, when they had attracted enough followers to move from mere radical political agitation to more militant actions they went into a nearly two year period of recruiting, organizing, and training in secret. In fact, even though they considered themselves to be working toward a revolution from the beginning, for nearly half a decade the activities of the founders of the Tupamaros were either completely ignored by the regular press or mentioned in such disjointed bits and pieces of social action and crime news that little official note was taken of them at all. We have to turn to radical literature for most of our information —and there, of course, we encounter a partisan approach and some of the adulation that has spelled much of the Tupamaros' success anyway.

Apparently, the organization germinated during a campaign to organize farm labor, engineered by a small, young, extremely radical element of the Socialist Party in Uruguay. A handful of students with legal training moved in among low-paid, migrant workers and earned acceptance for themselves by helping the workers through the bureaucratic processes of obtaining the fruits of their country's extensive program of social and welfare benefits —probably one of the most extensive in the world at that time. These activists were touched by, and seized upon, the scenes of poverty and deprivation they found. They got into food programs. They eased into occasional expropriations of truckloads of foodstuffs and distributed them among the inhabitants of jerry-built shacks in slum areas. Then they made these forays rather regular affairs.

Such activities are self-escalating. Even the use of the word expropriation does not eliminate the reality that these supplies were taken either by stealth, or literally at gunpoint. Guns were needed, so the rationale went, not to use in any offensive way, but to obtain the people's rights to what had "in reality been stolen from them by the capitalists who had used the workers' labor to produce them." And guns were needed for use in self defense by the expropriators in case the police, "the servants of the capitalists" came after them. So weapons and explosives were expropriated too.

At the same time something was also happening to the people among whom the fledgling Tupamaros were distributing goods. As we saw in the reception of the several millions of dollars in food the SLA extorted from the Hearsts, there will be enough people on hand to soak up such windfalls, although others, perhaps including the most truly needy, will refuse them because they see them as stolen. This was apparently true in Uruguay. But, among those who accepted the Tupamaros self-styled welfare there arose a variety of attitudes —ranging from guilt and fear to sheer gratitude and willingness to cooperate with them, if not actively follow their leads.

Depending on how frequently they participated in this game, or how active their participation gradually came to be, some of these people were hooked into at least the fringes of the Tupamaros camp. In short order, these fringes became rather thickly populated —even with people who had never received any of the supplies nor had any need to do so. There were those honestly touched by the idea of such abject and neglected poverty that only theft could lessen its ravages. There were those who, though not poor themselves, resented the extreme wealth the Tupamaros were seen as tapping. "Right on!" they said, at least to themselves. The underdog was having his day! Somebody is finally taking on the establishment! Some of these people would passively, if not actively, provide bits of support for what was going on. There were others who saw high adventure in it all —some of them would encourage, or take little parts, in the activities. And some of all of these were potential recruits to the several inner circles the Tupamaros were eventually to evolve within their organization.

Thus, when in July 1963 the organizer, and strategist, of the Tupamaros led a small band of committed militants in the seizure of a dozen automatic rifles from a sports club in the Uruguayan countryside, they had a sizeable following of people of all types who would help them evade the police. This incident was a shocker. It was reported in the press as both an ordinary robbery and as an act of subversion against what had been generally credited as being the most democratic country in Latin America.

Though their group was not widely known as an organization then, the police identified the founder of the Tupamaros as one of the young activists responsible for the raid on the rifle club. The police were not able to apprehend any of them. As they were to do time and time again in the future, the Tupamaros vanished and no one would provide any clue as to what had happened to them. The press seems eventually to have put the incident down as nothing more than a robbery, and the society in general was content to chide itself over the corruption and inefficiency which permitted such things to happen —or which created the conditions that it saw as making them inevitable.

Depending on your viewpoint, you could produce volumes on what was, or was not, wrong with Uruguay at that time. The same could be said of any other country, at any other time. A country's socio-economic or political conditions are one set of problems, while a precipitous slide toward terrorism as the answer to them is quite another. The true significance of this boldness, this fleeting appearance of revolutionaries unmistakably busy at their own trade, was distinct unto itself. The point that seems to have been missed by Uruguayans generally —though many have noted it in retrospect—was the revelation of the presence within the society of a group far enough along on the road of development as a revolutionary organization to stage this raid and successfully disappear into some enclave of acceptance within the population.

While official agencies were puzzling over what was really going on, the small band that was in time to become the Tupamaros was quietly moving up to a new stage of development. Having long adhered to the idea of displacing the capitalist system in Uruguay, the twenty or so militants comprising its nucleus had hardened their plans for doing so. No longer were they satisfied to serve as the armed branch for some leftist political party too intent on reaching socialism through legal political work to risk dirtying its hands with the illegal actions required to keep fear and dissatisfaction at the highest pitch. It was decided that they, themselves, were to form the vanguard force and lead the revolution of the people. Their idol was Che Guevara, the much romanticized Argentinian who became Castro's revolutionary lieutenant, authored treatises on guerrilla tactics, and was finally "martyred" trying to promote revolution in Bolivia. Parenthetically, the German-born woman "Tania," whose name Patricia Hearst so reverenlty took when she announced she had joined the SLA, was Guevara's mistress and revolutionary comrade-in-arms before she too lost her life to the cause.

And true to the dictums of the people's warfare doctrine Che Guevara espoused, these twenty or so young radicals appointed themselves to be the "Movimiento de Liberacion Nacional" (MLN) [National Liberation Movement] of Uruguay. They added a dash of historic patriotism to their image by devising their street name, "Tupamaros," from that of an Inca chieftain who had been cruelly martyred in a rebellion against the Spanish 200 years before. They provided themselves with a striking and distinctive insignia, a T centered over the outline of a five-pointed star, which they splattered onto walls and buildings, or which they left at the scene of an action as something of a calling card. This device was later to make the lone security guard or policeman, going his rounds at night, cringe with the thoughts of a knife suddenly thrust at his throat, or a gun silently shoved against his head.

Information as to all the Tupamaros did during their two years underground is sketchy. Their discipline was good and their secrecy very tight. Again, however, their subsequent actions leave little doubt that they were adding to, and perfecting, their organization, studying the manuals on propaganda and guerrilla warfare, and laying out their own tactics.

For, in a few short years after their 1965 proclamation of themselves as the Uruguayan National Liberation Movement they were to all but stand the country on its ear. By 1968 they had mounted an assault on the presidency—blowing up a radio transmitter over which the President was about to speak, and grabbing one of his ministerial level appointees as a hostage. Almost simultaneously they had launched attacks against the police and initiated their long string of bank robberies. By 1970, they were kidnaping representatives of foreign governments from their homes or offices in Montevideo and demanding political concessions from the government for their release. And they had killed a U.S. government official they had kidnaped, because their demands were not met. By 1972, they had overstepped themselves so badly that they had run through a spate of almost worshipful popular support and provoked a reaction from the right. Nevertheless, in the meantime they had completely demoralized the police, precipitated impeachment proceedings against the President, and led the country to the closest it had been to a military dictatorship in forty years. Perhaps the picture is best illustrated by the following headline and opening paragraphs of a story appearing at that time in an American newspaper not noted for its harshness with populist movements:

44

TERROR BY LEFTIST TUPAMAROS SPARKS
RIGHTIST COUNTER-TERROR IN URUGUAY

Montevideo — Marxist Tupamaro guerrillas have provoked a determined rightist counter-terror, and Uruguayans are wondering whether their proud democracy will be the victim of the terrorists' rivalry.

For at least two more weeks, the country will be under military rule, voted by parliament after Tupamaros assassinated four persons in mid-April.

Those on the extreme political fringes used to argue and pamphleteer without fear, basking in Montevideo's tolerant atmosphere. Now, they read down posted death lists in search of their names . . .

[Washington *Post,* May 2, 1972]

This is the sort of powder-keg situation one has to visualize terrorism capable of creating. As we shall discuss in more detail later, this is one of the eventualities possible when just a handful of people take it upon themselves to accumulate political power through the use of violence mixed with propaganda.

And when the Tupamaros emerged from their cocoon of secrecy in 1965 they did so with a completely interwoven combination of propaganda and urban guerrilla actions. Their propaganda campaign was so well conceived, and so convincingly communicated, that it would have put the whole of Madison Avenue to shame. Their street tactics were so imaginative, so daring, and so flawlessly executed that they would be the envy of the best fiction-adventure writer —and they were to become the subject of two full length movies, each thoroughly laced with Tupamaro propaganda.

Their propaganda was initially something on the order of a pre-game show —a warmup for the fans they were to attract among the people of Uruguay. And no football or soccer team, indeed no sport, has had a greater or more entranced following —composed of people from every element of society— than the Tupamaros eventually pulled unto themselves. Once they had a good start with this following they kicked off with the real game, a two-pronged strategy designed to ingratiate themselves with as much of the public as possible on the one hand and to embarrass and cripple the government and the capitalist system as much as possible on the other.

They poured out posters, leaflets and pamphlets publicizing themselves as a new political force crusading against high prices, unreasonable taxes, low living standards, injustices, and poor working conditions —matters which hit home with people. They attributed all of these problems to high profits by the wealthy businesses, exploitation by foreign corporations, misuse of government funds, military ineptness and waste, and police brutality. They sought out the negative aspects of every institution and policy in the land to thread into their literature. And they produced what served as documentary proof of their allegations. They put together teams of researchers, working in and outside the establishment, who dug up the dirt, and copied or slipped documents and correspondence out of files they had gained access to. As their charges were listened to, they were able to get increasingly more of them into the regular press, no longer having to depend on the limited impact their own literature could produce. In toto, they worked hard at painting a picture of the whole system being rotten with inefficiency, corruption, and completely insensitive to human rights and dignity.

On the other hand, they took great pains to make themselves appear as efficient, totally incorrupt, and meticulously sensitive to people's feelings and needs as possible. They made it clear they were not after little people, they were after the big shots. As they moved toward violent action they were careful to explain their purposes to the ordinary citizen and exerted obvious effort to see that he was not endangered or hurt. Even when they commandeered the citizen's property for use in some Tupamaro robbery or kidnaping they did so with great overtures of courtesy and concern for his safety and that of his property. For example, one or two pleasant-looking young men or women might slide into an automobile as it stopped at a traffic light, show a gun, explain to the owner that his car was needed for a short while but that it would be left where it could be recovered by the police and returned to him. They also designed and timed operations to avoid hurting or killing innocent bystanders or people simply working in a building or installation. And if they did hurt someone they made it a point to administer first aid, or to see that the individual was put where he or she could get medical attention.

On the other side of the coin they did just the opposite with the establishment. Whereas they spoke in gentle, persuasive words to people within the masses, they used harsh, authoritative ones toward the individuals they sought to portray as the villains.

They flaunted themselves in their assimilated role as the voice of the people, using tones of authority that would have been laughed at were it not for the violence with which they reinforced their statements and demands. For example, when they abducted the presidential appointee they left behind what they called a "communique to public opinion," a document which began pompously with: "Today Mr. Perreira Reverbel has been detained by a decision of the MLN . . ." Following a list of demands wrapped around public issues they had helped to create they intoned: "Mr. Reverbel will be released safe and sound when the leaders of our movement feel it opportune and if the afore-mentioned requisites are honored."

When they kidnaped what corresponds to the U.S. Speaker of the House of Representatives they spoke of having conducted him to a people's jail where they had him listen to witnesses to support their claims of police oppression against their organization. When they killed the American kidnap victim because their demands had not been met they issued a communique saying that he had been executed after trial by a people's court.

This switch in tones —from an exaggerated gentleness toward the mass of private citizens to a pompous hostility toward targets of their attacks— is, of course, part and parcel of the propaganda used to promote the legitimacy of a national liberation movement wherever one is proclaimed. It is the basic tenet of the almost universal guerrilla strategy for organizing the people, on the one hand, and destroying the position of the system on the other. The Tupamaros were good at it.

This was more than mere words, for this type propaganda preceded as well as followed attacks on specific targets. In other words, the first objects of physical attack were those which the Tupamaros had decided were already somewhat unpopular with the masses. The hostile propaganda was simply used to deepen this unpopularity and justify the level of violence they had chosen to use. Second priority for attacks went to people or institutions with the greatest potential for popular disfavor. The hostile propaganda sought to make them hated before they were hit with actual violence. The next priority went to those next most vulnerable to a hate campaign. Pre-attack propaganda attempted to set them up for violence which would appear to be completely justified in the eyes of the public. The process went on, as long as the campaign prospered, seeking eventually to focus hate on every institution standing in the way of the Tupamaros' own objectives.

This is easily observable wherever terrorism has flourished. In the villages of the world it is the despised landlord, or the local government inspector, whose head first appears impaled on a pike on the morning after terrorists have struck. In the cities it is the bank, the police station, or the utility company that is hit. As time goes on, and propaganda contending corruption, inefficiency, and insensitivity to the people's needs as its effect, the list of those eligible for attack always grows.

As we shall discuss later, this particular aspect of terrorism is of the utmost importance in any consideration of how, where, and when terrorists might decide to strike.

The Tupamaros were true to form. Both psychological and physical attacks were leveled against the banks —"which gouge everybody and stuff their pockets with the people's money"— and the police —"who enforce the laws with which the wealthy take the fruits of the people's labor." And, as sufficient anger was aroused against a new type of target, attacks were widened accordingly —pulling the support of the people in behind one series of attacks before a new series was launched.

As their movement gained momentum, the attacks of the

Tupamaros were based on better information, supported by more participation from ordinary people, and better protected from interference by the police. The Tupamaros' operations came to be masterpieces of planning and coordination. They pulled off feints and deceptions right according to their scripts. They provided themselves with police and military uniforms, badges and sets of identification, and they donned repairmen's clothes and drove utility company trucks and other service vehicles.

For example, a kidnaping might involve a complex set of events such as the following. A neatly dressed young man and young woman would commandeer a panel truck from a certain rug cleaning company. Following detailed instructions, they would drive it to a designated spot, maybe in a pleasant, quiet residential section, park it and go to their regular jobs. But, as they climbed out of the truck, a precisely timed automobile would drop off three other people wearing the uniforms of that rug cleaning company. Blocks, maybe miles away, in another residential section these would back the truck up to the previously studied residence of a kidnap victim, get the door opened on the pretext of rug company business, grab the victim, roll him up in a carpet off his own floor, and trundle him off in the back of the truck. At another house, again some distance from the kidnaping scene, this trio would pull the truck into the garage of a house, either taken over for the purpose or belonging to a sympathizer. In a short time this truck would emerge from the garage, be driven to another location, and abandoned. The people driving it would go about their business. Another stolen vehicle with a different set of operators would subsequently move the victim from this intermediate house to a Tupamaro hideaway. While all this was going on, people in the command and control elements would take care of the kidnap demands and whatever negotiations were to take place.

In some other case, the kidnapers might appear at a home, or at an isolated work place, with police credentials, and literally apprehend their victim before starting him off on a series of vehicle and guard swaps that would eventually put him in a hidden room or cellar. In still another instance, a utility tower might be destroyed by men wearing civil guard uniforms. They simply relieved and sent the official guards away before they installed the bomb, set it to go off, and left. No Mission Impossible script on television has been more sophisticated or has worked any smoother than some of the operations pulled off by the Tupamaros.

Yet, they were able to do so not because they were a great *army* in the sense of having a large, centralized base from which they could dispatch units here and there—and at which government forces could direct counterattacks. Quite the contrary, they had built for themselves an even larger, but decentralized base, located right within the homes, offices, and factories of the population where, as individuals or small teams, its member units could function almost in place —and where government forces could not even cast their information-gathering nets without entangling people who were merely on the fringes of the Tupamaro operation, or not involved in it at all.

The operational scheme for the organization was set up in a number of concentric circles. At the outer edges of this complexity there was no organization of any kind —not even the visible means for continuous contact with an organization. Here lay the passive to occasionally active support —people who might never do more than throw their political weight against the government official who sought to have the Tupamaros hunted down. In the next circle or so toward the center were individuals, even organizations, that provided anywhere from minor to major spurts of support, but never had any direct part in any activity of the Tupamaros —still no organizational affiliation with them.

Perhaps you could call the next circle of people the stringers —no continuous organizational tie, but sufficient contacts for them to pass information toward the center, or to carry out ad hoc activity assignments, as they might be required. As you moved further in you would begin to find small cells of people, who were not only sympathetic to what was going on —as were those in the outer circles— but who had accepted enough of the indoctrination of the movement to allow themselves to belong to a formal group. Depending on the level of indoctrination to which each had been brought at any given time, these cells were capable, for example, of missions involving minor uses of weapons, such as commandeering vehicles to turn over to cells with deeper involvement in actions. These more deeply involved cells would be composed of people whose commitment to the movement had reached a higher level, and who had been trained accordingly. And so it went, until through succeeding circles, the whole organization was masterminded by a core of people totally committed to the complete destruction of the society in which they were operating —and working seven days a week in that direction.

This type of organization —and the Tupamaros reached an advanced stage of it— is highly resistant to anything law enforcement agencies can do. At the outer fringes there is nothing for them to grasp. Their intelligence nets get cluttered with law abiding citizens —indeed, legislators, officials, and other public figures— whose various degrees of involvement may actually be nothing beyond their responses to the political situation as they see it at the time. Even as law officers encounter the rudimentary trappings of the organizational network they still tangle with citizens who have violated no laws —and others who can cause more trouble over charges of police harrassment than their actual involvement in the overall operation seems to merit.

When the police manage to touch the circles of formally organized cells they run into the built-in dead ends the cellular organization was contrived to provide in the first place. The cells having any active part in operations are extremely small and tightly knit —people within them know each other quite well and will detect an infiltrator very easily. On the other hand the cells usually know *nothing* of the overall operation beyond their own part, and they know little more than that about the organization as a whole —maybe nothing more than a single means of contact through which they receive their instructions. They will have been indoctrinated against cooperation with law enforcement agencies, and could tell them little even if they wanted to. People in cells further toward the center will go down shooting rather than fall into the hands of the police — and they frequently did in Uruguay.

This was the type of structure the Tupamaros set out to build. Toward this end they worked tirelessly, month after month, one year into the next, until they had honeycombed the society—either with people who would do their bidding without asking questions, or with others who could be counted on for varying amounts of support even if nothing but the "turning of heads" at the opportune moment.

At one level or another the Tupamaros recruited support from every element of the society. With as much commitment as they could get, in each case, they patiently equipped themselves with representatives of all of the professions, services, and industries —teachers, professors, social workers, lawyers, doctors, nurses, journalists, technicians, repairmen, etc. And in a pinch, they knew they could always kidnap whatever talent they needed and force its performance.

In summary, they made cooperating with them the thing to do. It was an exciting and glamorous thing for the young people, the intellectuals, or the radically inclined professionals to identify with the Tupamaros, or to be able to feel that they had a part in their successes as they could see them occur before their eyes. And for the political aspirant, being actively against the movement was unthinkable. In fact, the political climate became one in which even a decidedly conservative president could not muster the legislative support required to mount a law enforcement offensive against the Tupamaros until the situation was obviously out of hand —and the military had to be called in.

Again, the Washington *Post* article describes the situation as it had come to be in 1972:

A wealthy merchant family denounced the Tupamaros in conversation, but at the same time it rents a summer home in Punta del Este to the guerrillas as insurance against harassment.

A policeman whose unit took part in one of the recent attacks on a Tupamaro hideout called the father of a girl known to be a guerrilla. "I didn't fire a shot, come count my bullets," he pleaded, asking that the word be passed along.

Several lawyers admitted that despite the determined independence of the judiciary from the executive branch, a truly disinterested trial involving Tupamaros is almost impossible.

"The judges are either biased for or against them, or are intimidated," said one.

This was at perhaps what was the turning point for the Tupamaros. Their popular support had suffered rather badly in 1970 when they summarily killed U.S. AID advisor Dan Mitrione. They had counted on being able to portray him as an enemy of the people who was in Uruguay only to teach torture to police —thus justifying his execution. This was a misstep. Mitrione's reputation did not support their claims. Besides that, the Tupamaros snatched him literally out of the arms of his wife and small children as he was preparing to leave home for work one morning. Later, the image of a grieving widow and her fatherless children cropped up when the Tupamaros dumped off Mitrione's bullet riddled body for the police to find. The support for a crackdown on them began to emerge, but by the time it did they had a tremendous foothold against a police system which was badly mauled and had little spirit left for the task at hand. By 1973, the determination to deal with their violence, in the midst of the social, economic, and political chaos they had helped to create, was so desperate that stringent measures such as press censorship had been taken — and the job of restoring order was turned over to the military. Many of the Tupamaros fled the country to form alliances with the ERP in Argentina, the National Liberation Army in Bolivia, or the Movement of the Revolutionary Left in Chile — which is to say that Uruguay, in its battle with the Tupamaros, has lost much of its democratic fabric but the Tupamaro threat is not far off.

In the meantime they were demonstrating to other political extremists around the world how it all could be done. A number of leftist and terrorist organizations in the U.S. have claimed the Tupamaros as their models, including NACLA [the North American Congress on Latin America,] which published a comic book on their exploits, the BLA [Black Liberation Army,] the Weatherman group, and the SLA.

Indeed, the SLA did try to copy the Tupamaros, and much of the reason for the sometimes ludicrous touches to the tragedy they produced was their attempt to telescope the long, arduous preparatory work into a few months. None of this handful of radicals, pseudo-radicals, and escaped convicts, that came together in Berkeley in the beginning of spring 1973 were trained or experienced revolutionaries. Some of them had never read a line of a guerrilla manual six months before they were proclaiming themselves an army. It was probably in April of 1973 that their grandiosely-titled "General Field Marshall," Donald De Freeze, gave Mizmoon [Patricia Soltysik] copies of Latin American terrorist material he had been reading before he escaped from prison. And *she* was regarded as the brains of the SLA when it surfaced that fall. Both she and Nancy Ling Perry, who became essentially the voice of SLA, tried to organize workers "to unite and throw off their chains." Mizmoon tried with library workers, and Nancy with topless waitresses. The library workers rejected Mizmoon's efforts by voting down the union she proposed, and the topless waitresses laughed at Nancy's efforts to radicalize them. So they organized *themselves,* studied revolutionary manuals, bought guns, donned combat boots, and practiced shooting on a firing range. They, and their followers, went underground just as the Tupamaros had done —the SLA only for no more than a few weeks, versus the Tupamaros for years. And a year after it all started, the commander, brains, voice, and three soldiers of SLA were dead in the ruins of their last makeshift command post fortress.

Turning from the patterns that can be seen from incidents coming out of Latin America, we can see a different set coming out of the Mideast. Some of the various Palestinian groups have been in the business longer than any of those in Latin America. They operate across the borders of nations scattered over a large part of the globe. They are supported by governments, either voluntarily or as a result of intimidation. They usually don't bother with extortions from individuals, families, or corporations; they take on nations, or the world. And although not all of them have practiced terror continuously, when they have, it has been generally more compelling to public attention than any thing we saw in the discussion of the Latin American model. For example, no organization has devised an operation guaranteed to pull a larger audience for a single day —estimated at 500 million, worldwide— than the Palestinian's "Black September," with its attack at the Olympic games.

Moreover, despite some of the momentary revulsion this and some of the other acts of terror by Palestinian groups have caused, they have probably had more success with terrorism than anyone else. Certainly the reception their cause has come to receive in the family of nations —especially in the United Nations itself— suggests this to be true. Though they have so far failed to destroy Israel, their primary objective, they have cut out a commanding role in world affairs for themselves — almost entirely with a mixture of terrorism and propaganda.

Some people have complained that the Palestinians have been able to do this because the media have heaped coverage on them gratuitously. In all fairness to the journalistic profession, however, the incidents they have been responsible for have literally demanded media coverage. They have gone to the most extreme lengths to insure that notice was taken of the things they did, adding jolting embellishments to what otherwise might have been ordinary guerrilla actions. Not only have they forced media attention with the size and audacity of some of their attacks, they have flashed before the public eye in colorful garb, and with intriguing organizational names, that no one could really ignore or forget.

Black September, its very name converting an event of defeat into a fearful symbol of terror, literally burst into the news with an act of such suddenness and repugnance that it alone may have been a turning point in attention the Palestinian cause was getting. On November 28, 1971 a small assassination squad alerted the world to the recent formation of Black September by firing a barrage of pistol shots into Wasfi Tell, the Prime Minister of Jordan, as he stepped to the doorway of the Sheraton Hotel in Cairo. Before taking to their heels one member of the squad leaned down and lapped the blood pouring from his body.

The affair had been carefully planned to insure success. There were six members of the killer squad, five young men, dressed to blend into the cosmopolitan crowd of the center of Cairo, and a girl, a student in the city. If the pistol shots had not killed Wasfi Tell she had a grenade that would have. She did not have to use her grenade and slipped away as police chased and caught the five young men. In true terrorist fashion they admitted the killing and claimed it as an act of revenge for Tell's evil part in the destruction of Palestinian guerrilla forces in Jordan in September 1970—that was the "Black September" from which they had taken their name. Shortly thereafter, the success of the attack was announced from Beirut as the work of a new and secret organization dedicated to revenge for the defeat in Jordan.

The organization broke into the news several more times over the next ten months until September of 1972, they staged the attack at Munich. That too was carefully planned to insure success. They had thoroughly reconnoitered the Olympic Village, including having a man examine in detail a building identical to the one they planned to assault. As we noted earlier, the Black Septembrists who survived the fire-fight at the Munich airport were jailed in Germany but released when their organization hijacked a Lufthansa jet a few weeks later.

Wasfi Tell's killers were brought to trial in Egypt, but they and their lawyers turned the proceedings into a trial of Tell and King Hussein, claiming these two were traitors and enemies of the Arab people. They put one of the former leaders of the Palestinian Liberation Organization [PLO] on the witness stand to testify that the Jordanian regime was responsible for all of the disasters that had befallen their people. The various leaders of the Arab world outside Egypt saw to it that the defense had unlimited funds and eventually put so much pressure on Egyptian authorities that the five young men were released on bail and never brought back to trial. Shortly thereafter, two of them were given travel documents back to

Beirut. Two, the one who actually fired the fatal shots, and the one who drank Tell's blood, remained free but were not allowed to leave Egypt to rejoin their comrades for other Black September actions.

Whereas the organizers of the Tupamaros had to build their organization from the ground up, and had to create much of the popular dissatisfaction, the Black Septembrists had different materials to work with. Secret societies specializing in assassination are common in Arab history. Terror is a weapon that has frequently been used in the Mideast for political and military strategies. In fact, Black September itself bears a resemblance to the ancient Arab organization which gave us our word *assassin* —one who murders for political reasons. "The Assassins," or *Hashshashin* in Arabic, were young men who were organized into a fanatic cult by an Arab religious teacher at the time of the Crusades. Under his tutelage they became addicts of hashish ("those addicted to hashish" is the meaning of their organizational name) and went out in small teams to kill at his command. Their drugged and fanatic dedication was such that once given their orders nothing could stop them. They set out to kill or be killed. And, if one team failed to dispatch a victim, another picked up the mission and did so.

The young men and women of today's Black September are equally as dedicated and willing to kill or be killed. Whereas the original assassins were motivated by a powerful drug, the Black Septembrists are motivated by a powerful hatred. As Christopher Dobson points out in his book *Black September,* few people in the West can appreciate the intense feelings of injustice the Arabs have for the existence of the state of Israel on land they regard as rightfully theirs.

These feelings have festered in the refugee camps created when the first Arab-Israeli war ended in 1948 with disaster and humiliation for Arab military forces and left nearly 600,000 Palestinians displaced, rejected even by the Arab governments that could have taken them in.

Besides eking out a living, the main occupation of these people became the dreaming of revenge against Israel for driving them from their homes, and revenge against the rest of the world for letting it happen. As one generation passed these fierce feelings to another, new leadership bubbled up to put these dreams of revenge into action. Some of this leadership has been unscrupulous, and has been comprised of opportunists who sought power for themselves. At the same time most of the nations of the world have slowly aligned themselves into opposing camps over the fate of these people. Some of these nations, including Arab ones, have been as unscrupulous as some of the new leaders, and have pulled and tugged at the Palestinians trying to tilt the balance one way or another.

Over the past two decades the forces within this cauldron have boiled up a continued proliferation of political organizations and alliances, almost all of which have some guerrilla or other para-military branch. And in many cases they have had governments, again both Arab and non-Arab, standing at least partially behind them that were willing to support guerrilla operations for ends they had not been able to attain with regular military action. One of the inevitable accompaniments to these guerrilla operations has been pure terrorism—again supported by some of the governments with stakes in the struggle going on. Thus for all of the present decade, and part of the past one, various Palestinian organizations have conducted a series of kidnapings, assassinations, bombings, and aircraft hijackings that have not only influenced international relations but have provoked actual conflicts including open civil war in one of the Arab countries. It was the outcome of this last event, civil war in Jordan, which added coals to the fires of hatred and prompted the formation of Black September as a secret and completely terroristic organization.

And, in the chain-reaction sequence of events typical of the Mideast, it had been a particularly aggravated campaign of Palestinian terrorism against Israel and a half dozen Western countries that started the Jordanian civil war. Beginning in July 1968, this campaign climaxed on September 6, 1970 when the Popular Front for the Liberatoin of Palestine (PFLP) launched the granddaddy of airplane hijackings so far —four jetliners at the same time. This wild assault on international commercial aviation ended four days later with the blowing up of four huge aircraft, belonging to Pan Am, TWA, Swissair, and BOAC. The Pan Am plane was loaded with explosives and blown up in Cairo, after all of its passengers and crew had slid down emergency chutes. The other three were destroyed in Jordan also after everyone had left them, but only after the more than four hundred people that had been aboard had sat in their seats in fear of their lives for four days in the sweltering desert heat on an abandoned airfield.

King Hussein, who was already having trouble with clashes between guerrillas of Al Fatah, another Palestinian organization, and his own troops, was furious because PFLP had used his country in the hijacking and destruction of these aircraft. His army was more upset than he, because they had been held in check while the increasingly arrogant guerrillas had done everything possible to provoke them. The king turned his troops loose on both Palestinian organizations. Some four thousand of the guerrillas were killed, the refugee camps were shelled, and the Jordanian Air Force held off assistance by other Arabs when they tried to intervene. When the fighting ended with a cease-fire engineered by Egypt the Palestinian guerrilla forces were all but destroyed. The month in which all of this happened was the "Black" September after which they later named their secret terrorist group.

Even with his guerrilla organization in complete disarray, though, Yasser Arafat, leader of Al Fatah, was apparently not ready to adopt the terror tactics the competing PFLP had been using. He was afraid of what it would do to his carefully cultivated image as a negotiator in world political circles. Yet, it was his followers, militant young survivors who had managed to flee King Hussein's final mopping-up operations in Jordan, who insisted that terror was the only weapon left open to them. When they seemed not to be able to make this point any other way, they started leaving Al Fatah to join the PFLP.

The organization's ranks were already badly depleted and it could not stand this. So, the young militants were finally allowed to go ahead with their plans for terrorist attacks, but only under the cover of being a new organization that, while remaining a part of Al Fatah, could be disclaimed by it. This new organization, put together and trained in secret, was called *Black September*. And Wasfi Tell, on whom they blamed the destruction of their guerrilla forces in that black September of 1970, was the first target.

In the months that lay ahead, there were to be many others. For, the dramatic success of that assassination by a mysterious group with a catchy name had put the Palestinian cause back in the headlines. And those among Al Fatah's leadership who had doubted the wisdom of using terrorism changed their minds, eventually adopting it as a primary weapon of the whole organization. Thus, some of the international transportation and communication facilities available to them through support from Arab governments, and some of the millions of dollars paid either willingly by some governments, or as protection money by others, went to pay for such affairs as the attack on the Olympic athletes at Munich, the mailing of letter bombs to and from half the countries in Western Europe, the attack on the Israeli Embassy in Bangkok, the murders of the U.S. and Belgian diplomats in Khartoum, and the attempted murder of the Jordanian Ambassador in London.

This last attempt, though unsuccessful in that the ambassador was only wounded, offers an excellent illustration of how Black September terrorists were able to make some of their attacks and get away, moving from country to country. The ambassador, Zaid el Rifai was being driven along a busy and fashionable street in London's Kensington in his diplomatic limousine. A young man in a raincoat was standing alone on a traffic island at an intersection. It was as if he were waiting for someone. As the ambassador's car came even with him he pulled a Sten gun from underneath his coat and stitched its side with bullet holes. Before he had sustained more than a shattered hand el Rifai was able to throw himself to the floor of the car and the driver sped to safety. The young would-be killer ran down another street to an automobile waiting with its engine running and was whipped off into oblivion. Scotland yard later had reason to believe that he had been picked up by the authorities in France and asked that he be returned to England. Apparently, however, French foreign officials were interested in avoiding trouble with the Arabs and caused him to be released on some flaw in the arrest procedure. He quietly slipped out of France to Algeria.

Slipping in and out of countries in Europe and the Middle East, undoubtedly using Arab contacts and local sources of assistance, Black September attacked Israeli supporters by setting fire to Gulf Oil tanks in Holland, murdering five Jordanians in West Germany, blowing up the Streuber Motors factory in Hamburg, and damaging the Esso Oil Company pipeline also near Hamburg, all within a month in early 1972.

In May of that year the organization took to hijacking aircraft. Two men and two young women, using pistols and grenades, took over a Sabena flight from Brussels to Tel Aviv, but ordered the pilot to continue on his course. Their plan was to attack Israel directly by being in command of the plane when it landed at Lod, and threatening to blow it and all aboard, including themselves, to Kingdom Come, if the Israelis did not release over three hundred Palestinians from prison. The plane captain, a British Jew, had radioed his situation to Tel Aviv, and Israeli paratroopers, dressed as airport ground crewmen met the craft and deflated its tires before the terrorists knew what was happening. Then for twenty hours of talk and bargaining everyone aboard the plane was cooped up behind its doors. The terrorists, in full view of the petrified passengers, went about the craft installing plastic explosive, setting it to go off, and bidding each other a final farewell. Before they could detonate the explosive, though, the Israeli paratroopers, following a procedure rehearsed on an identical aircraft, stormed aboard and, in an exchange of shots lasting less than half a minute, killed two of the terrorists and captured the other two. One of the passengers was killed and several injured.

The two surviving terrorists, the young women, were tried by an Israeli court. The testimony they gave during this trial, showed each of them to be quite different in character and motivation, and provides some revealing details on Black

September's internal organization and methods of operation. One, a nineteen-year-old nursing student, born of an Arab family still living in Israel, displayed a deeply ingrained hatred of the Israelis. She had been recruited into terrorism by a fellow student, but seemed to have taken gleefully to it. The other, a twenty-one-year-old nursing assistant told of being raped by one young man and made a drug addict by another —a doctor. She was the doctor's mistress for a while and he then brought her into the terrorist organization. She claimed that she was forced to sleep with men in the group lest she be deprived of drugs and beaten. She said that she had no choice but to carry out any orders they gave her.

The two had been given intense indoctrinations, trained in explosives and methods of sabotage, and sent to join the two young men in Brussels. There they spent several days enjoying the shops, good restaurants, and night spots before they boarded the airplane with forged Israeli passports. Only after the plane had taken off for Tel Aviv did they find out where they were going and what their mission was. Before, they had only known that the body belts they wore contained plastic explosive and their cosmetic containers held grenades and pistols. The court sentenced the two young women to life imprisonment.

This whole affair was regarded by Black September as a serious defeat that had to be erased in some way or the organization would lose its terrorist credibility. The subsequent ad hoc alliance with the Japanese Red Army whose three "soldiers" carried out the massacre of the Puerto Rican pilgrims at Lod airport was, at least in part, intended to do this.

There are numerous variations of the organizational and operational patterns we have seen in the two models we have discussed—the Latin American one and the Mideast one. And, as we will see in the next chapter, there are also a number of ideological differences from which the nearly a hundred extremist groups around the world take their cues. It would be a mistake, however, to leave the impression that the level of violence of which a group of terrorists is capable, or the amount of blood they are willing to let, depends upon their ethnic or national origins. The mass killing at the Rome airport was by Arabs, but the one at Lod was by Japanese. Retaliations of jolting ruthlessness have been seen at the hands of Israelis. The Irish have spattered blood liberally, as have other Europeans. Incidents involving Latin American groups have shown absolute viciousness. And, it would be hard to top the butchering by the so-called Manson Family in the United States.

The point was made during our discussion on what terrorism is, is that typical terrorists are deliberately trained and disciplined to carry out the violence decided upon by their organizations. If there is a gauge by which one can measure a group's potential for violence it would be in the nature of this training and the degree of discipline it instills. Obviously, members of a group will be capable of doing damage according to the type of weapons they have —hand guns, rifles, shotguns, rockets, explosives, or perhaps even more powerful devices as time goes on— and according to the proficiency they have achieved with these weapons. We have to note, for example, that in the early days of the Weatherman organization several of its members blew themselves up trying to manufacture bombs in a Manhattan townhouse. Not withstanding the gun training and range sessions of the SLA, they fired an awful lot of ammunition without hitting anyone. On the other hand, we have seen much more proficiency from the Weatherman since, and no one can dispute the skills of any of the groups that stay in the business very long.

Physical training and weapons proficiency are only part of the training that will tell how dangerous a group can be. The other part of the qualifier tells much more —the discipline to carry out whatever violence their organization prescribes. We have said previously that terrorists get psyched up to commit violence. They come to believe in a cause with such fanaticism that all else —judgment, compassion, previously-held values— is jettisoned. We have contended that constant group rapping along a single line of thinking, with no let up for comparisons with other ideas, or with day to day realities, is one of the ways this is done. Communiques loaded with blind revolutionary rhetoric coming from some groups, or statements by their members on trial, attest frequently of this. The young Arab woman on trial in Israel claimed sex, drugs, and beatings were used in making her a suicidal hijacker. However exaggerated her claims might or might not have been, some of the visible lifestyles of terrorist groups attest to things of this sort. Reports of brainwashing inevitably emerge as explanations for the behavior of some members of terrorist groups. And, indeed, the complete turnabout in the lives of many of them suggest drastic changes have occurred in their ways of looking at things.

Scientist are not in total agreement that anything as thorough as the term brainwashing implies is really possible. There was a spate of interest in these matters following the Korean War, in which a number of American prisoners of war were induced to become turncoats, and join the cause of their captors. Two comments particularly relevant to our discussion of mind-changing by terrorist groups came out of some of this scientific interest. One, by Dr. James A.C. Brown, a specialist in psychology and psychiatry, commented that the Americans who became turncoats in Korea did so because they went into that war with a poor foundation in the ideology and belief system of their own side of the struggle. This view was criticized by some authorities, who said it failed to show much sympathy or insight into the minds of the prisoners of war themselves. Doctor Brown wrote:

> This may or may not be so, but from the practical point of view it shows clearly that political indoctrination is not a mysterious process, although certainly a peculiar one judged by experience of past wars, and that its success with the Americans and relative or complete failure with the British and Turks was due to the poor morale of the former and the better discipline of the latter. [*Techniques of Persuasion: from Propaganda to Brainwashing,* Penguin Books, 1963 p. 267]

The other relevant comment is attributed to psychiatrist Dr. L.E. Hinkle, and attempts to differentiate between the sorts of things described in fictional accounts such as George Orwell's thought-control in his book *1984* and the methods actually used in known cases of dictatorial political indoctrination in real life:

> They [the methods most commonly used] are not dependent on drugs, hypnotism, or any other special procedure designed by scientists. No scientist took part in their design, nor do scientists participate in their operation. [p. 268 of the above.]

Taken together these comments suggest that terrorists do not even need Orwellian systems or lab-coated scientists armed with needles of mind-changing drugs if they recruit among people who don't have a very good hold on the value system of the society in which they have been living. And, if we check out the individuals who make up the ranks of terrorist groups we find again and again that they were already somewhat adrift, or actually seriously alienated, from the society they are attacking before they joined up. Then, it generally appears that although street drugs and the breaking of sexual taboos may often be used, the methods are more those of the propagandist than the true scientist. And, as often as not the administrants of the propaganda will simply be true believers themselves, self or peer taught, in whatever doctrine they are following and preaching.

The writings and statements coming out of most of these groups tell the story rather well. In addition to the particular political doctrine they contain you can usually see the traces of a process for remaking a human being that outdoes any religious conversion ever recorded. It begins with a condemnation of the past self and everyone and everything connected with it. Self-criticism in the midst of a peer group is often a part of this. It will include the making of statements or the commission of acts, or both, that renounce the formerly held beliefs, traditions, and taboos. There will be a confession of guilt over ever having lived, believed, and loved as the individual formerly did. There will be the denial of the former self and all connections with it, and admission of internal conflict and disharmony that only a new self and new philosophy can dispel. A new name will usually be taken, one with some significance to the new identity —or one in itself symbolic of the new dedication. There will be an expression or demonstration of awe and gratitude toward the new comradeship. This will usually be accompanied by some show of humility over the humanity and love of the new-found comrades, and the size and beauty of the altruistic endeavor they have taken unto themselves. There will be an expression of hope that the newly joined can only live up to their standards. Then will come the declaration that he or she will try to be worthy, and will do whatever is required, no matter what it might be —even kill or be killed.

Presided over by a truly faultless and compassionate Lord, the process through which terrorists put each other could perhaps, indeed, save the world. Presided over by lesser beings, or followed in the pursuit of mere political doctrines, whatever they might be, it can result in the complete submission of body and soul to the most consummate evil.

That form of literature known as the novel is said to have come into being as a means of calling awareness to the life functions of common place matters through depicting uncommon or bizarre versions of them. Perhaps in a similar fashion we can illustrate the more commonplace routines by which individuals can come under the control of terrorist organizations by briefly examining one of the more bizarre versions of these routines —the one developed by the "kill through others" murderer Charles Manson for completely dominating people in what came to be called his "Family."

Many people probably remember the grisly past of this group only faintly, and can call it to mind primarily because one of its members, Lynette Fromme, recently staged an attempt on President Ford's life. Her quickly volunteered reason for this act was to get the Family back into the news in hopes of somehow obtaining a new trial for Manson. He is now serving a life sentence for ordering several terroristic murders in the late summer of 1969. As will be illustrated shortly, staged is the proper description for Lynette's action toward the President in September 1975 because it had all of the earmarks of having been more propaganda of the deed than anything else.

Maybe we are not accustomed to thinking of the Manson Family as political terrorists, maybe not even as terrorists. By everything that came out in their months-long trial in 1970, they qualified completely. They were autocratically run, in that Manson alone authored the political philosophy on which their violence ws based —a twisted and fantastic somewhat neo-Nazi theory. He methodically trained and disciplined his followers to carry out the violence he decided would further this strategy.

Then, when one August night in 1969 he sent four of his clan —three girls and one young man— into movie actress Sharon Tate's home literally to butcher her and four of her friends, he did so with the intent of striking terror in the hearts of people in the white community. He intended the crime to be so gruesomely spectacular that it would demand attention. And he planned for it to be blamed on blacks, and thus to help start the massive racial strife he was convinced would turn into a civil war that would eventually catapult him and his pure Aryan followers into power.* The young killers he sent in were trained and disciplined to do the job without question —even though the men and women murdered, some of whom they stabbed as many as forty or fifty times, were total strangers to them, and one of the women was about to have a baby. And they did it armed only with knives and one lone 22 caliber pistol —spattering and tracking blood everywhere, even tasting their victims' blood and writing on the walls with it. The next night, some distance from the scene of that crime, they entered the home of Leno and Rosemary La Bianca and killed them in a similar fashion. These young people did not kill for personal gain —money, for example— they did it because "Charlie" told them to. And they were trained and disciplined to do whatever Charlie told them to do.

Charles Manson had become, literally, their lord and master. They were convinced he knew what he was talking about, in terms of the Armaggedon he prophesied, and they

*For an excellent elaboration of Manson's strategy and philosophy, see *Helter-Skelter* by Vincent Bugliosi and Curt Gentry.

thought that somehow he was destined to be the savior of the world —some thought he was Jesus Christ, some Satan, some a combination of both.

Manson's is a complex personality, that is certain. Although at times he may appear simply insane, he is quite intelligent, and strong willed. More than half of his thirty-three years had been spent behind bars when he founded his notorius clan in 1967. He had little formal schooling, but he had become a keen observer of human nature. He read poorly, but he had somehow acquired some knowledge of the ideas of Nietzsche and Hitler —and he was impressed with them. He had periodically hovered around courses on various mind-control theories. He had tinkered with several offbeat religions and, in fact, knew quite a bit about the Bible. He could hold people in conversation for hours. He had a captivating personality, and a cunning of almost unbelievable proportion. And he had had practical experience in a number of types of crime —theft, forgery, and pimping.

With this background he was released from prison in 1967 and quickly gravitated to San Francisco's Haight-Asbury, wandered among the flower children, into the hippie community, and into the drug culture flourishing there at the time. Almost overnight he began the seduction and collection of young women and girls that was to lead to the formation of the Manson family. The very first of these was a college graduate, a library worker —later a convicted murderess. The next was Lynette Fromme, then a seventeen-year-old delinquent, who was to become Manson's second in command. She was suspected of involvement in several murders, but always managed to avoid prosecution for any major crime until she was charged with the attempt on the President's life.

In the two-and-a-half years between the time Manson picked up these two young women and the time he was arrested for the Tate-La Bianca murders he looked over and sorted through hundreds of runaways, outcasts, drifters, and drug experimenters —the confused and the alienated. Some he chose, some he discarded. Some chose him, some rejected him. Some he brought to the Family for a while and then drove them away. Some came for a while and then left. If he let them stay, and they chose to do so, they became increasingly under his control —until they would do absolutely anything he even so much as asked them to do.

Thus, the first principle in operation in his procedure was the selection of individuals who would be susceptible to his suggestions, people who had already made some sort of serious break with family, friends, and society, and were looking for something to hang onto. The second principle was the use of whatever was already bothering them to make their break with the outside world total and complete. The third was to give each of them something to hang onto, a new identity, a new pattern of behavior, a new set of ideas to believe in, and a new object for their affection and allegiance.

The selection out of the way, he worked on them with sex, drugs, music, religion, nature worship, fear, and a constant mixing of hate and love —hate of "them," and love of "us." And he did a masterful job of blending all of these in the daily routine of the Family's life, wherever they might be —in a house in the city, on one of the two ranches they occupied for months at a time, or in the wilds of the desert. He did it as he put them to work doing the menial chores necessary to their livelihood, he did it during meals, over which he always presided, and he did it on special occasions, with celebrations, parties, and drug or sex orgies.

Drugs and sex were always a part of their life. And Charlie always led the way. He made sure, however, that his drug doses were always much milder than anyone else's, and he always managed to be in control of the sex.

He put it all together into what can be seen as roughly three primary techniques: forging the break and isolation from the outside world; constant repetition of the replacement ideas and experiences for those former ties; and committed involvement in the Family's activities.

He pushed people into completing their break with their former lives by forcing them to do whatever he discovered they had inhibitions against —violence, theft, drugs, or sex. Sex was always involved this process. He initiated the new girls himself, before making them available to all of the others, male and female. And he used the girls to attract new males, as well as the more seductive males to attract new females. Whatever he found any one of them reluctant to do in sex, he forced them to do, and do it before the others. At the trial in 1970, one of the girls said, "Charlie helped us get rid of our middle class hang ups." He did, and he took steps to see that they remained rid of them —communication with the outside was simply cut off, not only did he forbid newspapers or literature except of his own choosing, he forbade clocks.

Repetition, though, was his strong suit. Unlike most terrorist groups, the Manson family did not have a stack of revolutionary or guerrilla manuals, nor did it produce piles of leaflets and communiques. Their politics and strategy were all in their heads —transferred from Manson's to the others' by his incessant talking, lecturing, and preaching. His political ideas were so far out —including the never openly stated but continuously insinuated idea that he was Jesus Christ come back to save the world— that they could have been passed on no other way. Not only is there plentiful evidence that this repetition worked, he consciously intended it to. He is reported to have remarked in court one day:

> You can convince anybody of anything if you just push it at them all of the time. They may not believe it 100 percent, but they will draw opinion from it, especially if they have no other information to draw their opinions from.

And he saw to the latter.

Finally, he got everyone involved, personally committed to the "new" life. The Family itself was total involvement. He had them so busy doing the work around the Family they did not have time to think or do anything else. One of their primary sources of supplies, food as well as clothing, was picking through garbage bins in nearby communities. That which they could not find there, or could not make themselves, they stole. Thus, as prosecuting attorney Bugliosi says in his book on them, they were led:

> Step by step [into] panhandling, petty theft, prostitution, burglaries, armed robberies, and last of all, for no motive of gain

70

but because it was Charlie's will, and Charlie's will is Man's Son, the final step, the ultimate definace of the establishment, the most positive proof of their total commitment —murder.

One, therefore, does not look to the personality of Lynette Fromme before she became part of the Family to understand how she came to point a gun at President Ford. Everything she did and said can be found right in the family album. As suggested earlier, her attack on Mr. Ford appeared to be a masterpiece of propaganda of the deed. It was weird, true, but that is the style in which she had been trained and disciplined.

Of course, we will undoubtedly never know the real truth about her staging of this affair, but it is easy enough to do some reasonably safe speculating. The specifics of the incident are that she thrust a forty-five caliber automatic pistol at President Ford and pulled the trigger. As she is said to have exclaimed at the time, "It didn't go off!" The reason for its not going off is simple, and probably intentional. There was no round in the firing chamber. That is, although bullets had been loaded into its magazine, none of them was in a position to fire. People familiar with this type of weapon know that to fire the first shot one has not only to fit a loaded magazine into its handle, but to work the slide atop its barrel so as to pick up the top round in the magazine and shove it into the firing chamber. Thereafter the slide throws itself backward and forward with each shot, as its name implies, automatically. This slide, though, is held in tension by a spring that is heavy, even to an adult man. The probability is essentially nil that a woman as slightly built as Lynette could pull that slide back the first time, especially standing in a crowd where she could not prop herself on some stationary support to get leverage. And those familiar with how long Lynette has been with the Family, and with the Family's habits of training with weapons, will realize she must have known all of this. The probability is that she attempted to do what a poker player might term as "checking locks." She created a situation which neither law enforcement nor the media could ignore, she pointed a loaded weapon at the President, but she arranged it so law enforcemnt, the establishment —even the whole society— could look bad for wanting to prosecute this frail young woman for attempted murder. There will undoubtedly be some public qualms over this, now or later. On the other hand, she set up a ruse by which law enforcement, especially the Secret Service and the FBI, could look a bit foolish and incompetent for not preventing such an apparently confused bumbling assailant from posing this threat in the first place. Some of that has already been plastered across the pages of our newspapers. Thus we have another of these damned if you do, and damned if you don't situations in which law enforcement —and hence the society— is bit by bit damaged without a full public realization of what is actually going on.

This is how terrorism works. Terrorists attack. A victim, whoever or whatever their target might be, sustains some damage which he cannot ignore, and he reacts. There is an immediate furor over the most spectacular aspects of the violence and the reaction to it. Then, as far as the public is concerned, the matter is relegated to past history. The victim nurses his wounds, and makes whatever adjustments in his life, or business, it all seemed to require. And the public is never engaged in the examination of what the longer-term threat of terrorism is. Yet it is the public, we the people, who finally absorb the damage the terrorist inflicts.

We are all somewhat like a ship's captain who sees two peaks of the iceberg that knocked a hole in the hull of his ship, but fails to concern himself with the parts of the ice formation less obvious than those standing in front of his face.

The two obvious peaks of terrorist operations are: a) the physical violence of an attack—kidnaping, assassination, bombing, or whatever; and b) the verbal element of the attack —the attempt to convert accusations of incompetence or wrongdoing on the part of the victim into a public issue.

Of course, in any appraisal of an incident we must consider both. They are visible and won't go away. But if the process is to stop there it can actually be counterproductive. In other words, if nothing of the whole affair is ever brought to the public's attention except these two peaks the proposition left in the public mind will stand precisely as the terrorists would have it stand:

$$\text{the degree of violence used} < \text{the evil toward which it was directed}$$

Again, that is exactly the impression the terrorists sought to create in the first place.

The mathematical symbol for *greater than* / *less than* was used in the above proposition because nothing else seems to illustrate so accurately the predictable picture terrorists will try to leave with the public. In other words, the routine is so pat we can express it as a formula without knowing what incident we are talking about. For, whatever level of violence they use on a given occasion, it will be explained on the basis that the evil it attacked was greater.

Look at the two peaks in the Hearst case. They are there. The kidnaping versus the great evils against which SLA claimed it was done. And the killing of Doctor Foster was done because of his crimes against the people. Black September killed and, no matter who was in their line of fire, immediately came up with justification in terms of monstrous evils they claimed overshadowed anything they had done.

Whether we accept any of these justifications or not, our attention is on them as we read of the violence the terrorists have brought down. Again, we are like that ship captain. We see only the violence itself and the justification, or issue, that the terrorists intended us to see. Yet, in addition to these two visible peaks there are invariably two other parts to the iceberg of terrorism: a propaganda effort and an organizing campaign. Thus, the whole of the iceberg looks something like this:

4) the violence	1) the "issue" raised	
		waterline
3) organizing operation	2) propaganda activities	

This is representative of the whole operation, the cycle through which the terrorist group is continually moving. It is the entirety of this cycle which produces the damage and poses the threat —and toward which responses must be directed.

You will note that the numbering of the elements of this cycle appears to be inconsistent with the experience of a terrorist attack as we see it in the press. For one thing, the numbering suggests that the actual violence is at the end of a series of activities, not at the beginning. This is true. This is why all of the cyclic elements must be considered if we are to understand the whole. The victim has been set up for the violence long before he is hit.

The issue has been chosen. It may be one already smoldering in the edges of the public consciousness, or it may be something the terrorist group feels should be made into an issue. A propaganda effort is launched, around the issue, and frequently around the eventual target. As we noted in our discussion of the Tupamaros, terrorists like to select targets that are already somewhat in public disfavor, or that can be pushed into such a position. Propaganda mentioning the potential target will usually be on the order of a hate campaign. It is simply easier to get away with hitting what the public has come to see as a bad guy, than one who will be considered an innocent victim. In the latter case, the after the fact propaganda will have to justify the act on the basis that, though innocent, the victim represents something evil. This is more difficult, so the bad guy type target is preferable.

There will have been a period of organizing. The terrorists will have organized, trained, and disciplined themselves. As often as not, they will be an arm or a splinter of some other extremist group —maybe the coming together of malcontents or splintered factions from several such groups. The Weatherman and SLA, in this country, and the various Palestinian groups, are examples. The organizing effort, though, is not all internal. Terrorists must have support and assistance, and above all they must have information —intelligence, if you will— money and places to hide, in order to dart out from a population, make an attack, and disappear back into that same population. The provision of such assistance takes propaganda and organizing work. It requires pulling help even from people who themselves would not knowingly engage in any aspect of terrorism. It requires information and funds that may not be seen by the providers as connected with the commission of violence—inside information that can be used to help make the issue and affix the bad guy image; and money for community projects through which to form a support base. Such organizational work may be extremely loose, but it may reach right into the potential target's own organization or premises.

In other words, the full threat of terrorism is not that some group is going to suddenly materialize, as if from outer space, and bomb a building or kidnap someone who has hostage value. The full threat is that the propaganda and organizing operations which precede one of these incidents have made the violence all but inevitable before hand. If these parts of the operation are left unchallenged, any action taken after the incident is going to run into what is literally a stacked deck —a propaganda game already programmed to make the victim look as if he got only what his sins earned him.

By way of a summary of how terrorism finally works we might apply the cycle just described to the development of a typical terrorist organization —a small, young one, for example. The cycle began as the potential terrorists came together around some issue they felt strongly enough about to be willing to take concerted action. They may or may not have had a particular political ideology in the beginning. Their initial association may have been completely spontaneous, or it may have been instigated by people with some knowledge and experience in extremist political activities. Or, the impetus may have been merely persuasive, reformist oriented, but was subsequently taken over by extremists —or hardened into a terrorist operation by the initial participants having fallen under the influence of extremist literature and ideas. Whatever the circumstances, the arrival of a group of people at the point of determination and preparation to launch into deliberate violence to further political goals is in itself indicative of more than spontaneity. The pattern is that they will already have gone through periods of self-indoctrination, propaganda work, weapons and tactical training, target selection, and support organization. These are the crucial phases of the terrorists' operation. It is to them one's attention must go not only in understanding how terrorism works, but in trying to devise ways for coping with it.

3.   Who Does It?

Convinced that only violence can change society, a small group
of fanatic young radicals has taken the dead-end road of
terrorism . . .
[*Life*, March 27, 1970]

Perhaps the most commonly heard answer to the question
before us now is a single, emotionally rendered word:
"Madman!" Certainly, it is tempting to leave it at that when
you contemplate some of the carnage and destruction their
attacks frequently leave. An emotional response is what
terrorism seeks to provoke. It is designed to cause people to
abandon rational thought, to dispense with factual consideration, and to react rigidly in ways that will not solve problems
but only lead to new ones. Emotionalism does not help in the
understanding of any facet of terrorism, least of all, in the
understanding of who does it. And the answer to this question
is extremely important as a stepping stone to the other
questions that lay in the way of finally saying what can be done
about it.

In an October 1974 article in the magazine *Commentary,*
Walter Laqueur, chairman of the Research Council at the
Center for Strategic and International Studies at Georgetown
University, set the stage for a rational consideration of the
immediate question:

> Seen in historical perspective, guerrilla warfare, per se, is
> neither good nor bad, certainly not more reprehensible
> morally than war itself. On many occasions it has been a

perfectly legitimate, sometimes the only possible, method of resisting national or social oppression. Such oppression has not gone out of fashion in the contemporary world and it has resulted in guerrilla warfare wherever physical conditions have been favorable. But at the same time it has become more and more obvious that what was once known as guerrilla warfare is gradually giving way in many countries to terrorist tactics, pure and simple, on the part of small groups (whether of the "Left," as in Argentina, or of the "Right," as in Italy, or raving mad, like the Symbionese Liberation Army) trying to impose their will on the majority in the struggle for power. . . .

These lines say a great deal to the task of sorting out who commits terrorism in a world where violence of various kinds occurs day in and day out.

We could hope for a world with no violence, but we could hardly expect to have it in the foreseeable future. We can deplore war, as Walter Laqueur obviously does, but we cannot dismiss it as a means by which nations may have to defend themselves for a long time to come. We can certainly take a stand against the unjust use of violence by governments, and governmental agencies, but we can hardly say that the mandates they hold to protect the lives and property of their people does not require them to use force. There is absolutely no equivalency, however, between a legally constituted police organization jailing a lawbreaker or, in fact, shooting one whose willingness to act violently leaves no other choice, and a band of private citizens deciding to deny the freedom of, or take the lives of, fellow citizens to make a political point. Some of the emotionalism inspired by terrorists has caused this type of comparison to be made only too often in recent times.

On the other hand, especially as Americans celebrating the Bicentennial of 1776, none of us can deny that "in the course of human events" there are time when people are suffering such intolerable oppression they have the right to use violence to try to overcome it. As Laqueur said, that sort of oppression has yet to be banished from the world.

Thus, any attempt to determine who is committing

terrorism is made with the risk of throwing the sheep in with the goats, no matter how conscientiously it is approached. There are some broad considerations, however, that if properly taken into account will reduce this risk. One of these is a realization that the mix of political extremism with honest intentions to overcome real injustices came together in the origin of most of today's political violence, wherever it occurs.

In 1970, in the midst of the first great upsurge of violence in the 1968-75 period we are examining, the media in the United States concerned themselves for a brief time with the question of who was involved in the violence in our country. It was typical of the coverage they gave the subject to provide a brief review of the upheaval on the campuses and in the streets with fairly frequent references to the radical movement that had germinated within the civil rights sit-ins and marches and burst fully into being during the massive protests over the war in Vietnam. Such stories usually noted, quite accurately, that the majority of the people who had taken to the streets were merely seeking redress for what they perceived as wrongs in society, but that there were some within their numbers who had become attached to the idea of revolution—and some among the revolutionists who had decided on courses of violence to accomplish their ends.

The Black Panther Party was in this last category. Several of their leaders said so in public speeches—even on national television—and their party newspaper carried the same message in fiery, rhetoric-laden headlines and gory, gun-slinging graphics. The Panthers put their words into action by literally "picking up the gun" against the police. Various splinter groups of the deliberately radicalized Students for a Democratic Society (SDS), however, initiated what has become the most sustained campaign of terrorism in the U.S. The paths these groups opened were the primary ones along which middle-class, college-educated young men and women took to acts of violence which no one would have thought they were likely even to contemplate. The blasts they let loose were as much of a psychological shock to the public as they were physical.

One such was the destruction, on March 6, 1970, of a $250,000 townhouse in Greenwich Village in New York. The four-story building was totally destroyed, several buildings nearby were damaged, and the force of the explosion was felt throughout the area. What at first was presumed to be a gas leak detonation was quickly discovered to be the accidental explosion of a large quantity of dynamite five members of the Weatherman faction of SDS had been using to make bombs— lethal assemblies of explosive stuffed into lengths of pipe taped around with quantities of nails. Three members of the crew of this crude bomb factory, two young men and a young woman, died in the blast. Two young women, though their arms, legs, and faces were cut and bleeding and their clothes were blown half off, escaped in the immediate confusion and became long-term fugitives. Both were already under indictment for their participation in what they had called "Days of Rage" in Chicago a few months earlier.

Prompted by this townhouse incident, *Life* ran a short pictorial on this and other explosions and bomb threats in the U.S. The article began with the paragraph from which the lines at the beginning of this chapter were taken. It read:

> A bomb set off in a public place is a message of hate addressed to whom it may concern. Madmen do such things; fortunately madmen are usually caught, perhaps because they are mad and want to be. In the past few weeks, however, bombs and bomb threats have taken on an altogether new and terrifying meaning in the United States. Convinced that only violence can change society, a small group of fanatic young radicals has taken the dead end road of terrorism . . .

This was, indeed, true. The ruins of the townhouse contained stacks of SDS and Weatherman literature. The five workers in this bomb factory were products of the split at the SDS national convention in June of 1969. They were among the more militant members of SDS who had been agitating for a guerrilla stance for months. Their particular faction split off in that direction at the convention, adopted the name Weatherman, gave their ideas a few trial runs in the fall, held a National War Council in December of that year and went underground. From this sanctuary of sympathy and support they began their bombing attacks, and into this sanctuary the two survivors of the townhouse explosion disappeared.

The weekly news magazines, of course, published roundups and commentaries on what they saw going on at the time. One of the pieces typical of this coverage was a three-page spread in the May 11, 1970 editon of *Newsweek,* headlined: "The Revolutionaries—A Guide to Who They Are, What They Want." Centered within the first two, facing, pages of this piece was a three-column photograph of a night-time gathering in front of the U.S. capitol in Washington with several people holding up a large cloth banner which read:

POLITICAL POWER GROWS OUT OF THE BARREL OF
A GUN

Mao

FREE BOBBY SEALE

The occasion was a demonstration in favor of Black Panther leader Seale, who had been arraigned in New Haven, Connecticut on charges of murder and kidnaping. The caption to the photo read: "Radical rally in Washington: Part crusade, part terrorism, part celebration of youth, part total communal ecstasy.'" It was a good photo, and a good caption. Between the two there was a fair thumbnail description of the situation.

Within sub-headed sections of the piece the magazine named some of the better-organized, harder-line groups that had sprouted and grown in the fertile soil of dissent of the late 1960's: the enduring, violence prone SDS splinter, the Weathermen; the prime agent of the splintering, the Maoist oriented Progressive Labor Party; the busily organizing Trotskyite youth arm, the Young Socialist Alliance; the fiery talking, police baiting Black Panthers; and the street-gang derived Young Lords—as well as some of the ad hoc groups that were to spring up, and try to attract the loosely organized radicals on the campuses, or die or merge with other groups. The opening paragraph of the *Newsweek* article began with an insight into the deeper backgrounds of some of the people within these organizations:

> In 1964, a small band of American radicals made their way to Cuba and, in the course of their stay, had a talk with Che Guevara. They told him how much they envied him: his revolution had worked, his countrymen by and large supported the cause. In the United States, they said, the revolutionaries' lot was a far less happy one: they were damned by the very people they wanted to liberate . . .

The conversation with Che Guevara went on. He is said to have replied to the Americans:

> I envy you. You North Americans are very lucky. You are fighting the most important fight of all—you live in the heart of the beast. [Capitalism was apparently the "beast" he meant]

This remark was enshrined in pages of underground newspapers all over the U.S. One interesting example was in the July 20, 1970 edition of *The Rag,* published in Austin, Texas. The paper gave over its front page to a poster of Che, overlaid on an outline map of South America, with his "I envy you . . ." remark, and a reproduction of the Uruguayan Tupamaro's star-and-T symbol, featured at the bottom of the poster.

Actually, however, this small band of American radicals totalled eighty-four, was not the first group to go, and did not make their way entirely on their own but rather had it made for them. A group of fifty-nine had gone to Cuba the year before—in 1963. Phillip Abbot Luce, author of the book *The New Left Today,* who was one of those to make the 1963 trip, and was chairman of the Student Travel Committee to Cuba which sent off the 1964 contingent, indicates both groups had the trips pretty much handed to them. He says the first trip was proposed in the fall of 1962 by the Progressive Labor Party. When the PLP representative approached the Cubans with the idea, Luce says they "jumped at the opportunity and immediately appropriated half a million dollars" to help finance it. This first trip was supposed to go in December of

1962, by way of Canada, where a chartered Cuban plane was to pick up the travelers. It was cancelled when the planners learned that the Canadians would not allow the Cuban plane to land. In June of 1963, when the trip finally got under way, what otherwise would have been a ninety-mile hop from the shores of the U.S. became a complicated journey through Paris and Prague, to circumvent the government ban on travel to Cuba. The 1964 visit *Newsweek* reported took the same route. Four of the 1963 travelers were indicted by the Federal government for making the trip and conspiring to send others on it. Nine were indicted for the one in 1964.

Further trips under the sponsorship of the PLP were not attempted, apparently because of concern for getting some of its members sent to prison. By the time the *Newsweek* article was written, a new effort had been mounted and over a thousand American young people had gone to Cuba as members of three Venceremos Brigades. Additional ones went in succeeding years. According to the Simon and Schuster book *Venceremos Brigade,* written by various participants in these trips, the National Committee which set up this program consisted of representatives from many organizations on the left. SDS was one of these. SDS had been recruiting people to go to Cuba to help harvest its 1970 sugar crop for six months before the first group departed. For example, in the June 18, 1969 issue of its national newspaper, *New Left Notes,* SDS called for 300 volunteers for the first brigade. Actually less than 250 went. The paper said brigadistas were being recruited from activists of the revolutionary movement in this country: blacks, Latinos, white-working class youth, students, and dropouts GI's. The paper said the brigades were to have three purposes:

> To politically, morally and materially support Cuba in the critical sugar harvest of 1970 with its goal of 10 million tons.
>
> To educate people about imperialism and about the international revolution against imperialism. This will be accomplished through a well-developed education and propaganda program . . .
>
> To gain a practical understanding of the creative applica-

tion of communist principles on a day-to-day basis. The New Left in the advanced capitalist countries has, in the last decade, clearly defined itself within the tradition of socialist and communist struggle began a century ago . . .

According to the book *Venceremos Brigade,* there was a bonus for many of the brigadistas in the chance to meet true revolutionaries, not only Cuban, but Vietnamese, Korean, Latin American or African who were often in Cuba.

The *Newsweek* article suggested that some of the people who had gone to Cuba were bent on revolution in the U.S., but no longer saw any hope of overturning this society without bloodshed and selective destruction of property. And four out of the five Weathermen members in the Greenwich Village bomb factory explosion had been to a revolutionary gathering in Havana on July 4-7, 1969. They opted for a strategy of terror shortly after coming home, and before the next July 4 two of their number would have shed the final drop of their own blood as they tried to put that strategy to work.

Elsewhere in the world, more seasoned terrorists, whom these American beginners might have encountered in their travels, had already been at work. From January to August, 1968, a group in Guatemala calling itself the Armed Forces of the Revolution shot to death the U.S. ambassador to that country and two senior military officers on the staff of the U.S. Defense Attache. In July of 1968, three members of the Popular Front for the Liberation of Palestine hijacked an Israeli airliner flying out of Rome and forced it to Algiers.

In August 1969, a TWA 707 was hijacked to Damascus and destroyed. In September, two revolutionary groups in Brazil cooperated in the kidnaping of the U.S. ambassador to that country. In the same month, revolutionaries in Ethiopia kidnaped the U.S. Consul General in Asmara. The next month one Swiss diplomat, and the son of another, were kidnaped in Colombia—both released 17 days later, after their families had paid ransoms.

As suggested earlier, 1970 was a particularly busy year for terrorists. In February a time bomb aboard a Swiss airliner exploded as the craft was en route from Zurich to Tel Aviv, killing thirty-eight passengers and nine crew members. Palestinians were suspected, but denied any responsibility.

On the very day of the Weatherman bomb factory explosion in Greenwich Village, the Guatemalan group that had killed the U.S. ambassador and two American military officers in 1968, grabbed the U.S. labor attache and held him until their government released two of their comrades from prison. During the month of March 1970 there were five more kidnapings and one unsuccessful attempt. A Japanese consul general in Brazil, a U.S. National Geographic team in Ethiopia, a Paraguayan consul in Argentina, the U.S. air attache in the Dominican Republic, and the West German ambassador to Guatemala, were all kidnaped by various leftist guerrillas. The West German was killed when kidnap demands were not met. The terrorists succeeded in freeing twenty-five prisoners with two of the other kidnapings. The Paraguayan was released although demands were not met. And the unsuccessful attempt was by a right wing group trying to kidnap the Soviet assistant commercial attache in Argentina. As if to round the month off, on March 29 Palestinian terrorists bombed the U.S. embassy in Beirut.

In April, members of the Popular Revolutionary Vanguard in Brazil attempted to kidnap the U.S. Consul General, and a U.S. Peace Corps volunteer and his wife were taken from a train and detained for five days by revolutionaries in Ethiopia. And Palestinians made an assault on the U.S. embassy in Jordan, causing some $100,000 damage.

On May 21, 1970 a surprise communique was sent out from a clandestine cell of the Weathermen. It was called a "Declaration of a State of War" against the U.S. and began:

> This is the first communication from the Weatherman underground.
> All over the world, people fighting Amerikan [sic*] imperialism look to Amerika's youth to use our strategic positoin behind enemy lines to join forces in the destruction of the empire . . .

*The spelling Amerika is deliberate and quite common with such groups. It is a try for symbolic reinforcement of their claims that the U.S. is fascistic.

It continued, saying the Weathermen had learned that "revolutionary violence is the only way." Thus, they said, they were adapting the guerrilla strategies of the Vietcong and the Tupamaros to the situation in the U.S. The communique also promised "within the next 14 days we will attack a symbol or institution of Amerikan injustice." On June 9 they bombed a police headquarters in New York.

This pattern was to be repeated several times during the year—Weatherman communiques, all signed by Bernardine Dohrn, and attacks, usually with bombs. Bernardine, a former national officer of SDS—and the holder of three degrees, including a doctorate of law, from the University of Chicago—became the voice of the Weatherman organization. In fact, she preferred Weather People, as the apparently increasing number of females recruited to its ranks put women virtually in control of the organization. She spoke in tones that seemed to be a mixture of high-school cheerleading and chanting that might have been appropriate at a satanic black mass. She described meetings with revolutionaries from other countries, in the Middle East as well as in Cuba, as if they were gatherings of sorority sisters, and piled on anything she considered an attack on the U.S. system as if it were a new score on some invisible board to which all of her listeners' eyes were riveted. Of the Manson Family's bloody murders of seven people in August of the previous year she said:

> Dig it; first they killed those pigs, then they ate dinner in the same room with them, then they even shoved a fork into a victim's stomach! Wild!

After the Hearst kidnaping, she sent what San Francisco newspapers called a guarded approval—gleefully praising the kidnaping of the daughter of a rich and powerful man in order to provide food for the poor, but saying she did not comprehend the execution of Marcus Foster . . . a Black person who was not a recognized enemy of his people.

In the last days of May 1970, by the time Bernardine's communique was being printed in radical papers all over the United States, a revolutionary organization known as the

Montoneros (Mountaineers), in Argentina, had kidnaped a former president of that country—holding him until mid July and then shooting him to death.

And two days before the Weathermen bombed the New York police headquarters in June of 1970, members of the Popular Front for the Liberation of Palestine kidnaped the U.S. political secretary in Jordan—releasing him unharmed a day later when the Jordanian government refused to meet their demands. Two days after that members of the National Liberation Action organization and the Popular Revolutionary Vanguard in Brazil kidnaped the West German ambassador to that country. He was released unharmed five days later, following the Brazilian government's release of forty prisioners. In the same month renegade Palestinian terrorists broke into several American homes in Jordan, searched and looted them, and raped the wives of two U.S. officials.

The next month guerrillas in Bolivia took two West German technicians hostage until their government released ten prisoners. The Weathermen bombed Bank of America offices on Wall Street. And the Tupamaros pulled two kidnapings and attempted another in Uruguay. They successfully took a U.S. public safety advisor and a Brazilian consul, and attempted the abduction of the second secretary to the U.S. embassy in Montevideo—all with demands that their government release 150 of their comrades from prison. The government refused. The American, Dan Mitrione, was killed ten days later. The Brazilian was released in February of the next year after his family had paid an undisclosed amount of cash ransom.

The Tupamaros continued their campaign into August with the kidnaping of a U.S. agricultural advisor they held until March of 1971 when he had a serious heart attack. They released him for medical attention.

In the first days of September 1970 the specific chain of events were started which would eventually lead to much terrorist bloodletting by the organization calling itself Black September—at Rome, Munich, and Lod, among other places. This was the month of reversals for Palestinian guerrillas from which the soon to be formed secret terrorist organization took its name. As we recounted earlier, on September 6 the Popular Front for the Liberation of Palestine provoked a disastrous campaign against all of the guerrillas present in Jordan by deciding to use the country's territory in connection with a multiple hijacking which resulted in the destruction of four huge jets belonging to airlines of three different countries. As if that might not have been enough, Palestinians also kidnaped two Americans, a cultural affairs officer and an army sergeant, in the same month. Before it was over King Hussein's troops and aircraft had made it indeed a black September for the guerrillas.

At almost the same moment, in the U.S., the Weathermen had pulled off a bank robbery in Massachusetts, in which a policeman was killed, and engineered a jailbreak in California. The latter was to take some of their members right into the Middle East and into direct communication with the Palestinian movement. On September 13, 1970, they helped Dr. Timothy Leary, high priest of the drug culture, escape from the California Men's Colony near San Luis Obispo where he was serving a term for a narcotics offense. A small team then disguised him, spirited him all the way across the United States, and flew him on a commercial airliner to a Black Panther sanctuary in Algiers. The Panther operation in Algiers had been set up in May 1969 by Eldridge Cleaver who had left the U.S. to avoid a parole revocation hearing. Several other Panthers subsequently followed suit and joined him there. According to Cleaver's writings the Algerian government gave his group the same facilities it provided to other liberation organizations from around the world. Thus, as the Weathermen installed Leary in Algiers, and as they and other Americans visited him and Cleaver, they also exulted in meeting and rubbing shoulders with revolutionaries from Africa, Asia, and Latin America, as well as from taking little trips among the Palestinian guerrillas in other Arab countries.

In October, while the Weathermen were setting off more than a dozen bombs—in Chicago, New York, Florida, California and Washington—their compatriots to the north, the Front for the Liberation of Quebec were kidnaping two government officials, one British and one Canadian. The kidnapers demanded the release of thirteen prisoners and $500,000 in gold, both of which the Canadian government refused. The Briton, his government's Trade Commissioner, was eventually released unharmed and his kidnapers flown to Cuba. The Canadian, Quebec Labor Minister Pierre La Porte, was found murdered a little over a week after his abduction.

November saw a kidnap attempt against the U.S. ambassador to Iran. And on December 1 the ETA (Freedom for the Basque Homeland), in Spain, kidnaped the West German consul stationed in San Sebastian. The demand was for the release of sixteen prisoners, but some lesser arrangement seems to have been worked out for his return three weeks later. On December 7, two cooperating groups of guerrillas in Brazil kidnaped the Swiss ambassador to that country.

Toward the end of 1970, in another of the weekly news magazines' spurts of concern with the build-up of terrorism, *Time* devoted a considerable portion of an edition to the subject of urban guerrillas. The magazine said that though the similarities among guerrilla groups seemed less a matter of conspiracy than a kind of contagion or psychological empathy, there was evidence of not only extensive communication between organizations, but exchanges of moral support and financial backing. It said there was no lack of spots where guerrillas of several continents could get together. And it cited Cuba specifically as having provided this sort of refuge, and as having trained more than 5,000 foreigners in such techniques as sabotage, bomb making, and murder from 1961 through 1970. Most of these people had come from Latin America, the magazine said, but there had been many from the U.S. Several Weathermen and Black radicals were mentioned by name.

The magazine put its finger on another aspect of the matter that is probably of more final importance than the get togethers in Latin America, the Mideast, and Asia:

One reason the new terror often appears to be epidemic is

that the tactics are so similar. The guerrillas all study the
same texts—by Mao or Che or Carlos Marighella.

[*Time,* November 2, 1970.]

This may be a great deal more accurate than the writer of those
lines realized. The magazine cited what it called a global cross-
pollination of radicalism through literature and communications. This becomes quite obvious when one studies the
reading lists and book and film reviews appearing in the
newspapers and magazines that revolutionaries and
revolutionary sympathizers the world over continuously turn
out. And it must be noted that the volume of propaganda and
instructional material these groups either produce or adapt to
their purposes from other sources, and thus surround
themselves with, borders on the unbelievable. The printed
material alone is astounding. Perhaps an idea of this can be
seen in a listing of the books, manuals, pamphlets, and
reproduced articles, etc, law enforcement officials found in a
house from which the very small SLA had fled. Newspaper
accounts gave us an idea of the weapons this group had and
sometimes mentioned literature, but it is doubtful that many
newspaper readers would imagine anything like this actual
accounting from one SLA hideout in Los Angeles::

On Organizing Urban Guerrilla Units
The Paper Trip
Credit!
100 Ways to Disappear and Live Free
Headin' South
National Liberation War in Viet Nam
Beat the Heat: A Radical Survival Handbook
For the Liberation, by Carlos Marighella
Dialectical and Historical Materialism, by Joseph Stalin
Theory and Practice of Modern Revisionists, by Jaques
  Grippa
Guerrilla Broadcasting
Marx to Mao Tse-tung
Oppose Book Worship, by Mao
The Police Weapons Center

Special Forces Demolitions Techniques
Quotations from Chairman Mao Tse-tung
150 Questions for A Guerrilla, by General Albert Bayo
Selected Readings from the Works of Mao Tse-tung
U.S. Cal. 30 Carbine
The Essential Stalin
Mao Tse-tung, A Biography, by Jules Archer
Tricontinental, spring 1973
Malcolm X Talks to Young People
"Revolution, Violent and Nonviolent" (from February 1968
    Liberation)
"Fingerprint Identification" (FBI Pamphlets)
"Mao Tse-tung: People of the World, Unite and Defeat the
    U.S. Aggressors and All Their Running Dogs" (statement
    of May 20, 1970)
"Mao Tse-tung: Where Do Correct Ideas Come From?"
"Venceremos"
Lenin: "Of the Struggle Against Revisionism"
Sandigan, Filipino Newcomers Service Center Handbook,
    San Francisco
"Letter to a Comrade on our Organizational Tasks," by V.I.
    Lenin:
In Defense of Self Defense
Operation and Care of 9mm Parabellum Automatic Pistol
"Ithaca Gun Model 37 Repeater"
"Buying a Used Gun"
"The Browning Hi-Power Pistols"
The American Rifleman, issues of January and July 1973
The Foundations of Leninism, J.V. Stalin
"Declaration of Regis Debray at his court martial in Bolivia,
    November 1967"
"Comrade George, An Investigation Into the Official Story
    of His Assassination"
Realistic Guide to Police, Fire and Aircraft Radio
The Firearms Dictionary
"The State and Revolution," by V.I. Lenin
Blood in My Eye, by George Jackson
"The U.S. Military Apparatus"

"The University-Military-Police Complex"
Mini-Manual of the Urban Guerrilla, by Carlos Marighella
U.S. Carbine Cal. .30 M-1, Parts
Simple Shotgun Repairs
"Statement by Mao Tse-tung in Support of the Afro-American Struggle Against Violent Repression"

Even though this list is of the collection of literature chosen by a very small group that was in operation only a short period of time, it is quite illustrative of the texts which *Time* said the perpetrators of the current epidemic of terrorism all study. We could add to the list above, and will cite some films and other materials, but those mentioned make the point.

The works of one of the authors that we saw in this SLA list are so widely used—and so pointed toward pure terrorism—as to warrant special comment. These are the instructional writings of the Brazilian revolutionary Carlos Marighella. His ideology does not differ from Mao's or Che's, both of whom *Time* also cited. He was, in fact, an enthusiastic student of both the Chinese and Cuban revolutions. But Marighella's writings are tactically specific, and technically practical. He wrote of assassinations, kidnaping, street fighting, ambushes, and sniping, all in how to do it detail. He advocated bank robberies for financing revolutionary operations and went into minute details on how they should be carried out. He wrote of the use of propaganda and the making of weapons and explosives from easily obtainable materials. And he was writing of things he knew about. He had been working at some form of revolution for over thirty years, had founded his own organization—the National Liberation Action—and was a practicing terrorist chief when he was trapped and killed by police in San Paulo in the fall of 1969. Indeed, the particular incident that led to this entrapment by the police was his kidnaping of the U.S. ambassador to Brazil on September 4, 1969.

As *Time* points out, Marighella's writings continue to live. His *Minimanual of the Urban Guerrilla* has been widely circulated among terrorists in many parts of the world. As testimony to the contagion some governments fear this *Minimanual* carries, it has been banned in many Latin American countries. And it was outlawed in some countries in Europe after being published there in 1969 and 1970. Though it has caused much concern among law enforcement authorities in the U.S., it has been reproduced and passed around liberally in radical circles in this country and extensively excerpted in underground newspapers in almost all of our large cities.

Time was correct in seeing the spread of the epidemic as more from this sort of literature than from a true master conspiracy. We have seen enough in these pages thus far to understand that there are ideological differences and strategy conflicts among the terrorists—even within individual countries—as well as cooperation, at least temporary alliances, and mergers and splits. We will look at additional cases of all of these as we go along. Also, there is no question but what there are secret agreements and working arrangements that are not visible to outsiders, and not likely to be. The situation still does not add up to the sort of grand conspiracy that might have offered us a simple explanation we could tie up into a neat package as most of us like to do. Nor does any admission that this cannot be done, of itself, advance our understanding of terrorism—and who does it.

Someone may say that it should be simple enough to name the organizations that commit terrorism. All one needs to do is to produce a list of incicents of terrorism and identify their perpetrators. It is not quite that simple. We have just discussed a number of incidents we have labeled as terrorism occurring from the beginning of 1968 to the end of 1970—1970 being, in our opinion, the height of the first great peak of the current epidemic. We can certainly pull out the names of the organizations responsible for these incidents and say they are part of the who does it. We can extend this process through the whole period we are looking at and produce a longer list of incidents, and a longer list of organizations. We have done both of these things. We will discuss the findings from them in general terms. The detailed results are contained in the appendix.

It would be a disservice however, simply to put down these results without some explanation as to how they were obtained, and why this or that entry is included and another is not. We noted in the introduction to this chapter that we are not dealing with matters that are completely cut and dried. What we have done is to go over all of the incidents coming to our attention that might be considered terrorism and weigh them within the terms of reference we have been discussing since the first paragraph of the first chapter of this book. We feel confident with our results, and believe they are useful in gaining an appreciation for the size of the threat terrorism poses, and for studying trends, and patterns of actions and outcomes within incidents. Since the list we compiled is based on such internal decision processes they are not likely to coincide completely with other lists even for the same time period.

And there are numerous lists. They appear piecemeal in periodic commentaries and reviews of the situation in the press. Some entries are carried in yearbooks of important happenings in the world. Magazines produce them from time to time, as do books such as this one. Data on terrorist incidents is collected by technical libraries, and libraries and library services catering to legislative bodies, and stored into machines for demand printouts. Research organizations, both government and private, compile lists of incidents, for publication as well as for use in studies they are conducting. Commercial security companies compile such lists for circulation among client industrial organizations whose personnel and property they are in business to protect against terrorism as well as any other type of threat. Then, of course, law enforcement agencies maintain lists.

Although many of the agencies and institutions mentioned above have official sources of such information, including direct observation of incidents in areas where they have representatives, the initial information on incidents usually comes to them all through the press. They build, revise, and correct from there. The press simply has a constantly operating, worldwide information network, and everyone uses it. After the first flash on an incident, further information and details are sought according to the importance of the people and circumstances involved. Thus, incidents are picked up or discarded according to the facts eventually developed. Everyone who is engaged in keeping up with such matters is always comparing his findings with those of others, but still compiling a list according to the needs and criteria of his own organization. No two lists so compiled are identical.

There are several reasons for the differences beyond those imposed by differences in the needs or resources of the various people putting the information together. And these reasons are actually of substantive importance to an understanding of any answer you might receive to the question of who does it. They involve matters which our political leaders, legislators, and diplomats have to deal with as they try to enact laws and reach international agreements to curb terrorism. These, in turn, are matters on which individual citizens need to be able to express themselves and take stands which they can themselves defend. The struggle in which terrorists kill innocent people, and destroy property which the citizen must finally pay for, is for the public mind.

The first of these reasons is not one we are likely to be able to do anything about—nor perhaps should we want to. That is the simple fact that there is no single, omniscient authority—human or machine—which can hand out a master list to which we can all refer. Even with all of our electronic means of communication and record-keeping, the world is too big, and human affairs are too complex, for there to be anything close to a hundred percent accuracy in such information. This is the least important of the reasons for the various listings not being in total agreement, but it is a reality.

The next reason for inconsistencies is both important and manageable. It is the practice by some compilers of picking up an incident as terrorism only if it can be labeled international—or transnational. In other words, applying the criterion of international to their accounting system they omit any incident which does not involve people or territory of more than one nation. This is not without logic. Especially in the early days, the only incidents of what could be considered terrorism to come to widespread attention were those that involved people or territory belonging to more than one nation. Many lists one picks up these days, indeed, begin with the assassination of U.S. Ambassador John G. Mein, on August 28, 1968, in Guatemala. There was even a way of looking at this type of incident as involving *three* parties, not just the obvious two: here, the United States and Guatemala. The third party was the terrorist organization. And some definitions sprang up in those days which still hold to the idea that terrorism is violence by one of two parties to an existing conflict against a citizen or property of a third party. Of course, in a sense, the assassination of the U.S. ambassador in Guatemala fit this line of reasoning, as did the murder of the West German ambassador there two years later—both by the same guerrilla organization. There had been a running fight between the Guatemalan government and the rather well supported, rural based guerrillas since the Mid 1950's. Thus the government and the guerrilla group were the two parties to a conflict, and each of the ambassadors was the citizen of a third party. We have to note that this reasoning automatically accorded the guerrillas a legitimacy they may or may not have been entitled to.

Further, in those early days we were still in something of a state of shock over the idea of the highest official representative any nation sends to live and work in another being deliberately murdered by people within the nation to which he had been sent. And we must realize Mr. Mein was the first U.S. ambassador in history to be assassinated. The fact that the assassins might have been killing citizens of their own country, and destroying locally owned property, for some time already seemed another matter.

And, of course, in the thirty months following Mr. Mein's assassination, at least sixteen other accredited representatives of eight countries were kidnaped, and/or killed, in seven host countries. The contagion *Time* spoke of seemed to have broken out and spread primarily toward diplomatic circles.

This was more illusion than reality. Notwithstanding the understandable concept of the internal affairs of a sovereign nation being matters properly the subject of its own concern, the infection at the international level had been transmitted directly—and predictably—from domestic terrorism. The texts terrorists read provide for it. Marighella, for example, speaks of kidnaping or killing foreign figures in the same breath with which he advocates doing the same to local ones. He goes on to explain that not only should actual opponents of the cause be selected as victims, but anyone who is important enough, or well enough known to provide a useful propaganda opportunity. A timely recognition that those who seek to manipulate murder, kidnaping, and sabotage into political power for themselves do not select targets in such terms as domestic and international could be important in very real ways. It might sound warnings before some of the incidents rather than after them.

Closely related to the line of reasoning that terrorism is only an international incident is the apparent attitude of some compilers that attacks against only governmental figures belong on a list of terrorist incidents. Again, this is understandable because for perhaps the first five and a half years of the epidemic the targets—at least in those incidents attracting wide attention—were all civilian or military officials of governments, local or foreign. However, the terrorists' textbooks would include business executives, entertainment personalities, and sports figures, as well as government officials. Look at the Munich example in 1972. Then, in mid 1973, there was a spate of attacks against business executives, again local and foreign. Some compilers don't carry any of these. Perhaps they don't for two reasons: a) the targets were not people for whom governments must provide diplomatic protection—the international angle; and b) the kidnap demands were usually for cash or economic concessions, not for what have been traditionally considered political ones.

Again, we must look at what the textbooks say. First, these manuals for revolution do not make such nice distinctions between political and economic matters. Everything has political connotations for the revolutionary who is trying to overturn the whole system. Second, robbery and extortion are repeatedly recommended as means for financing these operations. Any list that omits incidents of kidnaping by terrorists because only money was demanded fails to call attention to millions of dollars thus becoming available to their organizations for supplies, additional weapons and explosives, and even for recruiting and training activities. We have noted examples of cash ransoms up to $60,000,000 collected by the same organizations that kidnap and kill for more obviously political purposes.

Taken together, the international and strictly political criteria some compilers use give us a distorted picture of the terrorist situation—world-wide, as well as within individual countries. Such accounting does not alert us to the size of the financial resources the terrorists have gained, and we are not shown some of the hot spots of terroristic activity until they become major media events.

For example, one list picks up only one kidnaping in Argentina for the same period in which others pick up a dozen or more—and by the same terrorist organization. One list barely indicates any terrorism in Argentina at all during 1973, while another shows thirty-six incidents on which there can be no doubt. The truth of the matter is that terrorism reached epidemic level in that country by 1973. And there had been so many kidnapings and threats of kidnaping of business executives and their families in Argentina that many major corporations moved management operations elsewhere.

The distortion we are talking about is by no means restricted to Argentina. The same type of accounting picks up all of the incidents of violence by the Irish Republican Army in England, because that is international, but none in Ireland, because that is domestic. It results in some lists carrying the actions of the SLA and some not carrying them. We would have to contend, as we obviously indicated, that the SLA's actions were highly significant. If for no other reason, this is true because the Hearst case was the first political kidnapping in the U.S. The point that terrorism had reached that stage in this country is in itself significant.

More important, however, than any of these rather technical or legalistic reasons for discrepancies in the information that is available on terrorism is a political one—a blockage that interferes with governments openly agreeing, even within their own executive, legislative, and judicial structures, what groups we are all really talking about. This is the entanglement of pure rhetoric and propaganda into the efforts to determine which groups are terrorists, pure and simple—using violence to accumulate political power for their own purposes—and which are the bonafied creations of whole peoples rising up against national or social oppression. This is the point Walter Laqueur was getting at in the passage we quoted from him in the introduction to this chapter. As he suggests, few conscientious observers of history would be willing to say that there are not times when there is no other way for people to overcome truly intolerable oppression than through the violence of guerrilla warfare. Yet, it is quite obvious that many of the groups claiming to be involved in this kind of struggle today have no legitimacy outside the fiction of their own creation. The failure to cut through this fiction and arrive at clear agreements on the distinctions between these groups—again, even within governments of countries beset with terrorism—is at the bottom of our general failure to enact and enforce national or international measures for dealing with the epidemic of it.

This is finally the essence of the question we are now exploring. All of the organizations committing acts of terrorism insist they are using violence legitimately. According to them, it is those who take action against them that are using it illegitimately. Most of them claim they are a people, acting through the only means available to free or defend themselves. Those who raise a hand against them are enemies of the people, or as Marighella phrased it, enemies of the revolution, and to be dealt with accordingly. Even when the terrorists don't claim to be the people themselves, they say they are acting for the people. Che Guevara liked to think of it that way. None of the terrorists admit to acting in anything less than the interests of a people, even though, as with Guevara in Bolivia, the only people actually around obviously want nothing to do with them.

Part of the political blockage hindering the distinctions that are so desperately needed is, indeed, a constant muddling of this term "the people." Perhaps many political leaders don't like to push for a clarification of this term because they play games with it too. It would appear, however, that even they do not grasp the sense in which the term is used in the propaganda we have been looking at. There it is more of a military term than a political one. We have to know that usage before we can cut through the fiction within which it appears.

Guevara knew it, when he was packing off to try to start a revolution here or there, Marighella knew it, when he was laying down his instructions as to who should be the targets of the terrorists' guns. Both were avid students of Mao Tse-Tung, however, and Mao offers the clearest explanation of the term. In fact, he apparently offered his explanation because he felt a clarification was needed:

> . . . we must first be clear on what is meant by "the people" and what is meant by "the enemy." The concept of "the people" varies in content in different countries and in different periods of history in the same country. Take our own country for example. During the War of Resistance against Japan, all those classes, strata and social groups opposing Japanese aggression came within the category of the people, while the Japanese imperialists, the Chinese traitors and the pro-Japanese elements were all enemies of the people. During the War of Liberation, the U.S. imperialists and their running dogs—the bureaucrat-capitalists, the landlords and the Koumintang reactionaries who represented these two classes—were the enemies of the people, while the other classes, strata and social groups, which opposed these enemies, all came within the category of the people. At the present stage, the period of building socialism, the classes, strata and social groups which favor, support and work for the cause of socialist construction all come within the category of the people, while the social forces and groups which resist the socialist revolution and are hostile to or sabotage socialist construction are all enemies of the people. ["On the Correct Handling of Contradictions Among the People," speech, Feb. 1957, as quoted in Philippe Devillers' *Mao.*]

As an aside, it is no wonder the followers of the "People's War" strategy have no sense of democracy, or respect for democratic processes. More to the point of the present discussion, the rather militaristic usage of the terms "the people" and "the enemy" are main ingredients in the fiction within which many of the guerrilla groups around the world operate. They strike poses as liberation fighters against oppression while actually using violence to gain enough political power to impose political change of their own choosing—the will of the people notwithstanding.

The conversation *Newsweek* reported between the group of American radicals and Che Guevara is of itself testimony of this fiction at work in real life. You will remember their complaint was to the effect that the people they wanted to liberate were so ingracious as to damn them for their trouble. Yet, undoubtedly, some of the participants in that very conversation were later to use violence in the name of the people they were then so candidly saying did not support their doing so. Of course, the texts those young Americans were beginning to follow warned them that the people must be awakened to their need for liberation. In other words, if the mix of violence and propaganda is right, people can be led into a revolution.

Any question as to the possibility of this producing a counterfeit revolution had long since been dismissed through their complete acceptance of the propaganda they were taking from the texts. The situation is not unusual in the circles they were moving in, and it should not be seen as reasoning peculiar to their lack of knowledge and experience as revolutionaries. Their revolutionary idol and mentor's mind worked in similar fashion. In fact, three years before that conversation was printed in *Newsweek* Che Guevara had literally been damned by people of Bolivia he sought to liberate—the exact movements of his small guerrilla band were reported by peasants to the Bolivian Army until they were able to trap him. In his book *The Myth of the Guerrilla* Dr. J. Bowyer Bell, whose studies of the guerrillas had taken him right into their camps, writes:

What revolutionary logic, which immutable law of Marxist-Leninist doctrine could explain in dialectic terms an Argentinian out of Cuba by way of the Congo in the wilds of the Bolivian jungles memorizing the verbs of the wrong Indian language in order to convert a people, already possessing land, whose vision for endless centuries had turned inward?

There is no question but what Guevara was devoted—committed unto death—to what he was trying to do. He had been at it most of his adult life, not only in Cuba, the Congo, and Bolivia, as Doctor Bell indicates, but agitating to do so in his own native country and in several others in Latin America. There is equally no question but what Guevara's main interest was in using guerrilla tactics—and, indeed, pure terrorism—to impose political changes not of the least interest to the people on which they were to be imposed. In order to distinguish between terrorists and legitimate popular struggles this sort of thing needs to be laid out quite plainly.

And it can be done essentially in Guevara's own words. In Bolivia, he came to say the same thing the young Americans had said to him: he was totally without any mandate from the people in whose name he was trying to run a revolution. He repeatedly complained that not only would the people not support him, but they could not be trusted not to work against him. The situation was so bad he was considering using terror to bring them in line. Six months after starting his campaign to win them over he wrote:

> . . . our peasant base is still underdeveloped, although apparently a programme of planned terror will succeed in neutralizing most of them, and their support will come later. We have not had a single recruit . . .

In another five months the people he was not able to recruit passed information to the Bolivian Army that led to his ambush and death.

We saw a minor replay of Guevara's experience among the peasants of Bolivia in the SLA's adventures in a ghetto of Los Angeles.

There is hardly a more pathetic story about that little band of self-indoctrinated zealots than newswoman Marilyn Baker's description of the organization's sole claim to a ghetto origin trying to recruit support from among his own people. Mrs. Baker writes that, on several occasions, Donald de Freeze went from door to door in the ghetto trying to get people to join the army of which he was General Field Marshall Cinque. They turned him away. What little support he ever got, he bought with SLA bank-robbery money. In fact, he gained entrance into the house in which he and five others were to die, with a $100 advance for a single night's lodging in one room. When De Freeze was joined by his white comrades, carrying pipe bombs and automatic weapons, they took over the rest of the house which was eventually set afire probably by their own molotov cocktails. People in this case fled from the liberation army.

The National Liberation Army Guevara founded there in Bolivia was passed to the control of his survivors and, though never very strong, even with considerable outside help, was able to reach out in 1971 and assassinate the Bolivian consul in Hamburg, Germany.

There should be no difficulty in seeing either this group or the SLA as committing terrorism. Nor should there be with a group that grenades an airliner full of passengers, or one that sets off a bomb in a crowded restaurant, or another that deliberately opens fire on men, women, and children who only happen to be where they planned an attack. Whatever ties such groups might have with any people, there is no legitimacy in this kind of violence. Those who commit it are terrorists.

However, there are some admittedly gray areas when you start trying to identify which are pure terrorists and which are struggling peoples around the world. There is some reason for the disagreements on the matter among, and within, the nations of the world. Some groups are so entrenched in such long-standing political entanglements, or operate amid such general violence, that it is difficult to determine their status without fear of some valid contradiction. Sufficient lines can be drawn, however, to produce a long list of organizations that are committing terrorism, "pure and simple," as Laqueur said.

Undoubtedly, the average newspaper reader does not remember the names, locations, or even the number of these organizations that pass before his eyes as they attack here and there in the world. Their names are really a confusion of similarities and dissimilarities that almost defy the memory. They are names that are suggestive of identical political rhetoric, used by unconnected organizations, operating on opposite sides of the globe, or slight modifications of others in the same country; names composed of ominous-sounding words that telegraph more emotion than politics; or one or two word names that, on their own, signal neither emotion nor politics.

As examples, among other places noted, there is a National Liberation Movement in Uruguay, and a National Liberation Movement in Iran. There is a Peoples Liberation Army in Columbia, and a Peoples Liberation Army in Turkey. The popular Front for the Liberation of Palestine (PFLP) and the Popular *Democratic* Front for the Liberation of Palestine (PDFLP) are competing groups with Israel as their common target. The Angry Brigade was organized in England, and a Death Squad in Brazil. The Weatherman in U.S., and the Montoneros have operated for all of this decade in Argentina. There are the ad hoc or short-time appearances of such names as the Eagles of the Palestinian Revolutionary Movement, used by Arab hostage takers in Austria in 1973, and the New Year's Gang, the name under which a small group of New Left bombers operated in the U.S. in 1969 and 1970.

As to the number of terrorist organizations in the world, if we look at those figuring most prominently in attacks occurring within the current epidemic, that is since 1968, we find over seventy. Two or more can be counted in almost every Latin american country, perhaps a dozen in the Middle East, and a dozen or more in Africa. Another dozen plus can be identified in Europe, especially in France, Italy, Turkey, West Germany, Spain, Ireland and the United Kingdom—even one in Yugoslavia. And, even discounting groups that have long been engaged in open guerrilla warfare in the Far East, they can be found in Japan, Burma, Malaysia, Sri Lanka, and the

Philippines. You can count at least seven in the United States.

In the appendix is a chronology of what we considered significant incidents of terrorism during the 1968-1975 period. This chronology includes nearly 300 incidents occurring in a total of 52 countries. This is, however, only a fraction of the incidents that occurred in the period. For example, there were 190 political kidnapings in Argentina in the year 1973 alone, and we show only 56 incidents of all types in that country for the whole eight year period. If we had picked up all of the bombings in all of the countries during this period we would be dealing in thousands of incidents. Anything near a complete compilation would be impractical as an appendix to a book. What we have tried to do is to produce a representative sample—showing those that received the most media attention and some that received little, the common and the unusual, trends, time and geographical spread, and a representation of the different outcomes. The names, in full or abbreviation, of the organizations to which we were referring in the preceding paragraph appear within the descriptions of the incidents. They appear also in an alphabetical listing at the end of the chronology which includes the total of nearly a hundred terrorist organizations we encountered in the research for this book.

The bits of political rhetoric included in the names of most of these organizations is part of their propaganda—part of their effort to establish legitimacy. By using words which in some other context have attractive meanings they seek to distract the public from their real purposes. No one can say this does not work to at least some degree. They have us all mouthing part of their propaganda everytime these names are run through the media—giving them at least tiny increments of credibility toward being what they claim to be no matter how far from reality it might be.

The SLA is an example almost too obvious to mention. their literature explained that the "Symbionese" of their name was from the word symbiosis, and thus was a reflection that their ranks were "made up of the aged, youth and women and men of all races . . . a body of dissimilar bodies and organisms living in deep and loving harmony and partnership in the best interest of all within the body." Yet, their oldest member had just turned thirty. The only one of any race but white seen among their number was the escaped convict Donald De Freeze, installed as SLA commander by Nancy Ling Perry and Patricia Soltysik. And, other than De Freeze, the only blacks SLA seems ever to have dealt with in their operations they either killed, threatened to kill, or scared half to death—really doing nothing in the best interest of anybody. Their idea of liberation was the violent destruction of the system in which they were living for some open ended arrangement they never spelled out. Their army existed only in their words and on the scraps of paper they left behind.

They were simply a small knot of dissidents and adventurers who became so imbued with the idea of revolution that they took weapons and set out to force the acceptance of their ideas at gunpoint. Thus, someone might ask, who would take this little gang seriously as revolutionaries anyway—as having any chance of hurting anyone but themselves. That is just why they used terrorism, so someone would have to take them seriously. And some people did have to. Doctor Foster, for example. For him the hurt was total and permanent. The Hearsts, as another example. For them, maybe the hurt was not total, but it was permanent. Others took them seriously, too—their ideological allies, and cobelligerents, for example. For some of these, SLA was "Right on!"—to them, any blow against the system is a plus—for others, it was "Bug out!"—to them, the SLAers were fooling around with something they didn't understand and running the risk of ruining it for those who do understand it.

If they had been more successful, as have other groups in the world with similar names and goals, we would all have had to take them seriously. And perhaps they would be trading shots, or at least epithets, with other groups with slightly different names contesting for political dominancy over the same people or territory—maybe with two or more of the great powers of the world backing opposing sides. The struggle in Angola is an example. There opposing groups, all of which have used terrorism, are locked in the advanced stage of revolutionary violence called guerrilla warfare. It may never be possible to determine how much of SLA's symbiosis exists in this affair. Charges of foreign intervention, and accusations that indigenous people were fighting only because they had guns at their backs, have flown from all sides.

If the SLA had been still more successful, as have other groups once visible only as terrorists, it might be seated as a legitimate government among the family of nations of the world. This is another of our objections to the international line of reasoning for the identification of terrorists. Speaking of terrorism as an incident in which three parties are involved, and describing the perpetrators of the incident as one, the country in which it occurred as another, and the country whose citizens or property were the targets as the third, automatically accords the terrorists a status that otherwise might exist only in a name or in a stack of their own propaganda material. It takes them seriously to a degree that even their own guns might not have been able to achieve.

Thus, the proposition works both ways. The degree of success one of these groups achieves has to do with how seriously it will be taken, and the seriousness with which it is taken has to do with the success it will achieve. The interaction of the two will determine whether any one of the bands of terrorists we have among us today will reach a status of legitimacy in the world—and therefore, no longer be considered terrorists.

As with all things political, you have to pick a point in time and take a stand on the situation as it exists at that moment. You have to collect the best data you can and draw some lines. Some are easy—the small, obviously unrepresentative groups, trying to shoot, kidnap, and bomb their way into public recognition. Some are more difficult—the broader political movements that appear to have some legitimacy as actually representing peoples struggling against visible oppression. The task in the case of the latter is frequently complicated by high levels of violence and few if any viable political institutions through which the people involved can really express themselves. This is the gray area we mentioned earlier. It is within it, however, that the lines have to be drawn.

For example, of the nearly a hundred organizations we listed as being terrorist, we omitted the groups on both sides in what became essentially civil war in Angola. Perhaps someone will claim that one or more, or all, of these should have been included because of violent excesses of which they are accused. We felt, however, that the situation there had deteriorated to the point that it was no longer possible to speak of it in terms of mere terrorism.

We omitted some groups that have become governments that others might have included—such as the obviously authoritarian African Party for the Independence of Portuguese Guinea and the Cape Verde Islands (PAIGC), which is now the widely accepted government of Guinea-Bissai. Some will disagree with that, citing this group as having ascended to power by questionable methods, and as being in sympathy with terrorists elsewhere. Be that as it may, we did not list PAIGC as terrorist.

On the other hand we did include the Eritrean Liberation Front (ELF) as an organization conducting terrorism during the 1968-75 period at which we were looking. This group formed as armed guerrillas in the late 1950's, went through a period of behind the scenes organization, and began an insurrection to separate the pre-World War II Italian colony of Eritrea from Ethiopia and reorder the society of the province according to its own revolutionary ideas. The evidence suggests, as Ethiopia has claimed—both before and after the coup which deposed the late Haile Selassie—that the ELF was very much involved with other terrorists in Europe and the Mideast. The situation in the country is serious, and has anything but improved since the military coup of September 1974 dispensed with the monarchy. The ELF even has a Marxist competitor, the Eritrean Popular Liberation Front (EPLF), which announced in early 1975 that it was about to proclaim itself an independent republic. Both liberation organizations have been impatient with the military regime for not moving forward fast enough with the socialist revolution.

108

Some of the property owners have themselves taken to outlawry over the regime's nationalization of rural lands.

The ELF, though, has continued pure terrorist operations right through 1975. They have killed, or kidnaped and threatened to kill, indigenous civilians, police officers, and soldiers, and citizens of several other nations—Canada, Italy, the Netherlands, the U.K., and the U.S. They have blown up bridges and shot up government convoys. They have dressed in Ethiopian Army uniforms and taken over a prison to release some of their comrades.

Four of its members grabbed two nurses from a missionary hospital as hostages, killing one of them, a fifty-four-year-old Dutch woman, when she could not move fast enough for them—barefoot, over rocky ground. They forced down a civilian helicopter and held its American and Canadian occupants hostage, announcing they would be released by the ELF revolution command in exchange for prisoners held by the Ethiopian government. They have bombed, shot, and kidnaped Ethiopian and American soldiers, sailors, and civilian technicians working at a communications relay station in Eritrea.

Frequently making their announcements from Damascus, or Beirut, the ELF has demanded the closing of the relay station, a facility the U.S. has used for years as part of a world-wide communications network for keeping in touch with naval craft—and more recently for handling the diplomatic messages to and from its negotiating teams sent into the Mideast. The ELF has also demanded that the U.S. cease its assistance to the Ethiopian government.

Thus we included some organizations on our list, and excluded others. The ELF, the Eritrean Liberation Front, we included as one of the organizations that does commit unmistakable terrorism.

In fact, we counted thirty-five terrorist organizations around the world with the word *liberation* in their names. We found them operating in Africa, Asia, Latin America, the Mideast, and in North America—five in the U.S., including the

Armed Forces of National Liberation of Puerto Rico. Some called themselves fronts, some movements, one is an *action*, another a *command*, others use more elaborate military designations, such as *brigades*, *army*, or even *armed forces* as the Puerto Ricans do.

One of these liberation organizations is the Brazilian group Marighella founded, another is the Bolivian group Che Guevara founded. Twenty five others have similar origins and ideological bases—Marxists of one sort or another and thus trying to liberate people from imperialism, in Latin America, the Mideast, Africa, Europe, and the United States. This in spite of the fact, as Doctor Bell says in *The Myth of the Guerrilla*, most of these nations "not only feel unimperialistic but quite satisfactorily liberated." But then, the imperialism Marxists seek to liberate people from is capitalism, as explained in their texts. The remaining eight terrorist groups with liberation in their names have rather vague ideologies. Four appear to be nationalist or separatist rather then leftist.

Fourteen of the groups we counted use the word front in their names. This is a political term generally used to indicate a coalition of organizations with diverse ideologies come together for the achievement of a common objective. Over half are purely Marxist. One is the apparently very small New World Liberation Front in the U.S., which has organized in secret. Its only public acts have been terrorism. All fourteen have committed acts of violence for which no front can really claim legitimacy.

Seventeen use *peoples* or *popular* in their names. All appear to be Marxist. It is difficult to find evidence that any of them are as spontaneous as popular suggests. Some are competing for supremacy over the same body of people. None has a mandate for the violence it has used.

Eighteen have either *revolution, rebel, insurrection,* or *resistance* in their names. Most have Marxist orientations— some Castroite, some Maoist, some Trotskyite, at least one Moscow aligned, the rest apparently unaligned. And three are probably nationalist.

Twenty-seven use military designators in their names—

army, armed forces, etc. Some of them are so small—or were when they took their names—as to make the military terms as ludicrous as that of the SLA. Although he repeatedly states how much he admired Che Guevara, in his book *Revolution in Cuba* Herbert Matthews writes that Che had forty-seven men in his group when he gave it the ambitious name of National Liberation Army of Bolivia, with an Estado Mayor (General Staff), and issued his first war communique.

Twelve of the groups we counted were called *movements.* Two of these, one in Uruguay and one in Chile, have been so successful in attacking their societies as to have governmental armed forces called in to deal with them. Two of these were right wing. The others appeared to be leftists.

Fourteen groups used some form of the word *national.* One of these was the self-appointed Armed Forces of National Liberation of Puerto Rico.

Ten had either *socialist, left, red,* or *communist* in their names. One of these, however, was the Argentine Anti-Communist Alliance, a decidedly right-wing group that has attacked and killed scores in its self-assumed task of ridding the country of leftists.

We also encountered a miscellaneous collection of one or two-word names that did not match any of those we have just tabulated. There were twenty of these, including the White Flags in Burma, Siakhal in Iran, and Tudeh (Communist Party) also in Iran—all clearly leftist. It included some right-wing groups that have conducted their share of terrorism, such as the Phalangists in the Mideast, the Ordine Nero (Black Order) in Italy, and the Jewish Defense League in the U.S., as well as some only vaguely aligned groups such as the Freedom for the Basque Homeland in Spain.

We have noted some instances of cooperation between groups within countries, and across national boundaries. We have also noted some gathering points and commonly used communications centers, such as Algiers and Havana. Cities in most of the countries of Western Europe have served similar purposes, even if to lesser degrees, as have Moscow, Peking, and Pyongyang in North Korea. In fact, it was in North Korea that George Habash, leader of the Popular Front for the Liberation of Palestine, made the initial contact with the Japanese United Red army. The Japanese terrorists, of course, later received some training in Beirut and carried out the Lod airport massacre to avenge Black September's earlier defeat there.

Habash has also called international meetings of terrorists, in Ireland as well as in Lebanon. He has been said to have gathered representatives of the Irish Republican Army, the German Baader-Meinhof gang, the Japanese URA, the Liberation Front of Iran, the Turkish People's Liberation Army, Italy's Red Brigade, and the Ethiopian ELF together at one time or another. He claims to have provided some training for the U.S. Black Panthers, and has had contacts with the Tupamaros of Uruguay. The Tupamaros, in turn, have had contacts with groups as far away as Turkey and Japan. And, in 1974 the Tupamaros, the People's Revolutionary Army, the Chilean Movement of the Revolutionary Left, and Che Guevara's old National Liberation Army of Bolivia reportedly signed a formal agreement of limited alliance.

This is no more than a glimpse of the contacts, meetings, and ad hoc or more permanent alliances terrorists have made since 1970. The communications network any of them with the proper credentials can plug into is quite well enough established. There have also been splits as well as mergers and alliances. These have generally just produced additional organizations with similar capabilities. We might look at a rough "tree" of the Palestinian groups, and then glance at something similar on U.S. groups to get an idea of the process involved.

The Palestinian Liberation Organization is the umbrella, or framework, organization for the main Arab guerrilla and terrorist groups. It was formed in 1964 by a decision of the first Arab summit meeting in Cairo, and designed to provide a government in exile for the Palestinians. And the Arab governments allocated a large sum of money to provide it with a military arm—the Palestinian Liberation Army. Egypt originally had the greatest influence over the affairs of the

PLO. To counter this Syria decided to support an older, but little known group, Al Fatah—led by Yasser Arafat and formed in 1956 as one of a number of independent Palestinian fighting groups. Operating from headquarters in Beirut, Arafat's little organization got into terrorism in the late 1960's. In 1967, however, it made such a show of its forays of violence that Arafat was appointed the leader of the umbrella organization, PLO, as well as retaining control of Al Fatah. In 1974, when Arafat addressed the United Nations, he was the leader of probably between 15,000 and 20,000 guerrillas within the groups under the PLO umbrella.

In the meantime there had been some other formations under this umbrella. In 1968, the Popular Front for the Liberation of Palestine was put together by George Habash from three scattered organizations including the revolutionary Marxist-Leninist Arab National Movement, of which he had been the leader. It has become increasingly extremist and secret, and prone to the bloodiest of terrorism. It has apparently received most of its material support from Algeria and Syria, but Christopher Dobson's description of the PFLP newspaper's office with its "tail fins of rockets, spent cartridge cases, Che Guevara posters, Kim Il Sung's books, the coats-of-arms torn from the walls of the American and Jordanian embassies and pictures of "Lenin and Mao" give a more vivid idea of where its propaganda comes from—again, the same textbooks.

In 1969 Habash's chief lieutenant, Naif Hawatmeh, led a splinter off the PFLP and formed the Popular Democratic Front for the Liberation of Palestine, with an even more extremist stance than its parent. Another splinter became the PFLP-General Command, under Ahmed Jibril. This split was in protest to the involvement of innocent people in terrorism—a practice which the group has since taken up itself.

We described earlier how Black September was formed under the secret sponsorship of Al Fatah. Although that organization was its parent, it recruited from the more radical members of both PFLP and PDFLP. Then late in 1973, a Libyan Black September, sometimes calling itself National

Youth for the Liberation of Palestine, was formed from a nucleous split off the PFLP structure and some input from the original Black September. This group has appeared and disappeared several times since, always leaving an extremely bloody trail

Illustration No. 1

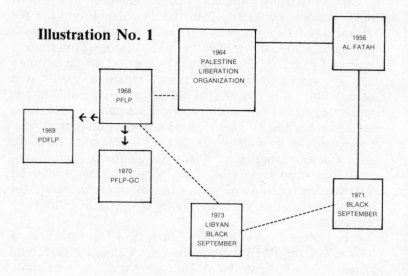

Switching from the Mideast to the United States we can see quickly how the Weathermen and the Symbionese Liberation Army came off the same original trunk. In the late 1960's the Students for a Democratic Society had taken in such an assortment of trained and experienced leftist organizers that it had become the center of an intense power struggle from within and without. Its well established communications network in the form of chapters and members on campuses all over the country made it a prize indeed. The main outside contenders were the Progressive Labor Party and the Revolutionary Union. The former, PLP, had been formed in the very early 1960's by two men whose Maoist orientations had caused them to leave the Communist Party USA. The latter, itself even more entrenched in Maoism than PLP, appears to be the product of a 1967 or 1968 splinter from the older organization. It had gone through a period of secret organization before it surfaced in California in time to make a bid in the power struggle that blew the SDS apart. Thus, instead of a takeover, PLP's push created some new, highly militant splinters, and left some less militant, but still quite radical chapters here and there to their own devices. PLP went into a decline from which it has never recovered shortly thereafter, but the splinters and fragments of SDS have generally survived—most even prospered—under new names. We show four particularly militant results of the struggle, one of which is the Weathermen we have discussed already. We will discuss the other three and some of the less militant fragments in the next chapter.

Important to developments we have described so far is the splintering of the short-lived terrorist group calling itself Venceremos from the Revolutionary Union. This is not a part of the Venceremos trips to Cuba program, but a small group, including founding members, that found RU not violent enough. In turn, two former members of both the Venceremos organization and the Vietnam Veterans against the War were founding members of the SLA.

Illustratin No. 2

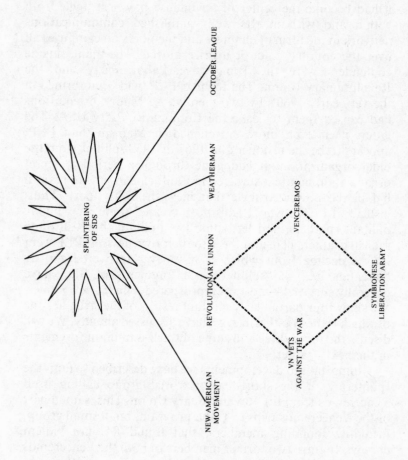

SPLINTERING OF SDS

OCTOBER LEAGUE

WEATHERMAN

REVOLUTIONARY UNION

NEW AMERICAN MOVEMENT

VENCEREMOS

VN VETS AGAINST THE WAR

SYMBIONESE LIBERATION ARMY

4.   Who Supports It?

> So in the Libyan fable it is told
> That once an eagle, stricken with a dart,
> Said, when he saw the fashioning of the shaft,
> "With our own feathers, not by others' hands,
> Are we now smitten." [Aeschylus]

Some time ago one of our famous astronauts did a TV commercial in which he asked: "Who needs America's railroads?" He paused only a second or so and answered the question himself: "You do!" If he had been asking the question we now have before us, "Who supports terrorism," he could probably have used exactly the same words: "You do!"

Indeed, the reality of this answer is probably no more obvious in the one case than it is in the other. In both, we are unaware of the relationships being suggested. That is, whether we realize it or not, the societies in which the terrorist groups germinate and grow furnish the support for them. The American society is no exception.

Of course, as the terrorists understand it, that is the way it should be. The texts they so commonly read tell them how and why to do it, but no money is included in the book packages. The books say that must come from the societies under attack. Mao's writings are almost estatic in places with his descriptions of how the people will participate in the revolution. Those that don't are counter-revolutionaries. And, "To put it bluntly", Mao wrote, "it is necessary to create terror for a while in every rural area" to deal with the counter-revolutionaries. After all, as he writes elsewhere in the same paper, "A revolution is not a dinner party."

Che Guevara romanticized revolution. There is little doubt but that he sincerely believed the peasants of Bolivia would have supported him, if they had only understood. Carlos Marighella looked upon those who did not support his urban guerrillas as enemies of the revolution, and wanted them shot.

If you produced a synthesis of what these three men wrote on this subject you would undoubtedly find their message to be: "Get voluntary support when and where you can, propagandize for it, build organizations to produce it, conduct yourself in a manner that will encourage it, but that which does not come forth from these means you must get by subterfuge, theft, or extortion—everything must come from the people and the land where the guerrilla is operating."

The fact that such a dictum has repeatedly been put into practice right around us seems to be a little difficult for most people to believe. For example, in the heyday of the underground U.S. press, when the number of wild-looking tabloids of radical politics and radical culture reached about 800 across the country, someone was always asking where the money to publish them came from. The question was almost always quickly amended with: "from Moscow, Peking, or Havana?" If any of us who were studying these papers at the turn of the decade ever found any outside money coming in to them it seems not to have been recorded.

The papers were getting the money for printing, for their hole-in-the-wall working spaces, and for their office and photographic supplies, from within the communities and cities where they were being published. Small amounts of it came from advertising revenue or subscriptions and street sales, but not much. They didn't carry much advertising and they gave away more papers than they sold. Most of their money came in the form of gifts, donations, personal allowances of staff members, proceeds from part-time jobs they held, even from staffers being on some government benefit program or other. Some frankly regarded their tabloids as guerrilla papers, and supplemented the voluntary support they got, with shoplifting and periodic light-fingered acquisitions of office equipment and supplies in businesses where they or their friends worked.

The money and other material support these young newspaper operators required were, of course, peanuts compared to that needed by full-fledged terrorists. However, the methods used to fill the requirements of both follow the same basic pattern. Some of the people who were putting out underground papers then have now gone on to terrorism. Some others have gravitated to organizations that support terrorism, either directly or indirectly. One of the five young people in the Manhattan townhouse explosion was a former editor—each of the other four was at least a patron of the underground press.

Just as people donated money to underground papers, some without knowing for what ultimate purpose their money was being used but some knowing rather well, people donated money that supported terrorism. Some of this is in the form of unilateral gifts of wealthy people who sympathize with the terrorists' cause. Some comes from benefits, entertainments of various kinds, or, in fact, passing the hat—all favorite forms for underground papers. We have seen also that even governments make contributions to terrorists, sometimes for specific acts of terrorism. Bank robbery and extortion have been primary means for supplementing voluntary support.

Financial assistance, however, is merely the tangible manifestation of a more important form of support that must precede it: psychological condonation. Money and supplies don't flow, nor do people provide information to support bombings, bank robberies, and kidnapings unless there is some feeling within their society that the terrorists are at least partially right in what they are doing. If there are not some elements of a population who agree at least with the general direction in which the terrorists are going, they will not be able to get the support and assistance they must have to continue operations. They will be caught. If there is not at least some flicker of a doubt in the main consensus of the population that what the terrorists are doing is totally wrong, they will be punished. Further, if there are not major elements of the population that have lost at least some of their faith in the sufficiency of getting changes in the society by legal means, those who support and assist the terrorists will be seen as guilty of unacceptable or illegal behavior and themselves censured, if not arrested and punished.

The record during the period of the epidemic we have been looking at rather speaks for itself. Those of us who have watched terrorists darting in and out of the Mideast know they are frequently not caught, unless they choose to be, and generally not punished even if caught. If we look at the experience with the Tupamaros in Uruguay that we described briefly in chapter 2, we will realize it was not because their methods were so infallible, or those of the police so faulty, that they ranged freely over the country for several years. It was because large numbers of respectable people of the society protected and helped them, and the vast majority of the population neither said nor did anything to indicate this was other than it should have been.

But we don't have to go outside the United States to illustrate the point. There are twenty-five known members of the Weatherman organization that have been vainly sought by local, state, and federal authorities for up to six years. You can read the wanted posters on them, and see their pictures and fingerprints. Two of them are survivors of the explosion of that Manhattan townhouse where they and three of their comrades were making anti-personnel bombs. With so much known about them, eluding arrest for such an extended period would be a record, even if they had simply hidden quietly away. But they haven't. They have continued to strike from coast to coast—setting off bombs in three widely separated cities in one day in 1975.

Of course, the Weathermen are not the only ones that manage to avoid arrest. There are numerous others wanted for offenses ranging from inciting riots to bombing and bank robbery. The much-publicized Yippie leader, Abbie Hoffman, has been underground for some time, still popping into print occasionally as the result of some clandestine meeting with a news or magazine writer. And police are still trying to round up the last members of the New Year's Gang that bombed the math lab in Wisconsin and killed a young man working in it in August of 1970. Some terrorists have been caught and punished in the United States. One of the gang we just mentioned was sentenced in November, 1973 to twenty-three years in prison—eligible for parole in 1979. Some have been caught and not punished. In almost all cases their apprehensions have resulted in highly vocal charges of brutality and injustice. Their trials have usually been turned into radical political exercises. Here again, the pattern has been the same everywhere.

Young people, characterized in the press as having good educations, being from good families, with good prospects for the future, are nearly always involved. And the characterizations are not inaccurate. As we have pointed out previously, it is difficult to find illiterates among the terrorists, and the truly poor don't seem to have much stomach for them. But, pick up a dozen of the news clippings running down their life stories and you can find a point in each at which you can snip it off and replace it with the comparable bottom part of any one of the other stories without changing the sense of either. The young people in these clippings are always ones who became concerned about something they felt was wrong in society. They tried to do something about it. They were unable to get anything done fast enough to suit them, and they protested. No one listened and they became activists. Then they became politicized, and fell into company with others of similar interests. They tried some new approach, perhaps one of the non-violent strategies being taught around the country. The chances are it only produced confrontations, because that is what it was designed to do. They then became radicalized—a term heavily used to mean crossing into the use of violence. Somewhere along the line they had run into the rhetoric and literature of revolution, and they became revolutionaries. When they took up terrorism as a tactic, it was only in furtherance of the revolution to which they had given themselves, minds, bodies, and souls.

The reality of this final position of revolutionary commitment usually mentioned in these stories can be seen not only in bombs but in pages of underground newspapers, in letters and statements transmitted to the regular press, and in leaflets and pamphlets by the truckload. Perhaps nowhere is it seen in such fully articulated expression as in some of the passages in the two-hundred-page paperback, *Prairie Fire*, sent out from the Weather Underground in 1974. They obviously took the book's title from that of a 1930 polemic written by Mao Tse-tung, *A Single Spark Can Start a Prairie Fire*, in which Mao argues in favor of the effectiveness of small guerrilla forces. Thirteen pages into the book, under the sub-head "The Banner of Che," the Weathermen wrote:

> We are at an early stage, going from small to large. This mass armed capability which will destroy the enemy has its beginnings in armed action. It matures unevenly, with setbacks and at great cost. It will not spring fullblown on the scene at the magical moment of insurrection. We cannot leave the organizing and preparation for armed struggle to some more perfect future time. It would be suicidal. There is no predetermined model for revolution—we are always figuring it out. But for some, armed struggle is always too soon, although it is under way here and around the world.

> We made the choice to become a guerrilla organization at a time when the Vietnamese were fighting a heroic people's war, defeating half a million troops and the most technologically advanced military power. In our own hemisphere Che Guevara urged that we "create two, three, many Vietnams," to destroy U.S. imperialism by cutting it off in the Third World tentacle by tentacle, and opening another front within the U.S. itself. At home, the struggle and insurrection of the Black liberation movement heightened our commitment to fight alongside the determined enemies of the empire.

> This defined our international responsibility and our duty as white revolutionaries inside the oppressor nation. We are part of a wave of revolution sparked by the Black liberation struggle, by the death of Che in Bolivia in 1967, and by people's war in Vietnam. This period forged our belief in the revolutionary necessity of clandestine organization and armed struggle.

The writers of this are, of course, among the educated, middle-to-upper class young fugitives we have been discussing. They wrote the book from their clandestine sanctuary within the American population, and they had enough support above-ground to get it printed and distributed nationally. At about the time this latest revolutionary gauntlet was being flung out, they set off a bomb in a public building.

Of course, each time such a bomb is set off, by this group or by any of some half a dozen other fairly active and similar groups, there is public consternation. Just as there was over the killing, bank-robbing, and kidnaping by the SLA. But there is, in truth, more consternation when the personal histories come rolling out, or when there is a collision with law enforcement agencies such as the Los Angeles shootout with the SLA. As Robert Moss says about Uruguay in his book *The War for the Cities*, the apparent or alleged roughness with which police handle these young terrorists seems to arouse, "a stronger public outcry then the murder of a policeman or the abduction of an ambassador by the Tupamaros."

Someone is sure to say, "Naturally we have a special concern for these young people, no matter what they do, they are our children!" There is something to that, undoubtedly. It isn't everything, though. It really isn't everybody's children who throw bombs. It isn't everybody's children who come to need help evading the police for months or years. In fact, except for what Eugene Methvin called "red diaper babies"— the offspring of old leftists—in *The Riotmakers*, the young people we were talking about cut all ties with their families when they take the step toward that final commitment to revolution. Their support as revolutionaries had to come from somewhere other than their families. They had to have the same sort of assistance and protection we saw the Tupamaros getting, that which we find wherever we find terrorism for any sustained length of time—supplied by elements of the society which are themselves somewhat radicalized, even if not to the point of actually throwing a bomb or using a gun.

Press accounts have suggested that sports activist Jack Scott had a great deal to do with Patricia Hearst and Emily and William Harris being able to forestall arrest for such a long time. And if we can depend on the stories by David Weir and Howard Kohn published in *Rolling Stone* magazine, Scott helped the fugitives extensively, drove them across country, and hid them out for months, but he drew the line on the weapons they were so enamored with. He agreed to help them only if they left those off.

Others than Scott most assuredly helped the SLA fugitives during the same period, and dozens of people around the Berkeley area undoubtedly encouraged the original members as they were studying their books, preparing their plans, acquiring their weapons, and training for their assault on society. Some came to their defense afterward.

Support of terrorism was demonstrated at the trial of Karleton Armstrong, the New Year's Gang member we cited earlier as having been sent to prison. He was originally charged with first degree murder for the bombing of the Army Mathematics Research Center on the University of Wisconsin campus in which a graduate student was killed. He was allowed to plead guilty to second degree murder and other lesser charges. According to the Congressional Committee on Internal Security's 1974 staff study entitled *Terrorism*:

> Armstrong not only admitted to the AMRC bombing, but also to his part in the December 28, 1969 bombing of campus ROTC classrooms; to the January 3, 1970 firebombing of ROTC administrative offices; to the January 4, 1970 bombing of the university's Primate Research Lab mistaken by Armstrong for the Selective Service office next door; to attempted sabotage of the power substation which provided electricity to the Badger Army Munitions Plant in Baraboo, Wisconsin; and to an unsuccessful aerial attack using a stolen plane against the Badger munitions factory.

After he had been convicted there was what the study called an unprecedented two-week mitigation of sentence hearing which provided the then twenty-nine-year-old Armstrong with a chance to tell the court and the public why he did what he did and to argue that his acts were necessary. During that hearing the Committee reports that:

> More than forty witnesses, many of them prominent scientists, historians and political activists, came to Madison to testify on Armstrong's behalf and sound the

core of his defense: The war in Vietnam was "immoral and illegal" and all resistance to that was justified.

The study says that among the 41 witnesses were Philip Berrigan, Daniel Ellsberg (who sent a tape), and Anthony Russo. According to these witnesses Armstrong had been driven to a desperate act by his frustration over escalation of the war and alleged war research conducted by the Army Mathematics Center.

The letter in which Armstrong and his comrades of the New Year's Gang proudly took responsibility for the bombing of the math lab put it a little differently:

> Today, August 24, the battle cry against imperialism was raised again as the Mathematics Research Center of the U.S. Army was struck by revolutionary cadres of the New Year's Gang.

> The AMRC, a think-tank of American militarism was a fitting target for such revolutionary violence. As the major U.S. Army center for solving military mathematical problems, it bears full responsibility for American military genocide throughout the world . . .

> We see our achievement as more than just the destruction of one building. We see it as part of a world-wide struggle to defeat Amerikan imperialism, that monster which is responsible for the starvation and oppression of millions over the globe, that monster which is a direct outgrowth of corporate captialism . . .

> For this reason, we declare solidarity with our revolutionary brothers in Uruguay, the Tupamaros, who are struggling to loosen the U.S. military and corporate grasp on their continent . . .

The closing paragraph of the letter said the group demanded the release of three Black Panthers being held in Milwaukee and the abolition of ROTC. They threatened revolutionary measures which they said might include kidnapping of important officials, and even assassinations.

As was true with Jack Scott and the SLA, it is not intended to single out all, or any, of the forty-one witnesses who appeared to argue for Armstrong in his hearing as the sole, or constant, supporters of the New Year's Gang. There is an even chance that some of those appearing knew little, if anything, about the group, but were carried into this situation by their own opposition to the Vietnam war. Perhaps that is even more illustrative of how elements of the population of a society come to speak and act in support of terrorism—for, that is the effect these witnesses finally had.

It is not the number of people who see themselves as revolutionaries and set up a chorus of bitter and unceasing criticism to justify a society's destruction that should alarm anyone. It is not the obviously inflated breast-beating and incongruous guerrilla warfare fantasies, or even the recognizable commonality of the textual sources of the strategy and rhetoric of the revolutionaries, that poses a serious threat. It is, instead, the number of voices joining in their chorus of damnation that belong to people with responsible positions in the society that must be seen as disquieting. It is not even the bombs the terrorists set off that are the greatest threat to the integrity of a society, it is the number of people who join them in the contention that they were justified in setting off those bombs.

There were apparently no more than four members of the New Year's Gang, including two ex-SDSers, one of whom was said to have come to the group from the Weathermen. Ten times this number of witnesses, all educated, professional people, joined in the argument that Armstrong and his comrades were justified in taking it upon themselves to protest their government's political policies with high explosives.

No one should miss the fact that anyone who comes to the defense of even one individual terrorist runs the risk of providing this sort of support to terrorism itself. The basic definition of terrorism with which we began our discussion in chapter 1 alerted us to expect terrorists, when brought to trial, to speak and act not primarily to win personal freedom, but to try to spread their organization's political ideas.

At the end of Chapter 1 we noted that we could also expect the main thrust of the terrorist's justification of his attacks to be what we called condemnation propaganda, designed to portray his targets as so evil and beyond redemption that they deserved the violence which he used on them. The British author Robert Moss speaks of the basic appeal of political violence being bound up with the rhetoric of vilification. He goes on to say this rhetoric is dangerous and pernicious because is is a positive incitement to violence. The two are almost synonymous. What Moss was describing is the prelude, ours is the postlude. One is more general in its scope, damning a society generally and hitting individuals or institutions in general. The other is more specific, focusing on the target of the attack which it seeks to justify. Look again at the passage we quoted a few pages back from the Weathermen's *Prairie Fire*, and then at the New Year's Gang letter explaining the bombing of the math lab for examples of both. You will also see that they overlap somewhat. And you can do what we were describing with the clippings on the life stories of young terrorists, clip off part of one and replace it with part of the other and not change the sense. Together they provide a fair idea as to the nature of the chorus revolutionaries have set up in the United States. Perhaps some of those who have lent their voices to it have not heard all of the stanzas that go with it.

The rhetoric, violence, and more rhetoric, are sequential. The support of any part of the sequence tends to support the whole. And the propagandists use one instance of support as justification or enticement for another. The depth of support coming from one set of people deepens, and the circles of people willing to provide support widen.

What we have really come back to is the almost invariable explanation of how the individuals in a terrorist group came to the point of accepting the use of violence themselves. They were radicalized. Then we can see something of the "which came first, the chicken or the egg," situation. Either, people who have already become somewhat radicalized support the terrorists, or anyone who comes to their support, for whatever reason, becomes somewhat radicalized in the process of supporting them. Those closest to the terrorists, or most involved in their support, will be radicalized to a higher degree. Those further from them, but still involved in their support, will radicalized to lesser degrees. Thus we can explain the growth of what we described as circles of greater or lesser involvement, in the support of the Tupamaros. Within the outer circles the support is so indirect that radicalization is slight indeed. There is little doubt, however, that under a sustained period of political violence the whole society either comes to support the terrorists, at least to the point of tolerating them, or it reacts and puts a stop to the violence— one way or another.

What happened in the case of Uruguay is that the society became extensively radicalized, with essentially everyone at least tolerating the prevailing terrorists, then something snapped. There was a reaction, a popular demand that the violence be stopped, and it was—by military force. No one knows quite what the price of that, in terms of extended loss of the democratic tradition, will finally be.

We have a big gap, however, in our attempt to explain who supports terrorism because we have described people who have given support after acts of violence had been committed, people after they had become radicalized. It is of more final importance to try to see how this process or radicalization was supported before it all burst into gunfire and bombs. In doing so we are going to speak almost entirely of what went on in the United States, but the experience was similar in other Western countries, and in the Orient, in Japan, particularly.

The critical point in the build-up process is that of radicalization. This expression, as we have pointed out several times, is not one we coined. It was originated apparently by people to whom it had happened. On the other hand, we have used the term radical frequently, sometimes all but completely interchangeably with revolutionary. The media have done the same thing. There were some examples in the paragraphs we have quoted. It is a practice that many of us who write on this subject finally succumb to. In a sense it is a copout. It is a safe generic for referring to people acting somewhere in a shapeless mass of human upheaval, obviously on the fringes of revolution but not clearly committed to it at the moment. In another sense, the word radical seems to add force and clarity to what is being said because the word revolutionary has been so overused in modern times (applied to everything from lipstick containers to trips to the moon) that you almost have to add real, or maybe violent to guarantee the communication of a political meaning. Perhaps that same feeling was also present among those in the depths of the ferment.

So, when we start trying to look at radicalization, and how it was supported, we have to define the term radical. It is not a bad word, nor is it really something that a society should be without. A radical, in the political sense, is one who advocates extreme changes in existing views, habits, laws, institutions, and methods of government. It is rather difficult to run any revolution without radicals. And those we speak of as radicals today are usually the first to point out that there were numerous radicals afoot in America in 1776. That, of course, is quite true.

Even beyond its founding days a society needs the impact of radical ideas or it becomes stagnant. On the other hand, undiluted, or unbridled, radicalism can produce chaos. Change made at a reasonable pace allows people to adjust to it. Sudden, drastic change allows them no time to do anything but comply or refuse to do so. Gradual change in a society is not likely to produce political violence. Abrupt change tends to produce it. Successive abrupt changes almost guarantee it.

What happened among young people beginning in the early 1960's was an awakening interest in change. Some of the proposals for change that came bubbling up were fairly moderate, others were less moderate, some properly classified as radical. But in the beginning the time-factor in the push for change was not so short. Then the word *now* became attached to some of the proposals for change. And they ceased to be proposals, and became demands. Things were heated up to the point that periodic violence was inevitable.

In a book called *Movement and Revolution: On American Radicalism*, Professor Peter L. Berger has portrayed this process in very practical terms. He identified three distinct, but related, currents swirling within the youth population in the early 1960's: youth culture, youth movements, and radical movements. This is an accurate appraisal, and it provides an useful framework for us to see how support, both conscious and unconscious, came from a variety of sources—some of which intended it to eventually produce violence, and some of which had no such intentions at all.

The youth culture essentially affected all young people, at least to some degree. For some it was only in style of dress, amusements chosen, or language used, but it tended to magnify the perennial difference between the young and their elders. Initially it was more economic than social in nature, and not political at all. It was simply the spontaneous creation of a generation experiencing the first, full impact of long accumulating technological advances that had for years outstripped the evolution of human working and living arrangements. Eventually there had to be some adjustments to accomodate differences in job opportunities and in the length and types of training required before a young person could take a place in the mature and productive strata of life. This time had come and some new bargaining had to take place between young people and the larger society.

This youth culture no longer exists in its original and totally youth-oriented form, for two reasons. One reason is that the bargaining process has resulted in the merger of parts of it with the culture of the larger society, and neither is really distinct anymore. The other reason is more important to our present concern: political radicalism seized upon certain elements of the youth culture and tried to mold and perpetuate them as the trappings of political revolt rather than merely those of a generation gap. Encouragement to use drugs, posters and clothing fads glorifying guerrilla warfare, the mixing of taboo language into political rhetoric, and the injection of all of these with the lyrics and accompanying artwork of popular music are examples.

Second to this broad-based youth culture, and more direct in helping to prepare the way for a marked spreading of radicalism, was the closely-following occurrence of numerous youth movements. In fact, these movements were usually *ad hoc* activations of that youth culture itself. This was inevitable under the circumstances. Young people, with more time on their hands, and already somewhat set apart from the larger society, yet drawn to each other by the new cultural experimentations, became a pool of energy and imagination. At their own instigation, and sometimes at the instigation of older minds, they became involved in issues of the day. Some of these issues were political, some were not. They were a real potpourri—including war, ecology, civil rights, hunger in the world, religion, education, and an almost interminable list of others. From the standpoint of the majority of youth, participants in these movements were not essentially radical, the changes wrought were more reformist in nature than revolutionary. There were usually distinct possibilities for rebellious surges because many of the problems around which the youth movements formed were beyond their capability of solving—some beyond anyone's capability in any immediate time frame. The young, loaded with idealism, and impatience, yet unencumbered with the responsibilities of actually being in charge, were thus often on a collision course with intense frustration from merely having their attention called to a problem they could not possibly solve. Thus, radical spokesmen, especially from the left, found college campuses convenient working grounds, and managed to manipulate students toward even greater frustration and thence to expressions of violence. Initially these outbreaks were simple vandalism, but they soon began to pick up some of the earmarks of terrorism.

The third current swirling around in the youth population in those days was found in existing radical movements. There was a variety of these too. They all had some political orientation, even if it did not appear at first. And they were inspired, for the most part, by people, young and old, who had some credentials as radicals. Some of these people were, indeed, of ages that would by no means allow them to be still counted as young, and had long histories of involvement in radical activities. Some were the offspring of older radicals, and simply brought their parents' radicalism with them. Some were teachers and college professors with pet theories on change—again young and old. Some were ideological drifters who had been in semi-hibernation in the backwood of political extremism, but who rose to the new scent of radicalism on the campuses and in the streets.

These three currents within the youth population naturally overlapped somewhat from the beginning. They were manipulated to overlap further. The radical movements fed directly on the other two. Radicals siphoned off recruits into a gaggle of youth fronts from old extremist organizations. And they tried to infiltrate, or at least mold and guide, the movements and organizations they could not take over. Issues were not important in themselves, but offered propaganda opportunities around which young people could be organized and propelled into confrontations with the system. They set up a call for a movement for a new society, never well-defined, but always intended at its hard-core center as a device for revolution not reform. It came eventually to be called simply "the movement," and the overwhelming majority of people jostling along in its ranks have never known precisely what it is all about.

The so-called underground press, itself a shapeless mass like this movement with which it was inextricably associated, was the prime vehicle for spreading radicalism—and, finally, for promoting and supporting terrorism. And, though the underground papers began with milder fare, the most militant of them gradually became the transmission system for the

Illustration No. 3

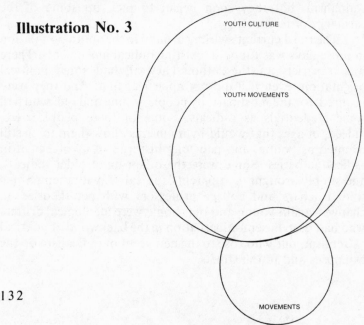

YOUTH CULTURE

YOUTH MOVEMENTS

MOVEMENTS

makings of terrorism. It was almost exclusively through their pages that the majority of young people who became fascinated with the idea of revolution were introduced to the mechanics of it. Before these neo-revolutionaries, and the potential terrorists among them, ever began to read the same revolutionary literature, they learned of the existence of this literature from the underground newspapers. Pictures and quotations of Mao and Che Guevara, and eventually the whole horde of revolutionary guerrilla heroes of the Twentieth Century, became the boilerplate of these papers. And the reproduction of Carlos Marighella's *Minimanual* was supplemented by their dumping into their pages excerpts of military manuals on the care and use of weapons and detailed instructions and diagrams of the home manufacture of explosives, bombs, and incendiaries.

Defenders of the underground papers among the older generation seemed to miss all of this, seeing only the breaking loose from old restrictions on writing and publishing, and characterized them as the new journalism, the alternate press, or at worst, the journalism of dissent. They supported the young people in publishing the papers and encouraged others to do so. The more squeamish among the ordinary citizentry tended to brush the papers aside as obscene or pornographic, sometimes confusing the underground papers with the sex tabloids sold at adult bookstores. Some of those who got past the bawdy language and sometimes sexually explicit pictures and drawings ran into radical and revolutionary political thrusts which they found too outrageous for rational consideration. Most people probably could not imagine anyone taking them seriously. The budding terrorists did.

The carnival appearance of the bulk of the papers was a distraction from the fiery messages they carried. They had the bounce and jump of mischievous kids to them. Even the names of some of the papers probably distracted some people from getting to the heart of their contents. They were often picturesque, drug or sex-related, sharply political, grotesque or mocking—as examples: *Chinook, The Great Speckled Bird, Kaleidoscope*, the *Marijuana Papers, Hooka, Good Morning*

Teaspoon, Intercourse, Organ, Outlaw Times, Left Face, Rising Up Angry, Guerrilla, Rat, and *The Great Swamp Erie da da Boom.*

Their forerunners were avant-garde publications typical of the mid 1950's. These earlier publications made sizeable cracks in the traditions as to what could and what could not be said in print—both in language used and subject matter dealt with. The underground papers started in the mid 1960's, however, pulled all the stops out. Nothing was taboo or sacred. And fired up with the fervor and experience of the civil rights movement and an increasing sentiment against the Vietnam war, the journalism of dissent argued next for more relaxed sexual mores and few restrictions on the use of drugs—especially the psychedelics. Underground publications began to pop up around college campuses and in burgeoning "hippie" enclaves in large cities everywhere. Beginning with cries of "racism" and "war," the papers sharpened their knives for eventually every institution in the society, calling for social justice, increased individual freedoms, and complete economic independence.

The number of these publications jumped from a mere handful in 1964 to more than 300 by 1968, over 400 in 1969, at least 500 by early 1970, and to probably more than 800 in late 1971.

At first there was an amount of spontaneity in the growth of the underground press. Newly developed printing processes, by which almost anyone could afford to publish at least an issue or two of some sort of leaflet, encouraged the flood of publications, and many of them showed individual creativity and versions of young people's newly found social awareness.

But, in short order, a form of political incest began to be practiced among publications scattered through most of the 50 states. Politically naive as most of their young writers and editors were, they not only copied from common texts, but from each other. The staffs of many publications gravitated towards highly politicized collectives and communes. Then, claiming unbearable frustration from trying to work within the system, they began to take their political cues from where many older observers had long-since decided the much-vaunted "New Left" was to finally take them: the "Old Left." For, in studying their literature, and listening to their speakers, it soon seemed obvious that the only thing new about it all was the people involved.

Perhaps one of the most succinct commentaries along this line, however, came from a young, obviously liberal-minded journalist—an ex-*Newsweek* writer, and a 1960's graduate of Antioch and Columbia, who after traveling and living among them wrote a book on underground newspapers which he called *The Paper Revolutionaries*. This young man, Laurence Leamer, writes very approvingly of the people he met in his travels, and describes how they shared information, food, and lodging with him—how "all across the country underground-press people treated me with what I found to be an overwhelming openness and frankness." He speaks sympathetically of the many things he saw the radical journalists trying to do. Yet, he expresses no little dismay as to why all of the underground papers were so preoccupied with Marxism, "a belief that in this past half century has been abused and warped almost beyond recognition." One of his answers was that the New Left had no basic beliefs of its own. As Leamer explains:

> When young radicals, in their search for tools to create a truly radical New Left, came upon Marxism they came upon it not as one of these essential but limited tools for understanding contemporary society, but as the ultimate font of wisdom.

It was not surprising that there developed within the family of underground newspapers a non-stop discussion of change by any means necessary. The inclusion of material from the texts of guerrilla warfare, and the recipes for making bombs, left no doubt as to what that finally meant.

The concept that the papers were a family although still loosely associated, was soon authenticated in the creation of their own wire services and press associations. The oldest is still Liberation News Service (LNS), by admission of its own staff, more a propaganda instrument for revolution than a news outlet. And LNS staff members could eventually be found clad in guerrilla fatigues and combat boots, sitting in dingy, doors-bolted, basement quarters, pumping out packets of printed and pictorial materials to subscribing underground newspapers all

135

over the U.S. and several foreign countries

The first press association of these newspapers was originally named the Underground Press Syndicate—later the Alternative Press Syndicate (UPS), as it tried to move further into the larger society. UPS, an open advocate of political agitation in the most extreme sense, served primarily to spread the underground newspaper movement. It did quite well by helping to get them started in nearly all of the fifty U.S. states, and instigating or tieing into underground press efforts in England, West Germany, France, Italy, and Japan, as well as in a few other countries.

These and similar organizations and associations spread the idea of underground journalism into the military services, into high schools, prisons, factories, and finally into some business offices and suburban communities.

In fact, at the peak of their publishing fever—in 1972— UPS contended the papers had a readership of over twenty million and that one in three persons in the fifteen-year-old to thirty-year-old age bracket was regularly exposed to underground publications. There was little reason to doubt this. UPS also claimed that the underground press had influenced the conventional media in their attitudes toward society and, that on such issues as the Vietnam war, drugs, ecology, rock music, and sexual attitudes, it had often been the major trendmaker or issue maker. There was little reason to doubt that either.

In fact, although the underground press and the radical movement did not invent drug abuse, it was quite an effective trendmaker with drugs. Drugs became the keystone of the counterculture. They encouraged marijuana—using its leaf as the most common single symbol of their publications. They also encouraged LSD, mescaline, and a number of other hallucinogens, as adventure-attractions to the counterculture, and experimentation with drugs as part of the initiation into it. Only a few of the papers ever encouraged the use of hard drugs, although it appears that the continuous printing of the imagery and language of drug users contributed to its spread in all forms. They probably downplayed hard drugs for other reasons, but an often stated one was that a real addict is no good in the movement.

On the other hand, the use of drugs made young people initially available to that same movement. The papers explained this at one time or another. *Argus*, published in Ann Arbor, Michigan, said drugs were a way of moving from a generation gap to a war. That may sound far-fetched but the war it was talking about was inter-class conflict: the have-nots or outs taking on the haves or ins. Most of the troops were of the have or in class. To become angry or alienated enough to attack their own kind, and to attack a system as strong as they saw theirs to be, they had to be provided with the status of being part of a separate culture. There had to be a real cleavage for the strategy to work. In a society as permissive as the American one had become it was not too easy to find something with which to manipulate this cleavage. Sex would not be strong enough, although as the underground magazine *Other Scenes*, put it, "Sex is one of the things that gets the other generation up tight . . . it's one of the things revolutionaries use as an inexpensive, effortless tactic to upset people." However, society was able to tolerate the new liberal sexual customs, and absorbed obscenities the same way. Hair, and "freaky" clothing caused some uptightness, but not enough for the desired clashes. Drugs would. The society would react to drugs. And, as the Chicago *Seed* explained, harassment from the older generation, and arrests, were new experiences for young whites, who "otherwise might have gone on thinking that a cop was just that guy in uniform who directs traffic, and that jails are really full of *criminals*."

In addition to creating issues the underground press became a primary tool for organizing around issues. The underground press carried column upon column on organizations and organizing techniques, whatever the issues. In addition to these columns, which kept a parade of organizations in the news, most papers carried what amounted to directories of the radical communities in their areas. Some took up as much as a quarter of a tabloid page. They featured the various services and sources of assistance such as drug rescue, havens for runaways, and medical care or free food. The larger part of most directories, however, was given over to lists of names, addresses, and phone numbers of political organizations in the areas. The papers encouraged readers to contact these organizations, join them, or support them.

As part of a research project in 1972, we selected the directories of sixteen sample papers from various sections of the United States and rank-ordered the political, or quasi-political, organizations in them according to the frequency with which they appeared in the entire sample. The following list was developed, and should provide some idea of the scope of these directories.

Black Panthers
Vietnam Veterans Against the War
United Farm Workers Organizing Committee
Peoples Coalition for Peace & Justice
National Peace Action Coalition
Weatherman
Young Lords Party
American Civil Liberties Union
Mayday Tribes
Yippies
La Raza Unida
Venceremos Brigade
Student-Mobilization Committee
Industrial Workers of the World
League of Revolutionary Black Workers
Young Socialist Alliance
Black United Front
Tupamaros
War Resister's League
New American Movement
FLQ (Canadian)
Vocations for Social Change
Gay Liberation
Committee of Returned Volunteers
Peace and Freedom Party
Berkeley Free Church
Women's Liberation

New Mobe
Republic of New Africa
Seattle Liberation Front
National Lawyer's Guild
Young Patriots Organization
Movement for a Democratic Military
Insane Liberation Front
Peoples Party II
John Brown Revolutionary League
American Servicemen's Union
Students for a Democratic Society
Los Siete de la Raza
The Rainbow People's Party
White Panthers
Socialist Workers Party
Palestinian Guerrillas
National Liberation Front (Vietnam)
Nasha Institute of Survival
Afro-American Patrolman's Association
Africa Research Group
Committee of Concerned Asian Scholars
Youth Liberation
North American Congress on Latin America
Radical Education Project
Union of Radical Sociologists

Nonviolent Direct Action Group
Communist Party
Medical Committee for Human Rights
Southern Christian Leadership Conference
Young Workers Liberation League
Universal Life Church
Black P. Stone Nation
Veterans and Friends for Peace
Alabama Black Liberation Front
National Committee to Combat Fascism
Black Liberation Army
National Organization of Women
Chicano Moratorium
Women's International Terrorist Conspiracy from Hell

Women's International League for Peace and Freedom
Youth Against War and Fascism
U.S. Committee to Aid the NLF
National Welfare Rights Organization
Revolutionary Army
Asian Alliance
Mattachine Society
December 10th Committee
Daughters of Bilitis
Movement for Puerto Rican Independence
Southern Conference Educational Fund

The underground press, and the movement generally, fattened on the manipulation of the Vietnam war issue. In truth, there is probably no better example of the manipulation of an issue than Vietnam. For, in the beginning the anti-war movement was not primarily a radical one. Its main theme was simply peace. The overwhelming majority of people involved in its demonstrations displayed no inclination for anything other than peace—and the placards, flags, and literature present at those early demonstrations were testimony to this. However, before this movement was deflated by the U.S. withdrawal from Vietnam, and its remnants trundled off into the backrooms of purely radical circles, the number of placards bearing pro-North Vietnam slogans, the frequency of the carrying of Viet Cong flags, and the amount of heavily ideological literature showed a tremendous radical influence. Many of the people who had appeared at the early demonstrations had either fallen away or become no more than foot troops, giving service—whether they knew it or not—to political lines developed for them by radicals in the background.

More than a few people who were themselves strongly against the war found, in trying to talk with the core of politically committed radicals who comprised the van of this movement, much that they could not stomach. They were against the inhumanities of war—whichever side committed them. The radicals' opposition was revealed as not being against inhumanity in general. They had no objection to that, as long as it was being practiced by the right people from their

140

point of view. They were opposed to what they called American imperialism, and they were pushing for changes in policy that would hinder the U.S. military effort, not that of the Viet Cong or the North Vietnamese.

And, indeed, as the U.S. was pulling out of Vietnam, various factions of the radical core began switching their antiwar arguments to anti-imperialist ones. In February of 1973, one such group, calling itself the "anti-imperialist coalition propaganda committee" wrote in the Atlanta underground paper *Great Speckled Bird*:

> Many people have raised the question of what happens to the antiwar movement when the war ends. If its only purpose was to end the war, the obvious answer is that it dies. If, however, its opposition to the war was one aspect of an overall anti-imperialist politics, then it should broaden and grow instead.

Three paragraphs later, they explain:

> Imperialism is not just a foreign policy of the US (or other) government. It describes the economic system and, derived from that, the political system of the monopoly stage of capitalism.

From the remainder of the article it becomes clear that this new explanation of the meaning of imperialism was necessary because the group's previously announced definition tied it exclusively to the Vietnam war. And that is not what those at the deep core of the movement were finally after. In their books anti-imperialism translates as anti-capitalism, and their goals were more on the order of the terrorist organizations we looked at in the previous chapter. In other words, the movement was more on the order of a peoples liberation movement, and it needed to diversify.

It did so in two ways. First, it began to put more emphasis on such issues as consumer rights, ecology, housing, and energy, in the place of the war, and to attack business, where the military and law enforcement agencies had formerly been the main targets. Second, the movement and the underground papers switched their orientations from being primarily toward youth to broader segments of the population, especially toward working class people. Some of the old underground press died, either because they were no longer needed, or because the journalists were not properly oriented. New tabloids cropped up, with more subtle approaches, and softer sells than before. These were usually being put out by some of the more thoroughly trained radicals who had been recruited during the heyday of the totally youth-operated underground press.

And the three circles we drew originally were gradually changed until they would have looked something like this: Within and underneath the organizations, alliances, and *ad hoc* arrangements generally represented in the overlapped and near-overlapped areas of these circles is the support for terrorism in the U.S. today—tucked into clandestine cells which form what you sometimes see referred to in the media as the underground. These cells house and protect the activists of terrorism, the bomb-throwers, arsonists, and kidnapers. They maintain the network of communication and transportation that makes it possible for the activists to move and strike as they do. Without activities above-ground that draw their support from areas of the circles where there is no overlapping,

Illustration No. 4

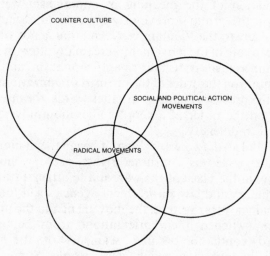

however, the life system they depend on would not continue to function. Thus, again, we have people knowingly supporting terrorism, and we have others who are supporting it without having any idea of doing so.

The underground press had a big hand in creating this situation. It could not have done so, however, without a tremendous amount of hard, organizational effort on the part of people who were willing to work long hours, days, weeks, and months in one place, or to jump into a car, or onto a plane and go where other work needed to be done. A major part of the job was done by the Students for a Democratic Society (SDS) and the numerous splinters its destruction left behind in 1969-70.

In a way the SDS stands astride the overlapping circles we drew to represent the youth-currents of the 1960's like a modern colossus, one foot in youth movements, one in radical movements, the prints of both feet still visible in youth culture. SDS would not have happened if there had not been that overabundance of youthful energy and idealism trying to bargain with a world not yet caught up to its own changes. SDS started out as the "neighborhood kid gone to college" of youth movements. And it became the "take over the campus or burn it down" fraternity of radical movements.

In his book *The New Left Today*, Phillip Luce wrote SDS "was the 'new' left." Nobody should disagree much with that. The New Left emerged with SDS's Port Huron Statement in 1962 and, although the term continued in use for a while, it was smothered before the SDS national convention of 1969. The SDS's within-a-decade rise and fall as focal point of collegiate political thought, and activity spanned the events which led to the epidemic of terrorism that erupted beginning in 1968. It produced the most active and fully-committed terrorist organization operating in the U.S. since then. The radical enclaves and projects SDS instituted have produced the main sources of support on which terrorism has fed in the U.S.

SDS was founded in 1960 essentially through renaming the old Student League for Industrial Democracy, itself created in 1905 by such men as Upton Sinclair, Walter Lipmann, and Jack London. SLID was a moderate socialist organization with a non-communist ideology. In its initial constitution, SDS invited "liberals, radicals, activists, and scholars" to join its chapters but specifically denied membership to communists.

Nine years later, after having opened its doors to any ideology, it was torn apart in a near-riot convention by Marxists and anarchists who together controlled the majority of the votes in the assembly. The remnants of the national staff and representatives went off in different directions to run their own revolutions. The local chapters and community action projects were fought over, abandoned, or plugged into by warring factions of every kind. And the pickings among the ruins of SDS were fat indeed.

SDS had gotten off to a fairly slow start in the early 1960's, having initially only a couple of chapters and a total national membership of about two hundred, but by 1965 it was claiming a membership of two thousand in seventy chapters. By mid 1968 it was claiming 30,000 members on 300 campuses, and reporting a national headquarters income of well over a $100,000 a year.

The pattern of its interests and activities, and its trail from moderate political involvement to extremism and the deliberate use of violence for political purposes, ran a close parallel to the individual's evolution along the road to radicalism. The organization went through five distinct periods:

1960-1962—Organization and the formulation of concerns about the affairs and conditions of the larger society.

1962-1965—Efforts within the system toward a broader participation in democratic processes, but edging into dissent.

1965-1967—Change from dissent to active resistance to the system. The adoption of a "from the bottom up" insurgency style of operation.

1967-1969—Initial steps toward actual conflict with the system. Moved toward a conviction that violence was necessary.

1969—Revolutionary declaration. Everyone has to make a

committment one way or another. The organization did not hold together through that last year.

The most critical period of SDS's development in terms of its growth, and in terms of its heading toward a commitment to violent revolution, was that of 1965-1967. Beginning in the previous period the organization had been having considerable success with community action projects in ghettos and low income areas in eight or ten cities on both coasts and in the Midwest, and in the mountains of Appalachia. It had received some grant funds, and membership was rising rapidly. There was an urge to move to national issues, and the first anti-war march on Washington was sponsored in 1965. It was a huge success, brought the organization into contact with large numbers of young people, and swelled its coffers. This prompted the increase of the national staff and the acquisition of a printing press. It was a heady period, in which SDS formally did what it had already done informally. It opened its membership to all ideological comers by removing its constitutional prohibition against communist membership. It had already begun to take an active interest in Marxism and the strategy of guerrilla warfare and the professionals of the Old Left swarmed around the national leadership of the organization.

In the next period—1967-1969—the writings of the guerrilla leaders of the world supplanted those of the social and political reformers for SDS. Che Guevara was consecrated as a martyr to the cause of national liberation movements, and SDS's traveling representatives extended themselves into the international circuit. Often, in the company of top American old left officials, SDS leaders and representatives visited North Vietnam, Cuba, Czechoslovakia, and the Soviet Union. Visits and correspondence were exchanged with New Leftists and revolutionaries in France, Germany, Sweden, and Japan. Student riots became a common affair both in the U.S. and in several foreign countries. A strike was held at Berkeley in favor of Third World revolutions. The SDS chapter at Columbia University rallied enough students to take over some five campus buildings, hold three school officials hostage for twenty-four hours, ransack the president's office, and set in motion a campus riot that lasted for nearly a week and ended only in a violent and chaotic clash with more than a thousand police officers. The disruption of the Democratic National Convention and additional campus violence were then pre-ordained. The coverage by the media of this violence simply fed right into the build-up for real terrorism. Incidents of political violence had been doubling each year since 1965. In 1968 they jumped eight-fold, and attacks against police jumped more than ten-fold.

In January 1969 high voltage power line towers were dynamited in the Denver, Colorado area. An SDS member was indicted for the incident, and his name became an entry on the FBI's most-wanted list. In the spring of 1969 the SDS national council announced formal support of the Viet Cong side of the war in Southeast Asia. By summer SDS had become a major force in the recruitment of young people to go to Cuba in the Venceremos brigades.

SDS members had been involved for some time with Progressive Labor Party strike activities, mixing with pickets under the name Worker Student Alliance, and the PLP had become a powerful influence on the whole SDS structure. Then at the SDS convention in June of 1969, this Maoist group, which SDS leadership had originally invited into the organization, made its play to take it over. If it had been able to do so it would have fallen heir to the network of more than a hundred SDS chapters and local projects scattered literally all over the country.

What happened was that the heavy-handed and well-planned PLP surge ran into two other factions within SDS, one led by the then national secretary Mike Klonsky, and the other led by Mark Rudd, the chairman of the Columbia University chapter at the time of the takeover there, and Bernardine Dohrn, the national inter-organizational secretary. PLP failed in the takeover attempt, and managed only to retain some strength in local chapters, primarily in Boston and San Francisco. Mark Rudd and Bernardine Dohrn had gathered together the nucleus of the Weatherman organization, and had walked away with the SDS mailing list, the money, the top leadership, and control of the national office on West Madison street in Chicago. The Klonsky faction was left momentarily with little of anything. Running under the name Revolutionary Youth Movement II (RYM I was the Weathermen faction) the Klonsky group was eventually to found the October League, an openly avowed Marxist-Leninist combat party dedicated to agitation in the working-class communities. It has, indeed, successfully launched many of the wildcat strikes that have occurred since its formation.

Another extremist organization that was to emerge during 1969, and to take much of its strength from the forces involved in the destruction of SDS was the Revolutionary Union. This group was founded by: a twenty-six-year-old member of the SDS national interim committee; a twenty-five-year-old former PLP member, and the chairman of the Progressive Labor club at the University of California before being expelled from campus: a thirty-five-year-old Stanford University English professor, who had been deep into the study of Marxist-Leninist strategy for several years; and a fifty-four-year-old ex-Communist Party functionary and ex-Progressive Labor Party leader. The Revolutionary Union had been germinating for about a year in the San Francisco Bay area when it surfaced in early 1969 and was brought into an SDS national council meeting in Austin, Texas in March of that year. There had been considerable interaction between this group and the RYM factions of SDS and the latter decided to bring the Revolutionary Union into play in the upcoming fight with the Progressive Labor Party. The Revolutionary Union was obviously helpful in that struggle but came away with some additional strength it had drained from SDS in the fight.

Both the October League and the Revolutionary Union now publish nationally circulated publications —somewhat resembling the old underground newspapers, published by some of the same people, but aimed at working-class readership. They vie for the leadership of what they see as the coming revolution in the U.S. and each claims it is forming a "new" communist party to assume this leadership role. Neither seems to have been overtly involved in terrorism, but both subscribe to the use of violence to carry out the revolution "when the right time comes." Both support terrorism with the most extreme vilification of the U.S. system in speeches and in reams of literature.

Then, there was a split off the Revolutionary Union, led by the Stanford professor who was one of the organization's founding members. This man, Dr. H. Bruce Franklin, was impatient to start the revolution immediately. And, pulling together a faction from inside the organization and joining it with an assortment of other extremists from the outside, he broke away and formed a more militant group called Venceremos. As we noted in an earlier reference, this was not one of the brigades going to Cuba. It was a distinct, but short-lived organization, that armed itself and set out on a brief career of terrorism its own. Their most notorious operation was setting up the escape of prison inmate Ronald Beaty who they hoped to recruit to their own ranks. They ambushed a prison car, moving the inmate from prison to court for an appearance as a witness to another crime, and spirited the inmate away, killing a corrections officer in the process.

If we take another look at the diagram we used at the end of the preceding chapter we can begin to see how some of the splinters from the explosion within SDS went on to form other organizations—all comprising one family tree of groups in the U.S. that either engage in terrorism or support it directly or indirectly.

You will note that we have had something to say about all of the organizations connected by solid lines excpet the New American Movement. This organization was founded in 1971 within a portion of the pro-Vietcong PLP-SDS anti-war movement that had just about lost its powers of leadership. The document that led to its founding was signed by a member, of the faculty at Berkeley, a young-woman member of the National Student Association delegation to Hanoi with the so-called People's Peace Treaty, and a young man who was a former SDS national interim committee member and Weatherman. The latter two soon became editor of the new organization's newspaper and coordinator of its field staff respectively. The New American Movement tried to pick up somewhere short of where SDS left off. It did not espouse

Illustration No. 5

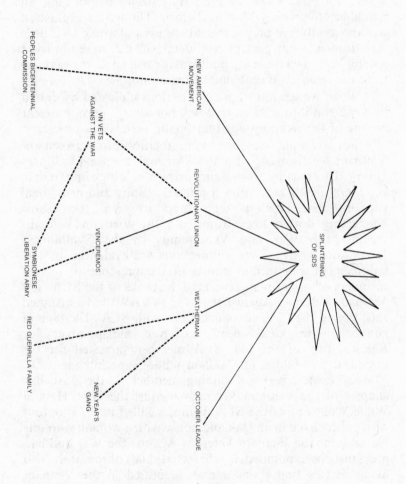

guerrilla warfare, at least initially, but it did seek to build a mass organization with which to bring Marxism to power in the United States. It hoped to present itself in such subtle ways, to the working class people of America, that its eventual goals would not drive away the ordinary citizen—whom they felt would be offended by Marxist rhetoric. Though it still exists, it has apparently had only marginal success and would have little significance in our present considerations if it were not for it having been the launching platform for still another organization: the People's Bicentennial Commission.

When we get into those connections indicated by dotted lines we run into an area that will not always permit a clear picture of the relationships that finally exist, or did exist.

For example, we show some relationship between the Vietnam Veterans Against the War and the Revolutionary Union. This is more from a similarity in ideology apparent in the literature of both, plus a mutual affinity and occasional support observable in their literature. We then show connecting dotted lines from both the Vietnam Veterans Against the War and Venceremos to the Symbionese Liberation Army. These connections are evidenced by law enforcement and media reports of the presence of former members of both organizations in the ranks of the SLA. The Vietnam Veterans Against the War (VVAW) have disputed this, saying they had no connections with SLA. The type of connection we cited seems, however, indisputable. Joe Remiro, one of the two SLA members arrested for the organization's killing of Oakland school superintendant Dr. Marcus Foster, was a founding member of the East Bay chapter of the Vietnam Veterans Against the War. He and Willie Wolf, one of the SLA members killed in the shootout with police, lived in an Oakland house with a woman who was working for the Vietnam Veterans Against the War and had previously been nominated to be its national coordinator. Also living in this house was a man identified in the Vietnam Veterans Against the War newsletter as one of its sub-regional coordinators. Remiro had also been a member of Venceremos, as had the woman mentioned above. SLA member William Harris had also been a member of the Vietnam Veterans

Against the War. According to testimony of one former Venceremos member the Hearst kidnapping corresponded almost to the letter with a plan commonly discussed in such circles. Finally, SLA member Thero Wheeler is reported to have been an extremely enthusiastic Venceremos member while in prison.

The suggestion that the New Year's Gang emerged with traces of SDS-Weathermen origins has already been mentioned. The Red Guerrilla Family, also a West Coast group using bombs, was included in our diagram in accordance with information provided to the U.S. Senate Sub-Committee on Internal Security in testimony from a Los Angeles police sergeant. As may be gathered from the following documentary introduction written by the police sargeant, one could have added additional organizations, such as the New World Liberation Front, to our diagram. We feel however that those shown are sufficient to illustrate the splintering and organizational relationships we have been discussing. As a matter of deepening anyone's appreciation of the number and types of organizations in the U.S. that condone or support terrorism, here and in other countries, the cover note under which the police sergeant presented his documentation is useful:

The documentation submitted herewith serves to establish the numerous interlocks that exist between openly terrorist organizations like the Weather Underground and the Symbionese Liberation Army and the New World Liberation Front, and other leftist organizations which do not publicly engage in terrorism.

Thus, we find the Bay Area Research Collective in its bulletin and flyers openly supporting the SLA, and carrying bombing communiques of the New World Liberation Front and the Red Guerrilla Family. We find the Los Angeles Group for Latin American Solidarity (LAGLAS) supporting a Venceremos Brigade-sponsored benefit for Chilean political prisoners, and cooperating in other projects with a wide array of groups, including the U.S. Justice Committee for Latin American Political Prisoners (USLA), the Committee on Brazil (COB), The Cal State LA Latin American Society. We find the Prairie Fire Organizing

151

Committee engaging in a united front action in support of the SLA prisoners joined by organizations like the National Lawyers Guild, the Bay Area Research Collective, the United Prisoners Union, and the Prisoners of War Offense/Defense Committee. And we find the Prairie Fire Organizing Committee (Weather Underground) participating in a united front meeting in support of the pro-Communist guerrillas in the Arabian Peninsula—with organizations as diverse as the Palestine Information Committee, 3d World Newsreel, The People's Struggle in Oman, Iranian Students Organization, Eritreans for Liberation in North America, African Youth Movement, Progressive Greek Students Organization, People's Democratic Association, Organization of Arab Students, Friends of Indochina (formerly the IPC), etc.

The brochures and flyers submitted herewith were either picked up in the course of raids on suspected bombers, or else came to our attention in other ways. Also included are some clippings illustrating interlocks.

Even with this rather lengthy list, that is not all. We noted some locations around the world where groups have offices or support installations. The truth of the matter is that there is hardly a revolutionary group of any size anywhere in the world that does not have either an office in the U.S. or one or more organizations operating in its behalf—gathering funds, supplies, even guns at times, or simply publishing information to encourage private support. Among these it is not surprising to find representations of the various obviously Marxist organizations of the traditional old left and those created within the chaotic period of the New Left we have just been discussing. One would also find others, even religious bodies, giving money or psychological support to extremists of the left or right. And finally one could find a blanket organization called Liberation Support Movement with offices in New York, Berkeley, California, and British Columbia in Canada. This apparently well financed group publishes a slick-paper quarterly of about thirty-five or forty pages providing a running account of its support to revolutionaries around the world. It says of itself:

Liberation Support Movement (LSM) is a non-profit, anti-imperialist organization formed in 1967 to advance the cause of international socialism. We believe that LSM's research, informational and material support work combine to help accelerate the process by which super-exploited and oppressed nations, peoples, and classes are freeing themselves from imperialism in order to build non-exploitive, socialist societies. Also, by working to increase collaboration among progressive forces on all continents, we hope to contribute a necessary internationalist dimension to the struggles which will continue to grow within North America as imperialist control of the "free world" disintegrates.

Perhaps it will not be surprising that this group, writing from its U.S.-Canadian offices, supports the opposite side from that championed by the U.S. government in Angola.

There is still one organization shown on our diagram that we have not discussed. It is fitting that this one, the self-appointed Peoples Bicentennial Commission, be left until last. For, with it we have come full circle from our statement at the beginning of this chapter that whole societies are pulled into supporting terrorism, to the discussion of an organization created to manipulate that kind of support out of the American public.

The Peoples Bicentennial Commission is an offshoot of the SDS-New American Movement which calls for a second American revolution to institute "economic democracy." According to this group economic democracy would entail the government taking over corporate properties and leasing them back to private interests.

Jeremy Rifkin, the thirty-year-old self-styled radical who is usually the spokesman for this scheme, was a founding member of the New American Movement and on its staff when he was first writing about PBC. Indeed, in an article in the November 1971 edition of the organizational newspaper, *New American Movement*, he detailed the idea for using the bicentennial as a means to organize local New American Movement chapters around the country. He argued that the revolutionary heritage of the American people could be used as a tactical weapon to attack the system and its institutions.

153

John Rossen, the sixty-to-seventy-year-old professional agitator who evidently originated the Peoples Bicentennial Commission idea, was one of the old leftists we spoke of as swarming around SDS. He was SDS's landlord in Chicago and the owner of the building in which the national offices the Weathermen took over in 1969. He was financially instrumental in SDS obtaining a printing press in 1968. And he was a speaker at that closed-door, press-barred convention in 1969 when SDS was splintered. He was on hand for the founding of the New American Movement in the fall of 1971. The year before he had published several articles in a periodical he called *The New Patriot* in which he proposed the basic blueprint for the Peoples Bicentennial Commission. In it he also displayed some of the symbols and artwork which are still being used by Rifkin in the Washington office. Rossen's thesis was that the way to "radicalize America is to Americanize radicalism." In *The New Patriot* he indicates he took this idea from a concept called revolutionary nationalism that he says was brought to his attention by Regis Debray, the French author-journalist who was Che Guevara's Boswell in Bolivia.

The propaganda used by the Peoples Bicentennial Commission is the kind we have found terrorists using. But it is skillfully produced and offers one of the best examples we have seen of how such propaganda works. The underground papers had so many freak shows going on people missed the build-up to bombs in the streets. The Peoples Bicentennial Commission literature has so much authentic-looking 1776 memorabilia spread over it that most people seem to miss what it is getting at.

With rare exceptions, the media have simply printed or broadcast whatever the Peoples Bicentennial Commission has given them. And Rifkin has been portrayed as all but the reincarnation of one of the founding fathers. This has been done by media all across the political spectrum, not only by the ultra-liberal journalists. *U.S. News and World Report* and *The Wall Street Journal* have jumped on the bandwagon—although, *U.S. N & WR* did administer a mild wrist slap when Rifkin and his group inspired an attempt to disrupt the bicentennial observances at Concord, Massachusetts in April of 1975.

Only in a few instances have the media peered through the screen of traditional Americanisms to reveal the background and goals of the group. Columnist James J. Kilpatrick, for example, did, calling it all "hogwash and Marxist hogwash at that." But he had previously praised them as the sort of young patriots this country needed more of. Jenkins Lloyd Jones, editor and publisher of the *Tulsa Tribune* has written a couple of scathing columns on the group. And more recently *The Chicago Tribune*, which initially lavished coverage on them came out in December 1975 with a lead editorial in which it complained that the Peoples Bicentennial Commission had gotten most of the bicentennial publicity even though "Messrs. Rifkin and Rossen and their colleagues" are not really the patriots they pose themselves to be but "imposters whose purpose is to destroy our economic system." This piece also cited the origin of the idea as having apparently originated by Rossen, "a Chicago theater owner who has often been identified as a former Communist Party organizer and who headed a pro-Castro rally here in 1961."

The answer to the question as to whether or not the Peoples Bicentennial Commission supports terrorism can be taken directly from the writings of both Rifkin and Rossen. And as a bonus, we get to see some of the manipulative handiwork of the propagandist in the bargain. A sample or two will illustrate the points of our discussion here. In a nicely turned out volume entitled *America's Birthday*, published in 1974 by Simon and Schuster with a Peoples Bicentennial copyright, there are numerous "sanitized" paragraphs identical to Rifkin's basic thesis which was written for the radical paper *New American Movement*. The obviously far leftist words and names, that might frighten away the average-American have been removed. Parenthetically, at the time he wrote those original paragraphs he was listed in the newspaper *New American Movement* as one of seven people appointed to a committee to do just this sort of sanitization job on that organization's literature.

For example, in the Simon and Schuster book there is a paragraph that begins at the bottom of page 13 with:

A genuine understanding of American democratic ideals is what links the American people with the struggles of all oppressed people in the world. . .

The end of the paragraph, on the next page, reads:

. . .Solidarity comes from understanding the collective nature of our separate struggles and the cry for humanity that is shared by all.

Now, if we refer to the top of page 10 in the November-December edition of *New American Movement* we find, in an article entitled "bicentennial" by Jeremy Rifkin, this paragraph:

A genuine understanding of revolutionary ideals is what links Thomas Paine, Sam Adams, and Benjamin Rush, and the American people, with Lenin, Mao, Che, and the struggles of all oppressed people in the world. . .

And the paragraph ends with the sentence "Solidarity comes from," etc., worded precisely as the one above.

The Rifkin-Rossen modus operandi is primarily the sending out, to schools, churches, and community organizations around the country a very professionally produced packet of tabloids purporting to show people how to reexamine the governmental and economic systems to see if they still conform to "original principles." A careful analysis of this packet shows it to be, in fact, a do it yourself vilification kit, designed to agitate and radicalize the readers of its pages. This packet, being sold to subscribers for ten dollars is supplemented with an irregularly issued periodical entitled *Common Sense* which continuously rephrases the call for the abolition of the corporations and the creation of economic democracy. *Common Sense* also always includes a section reporting on the projects of local Peoples Bicentennial Commissions. These are usually vilifications, angry protest demonstrations, relatively minor acts of vandalism, or verbal attacks on commercial institutions, never anything so violent it might actually be classified as terrorism, but frequently just short of it.

We have to agree, with Robert Moss, that this sort of

vilification incites violence, and that it prepares people to justify violence. Should we doubt any knowledge or interest in such matters on the part of the Rifkin-Rossen team we can turn to the first book published by the Peoples Bicentennial Commission: *How to Commit Revolution American Style*, by Jeremy Rifkin and John Rossen, 1973. This is a book they don't advertise these days. And, although it carries the name and address of the Peoples Bicentennial Commission office in Washington, it is not available there. Perhaps one of the reasons is that the publishing house which printed it is not one with many books on the family bookshelf: Lyle Stuart, Inc. —a house that deals mainly in sex or radical/revolutionary materials and issued one of the notorious bombmakers manuals, *The Anarchist Cookbook*. The primary reason, though, must be seen as its contents and the association it puts its authors into. For, it is an anthology, and contains not only a section by Jeremy Rifkin and John Rossen, but other sections by people who have been noted for their SDS, New American Movement, or other New Left affiliations. And specific views on the support of terrorist organizations in other countries are contained in Rossen's section, especially. Rossen uses a title he indicates came from what Debray had to say on revolutionary nationalism and he develops some of his ideas about running a revolution in the U.S. by making it the patriotic thing to do. But he gets down to cases when he uses examples from other countries to illustrate what he is advocating in the United States. Under "Revolutionary Nationalism and the American Left," he writes that what he has in mind is already happening elsewhere:

Nor is the new movement in our hemisphere limited only to South America. In Cuba, Fidel, who was an early revolutionary nationalist . . . is clearly aware of this powerful new current and its effect on world revolutionary strategy. Recent issues of Gramma carry lengthy reports on the new revolutionary ideology of the Peronists in Argentina (for decades denounced by the Left as fascists) about the new strategic vistas opened by the electoral victory of Salvador Allende in Chile, and about the significance of events in Bolivia and Peru.

In the Caribbean islands, new Black liberation movements

are popping up all over. In Canada, the Quebecois Liberation Front has brought the fires of revolutionary nationalism right up to the U.S. frontier.

On the European continent, similar fires are scorching the hides of the imperialists. In Spain, Franco's fascist empire, kept afloat for nearly three decades with the aid of the U.S. imperialist Establishment, may be smashed on the rocks of Basque and Catalan revolutionary nationalism, aided by the revolutionary new patriots within Castile itself. In northern Ireland, the Catholic minority represents a form of revolutionary nationalism; and closer to home for the British imperialists, the renaissance of Scottish and Welsh nationalism forebode new headaches for No. 10 Downing Street.

In the Middle East the Palestine Liberation Movement and in Africa the struggle to free Angola stand out as the revolutionary nationalist bastions of the anti-imperialist front. In the Philippines, the resurgent anti-U.S. imperialism movement is clearly another manifestation of the new revolutionary nationalism.

In Asia, the entire continent seethes with the new movement. The victory of the first stage of the Chinese Revolution can be said to have struck the sparks that set off the whole world-wide phenomenon of revolutionary nationalism. And the most heroic, the classic example of the power, the invincibility, of this historic movement is that of the revolutionary nationalism of the people of Vietnam. [*How to Commit Revolution American Style*, pp. 149-150]

After a careful reading of these admittedly difficult paragraphs, and a rereading of the one of Rifkin's cited a few pages back, turn back to page —— and read again the passage from the Weathermen's book *Prairie Fire*. Look again at the New Years Gang letter attempting to justify the bombing of the math lab, at the Liberation Support Movement statement or the police sergeant's note or at statements by the SLA and other terrorists we have mentioned in previous chapters. Then answer the question as to whether the Peoples Bicentennial Commission is not finally the type of organization that supports terrorism and one designed to lead the American public into doing the same thing.

5. Where Can It Lead?

Thereafter mighty forces were adrift;
the void was open, and into that void
after a pause there strode a maniac
of ferocious genius. . .

[Winston Churchill]

Those who support terrorists encourage a macabre form
of political gambling in which bets are made and raised in
terms of death and destruction. For, the outcome of a given
terrorist attack is no more predictable than that of a single roll
of a pair of dice. And the accumulated result of a series of
attacks, or of a sustained terrorist campaign, is no more a
certainty than is what will be left on the table to win, or whose
hand will be holding the dice, when the last roll is made.

There is no certainty with which to predict where any
revolutionary upheaval will finally leave a society. Fighting a
war against an open attack by some outside force may pull a
nation together, but internal political violence divides a people,
even to pitting member of families against each other. It strikes
down reason and moderation. It creates voids which can be
filled by whoever and whatever is strong enough at any given
time to step in.

Terrorism may never get to be more than a nuisance in an
area, or country, or, as we have seen, it may become extremely
costly—not only taking lives and destroying property, but
badly damaging the societal fabric that holds a people
together. The terrorists may bring some valid problems to

public attention, they may create problems where none existed before; or they may never articulate anything that makes any real sense.

A given terrorist group may succeed in achieving a status as a political force to be reckoned with, and manage affairs under its control effectively, or it may succeed in achieving a standing but produce conditions more intolerable than it claimed the original ones to be. Terrorists may succeed only in setting up a society for other forces to take it over. They may fail, and be destroyed; or they may fail for the moment, only to rise again later. They may become over-confident and raise the level of violence for a quick victory; or they may become desperate and use a higher level of violence to try to avoid certain defeat. We will try to look at some of the possible directions toward which terrorism can lead.

At the end of each of the past few years a number of news writers have made attempts to recap the toll terrorism took during the year. To some degree such stories are supplementary to the traditional end-of-the-year roundups of the human and material costs of accidents. And well they should. For, although the number of people killed by terrorists does not even approach that of the deaths from accidents of various sorts, or the number of people killed in the course of general crime, the total physical, social, economic, and political damage inflicted by terrorists is not actually assessable.

As 1975 was drawing to an end it appeared that the number of people killed in terrorist incidents would hit the thousand mark. The figure was probably higher. The media are not likely to report even this number, however, because the incidents have become so common in some places in the world they have to be really spectacular to get any attention outside the local press. In Argentina, for example, the average reached more than two a day—people killed by terrorists from both the left and right extremes of the political spectrum.

Some forty or fifty people were killed in incidents during 1975 which drew wide international attention. And there was an average of about one a month of what the press has come to call "major incidents"—in France, Israel, Sweden, Malaysia, Spain, Ireland, the Netherlands, Greece, England, and the

United States. Perhaps the most violent of those to receive major attention were: the Baader-Meinhoff Gang's seizure, bombing, and burning of the West German embassy in Stockholm, in April; the Palestinian attack on a Tel Aviv hotel in March, during which eight hostages were killed; and a Palestinian attack on Jerusalem in July, in which explosives loaded into a refrigerator and set off in a downtown market area killed fourteen and wounded thirty-two. Incidents in the U.S., or those involving U.S. citizens, included the as yet unattributed explosion, in December at La Guardia airport, which killed eleven and injured fifty; and the murder of a CIA official in front of his residence in Greece.

In many of the highly publicized incidents the terrorists did not fare so well. In most cases the terrorist groups launching the attacks seemed to get little or nothing of what they sought. The majority of the terrorists demands were not met. In only one case, drawing wide attention, were the terrorists' demands completely met, that being the release of five imprisoned members of the Japanese United Red Army when some of their comrades seized the American consulate in Kuala Lumpur. The Japanese government released the five, flew them to the Malaysian capital in a commercial jet, then flew all of the terrorists to freedom in Libya in exchange for fifty American, Australian, Japanese, and Malaysian hostages being held in the consulate.

In a good half of the major incidents during 1975 all of the participating terrorists were either killed or captured. And, as had been true in previous years there were many vocal denunciations of terrorism and several proposals for international cooperation to put an end to terrorism. Individual setbacks did little to discourage the movements to which the terrorists belonged, or to dampen the enthusiasm of those who supported them. On the whole, despite severe denunciations, the causes for which the attacks had been launched, actually prospered. There is no better example than the increasing ascendancy of the Palestinian cause in relation to that of the Israelis. And in Africa FRELIMO (Front for the Liberation of Mozambique) became the government of Mozambique apparently only to continue the pattern of terrorism it had established in battling COREMO (Revolutionary Committee of Mozambique) for the dwindling hold Portugal had over the country.

Not in a single country, nor in a region of the world, has terrorism been dealt a serious blow. The trend seemed to be that terrorism was leading to more terrorism, and then to near, or all-out civil war in a number of places. This is to be expected. Unchecked, these are conditions terrorism can lead to.

It is probably elementary to observe that it can also lead to increasing tensions in the world, not the lessening of them. This increase is perhaps so gradual, that it is not commented on in the press, and if so, not attributed to terrorism. For example, the end-of-the-year compilations we mentioned earlier seldom mention any of the side or accumulative effects. This seems to be true even when an incident is reported to have had wide effects on the larger political scene in a country. For example, the kidnaping of one of the candidates for mayor of West Berlin in February of 1975 caused a renewal of calls for cracking down on terrorism, even restoration of the death penalty in Germany, which in turn could lead to a voter swing to the right in the 1976 elections. After terrorists had killed the chief judge of the West Berlin courts in a kidnap attempt, this incident seems immediately to have tipped a municipal election toward the conservatives. It occasioned some overdrawn comparisons between the uneasiness terrorists were causing throughout West Germany and the chaos that destroyed the Weimar Republic in the 1920's and set the stage for Hitler.

However far-fetched the Weimar Republic comparison might have been with respect to modern Germany, it is not an exaggeration as to what terrorism might eventually lead to. The term law and order has come to be associated with the bumbling right-wing demagogue in much of the American press and popular literature. However, law and order is what governments are basically constituted to maintain. Even in the most permissive societies they are not expected to let things get out of hand. If they do, it is only a matter of time before there is a reaction from the population—demands for changes in leadership, laws, law enforcement agencies, etc. If things get worse, there will be a more drastic reaction. A people will not put up with chaos. They will opt even for totalitarianism instead.

Short of these dire conditions, most governments will have taken some measures to put down the terrorists and restore order. These may include a variety of actions and programs, including some that are more conciliatory than combative. Even the most benevolent government administrations, however, will be forced to take repressive measures eventually, and some slightly repressive ones even in the early stages of terrorist activities. Security checks at airports to curb hijacking of planes is an example. As the frequency or seriousness of the terrorists' attacks increases, governments are pushed toward more repressive measures. Not all terrorists subscribe entirely to the Marighellan theory which claims that provoking a government to intolerable repression will deliver the situation automatically to the revolutionaries. Nevertheless they all trade in provocation one way or another. In fact, the majority of the Marxists who use or support terrorism—and that, of course, includes the followers of Mao, Guevara, and Marighella—seem to harken to Lenin's warning that terrorism is effective only when linked with a program for organizing the masses of people toward acceptance of the idea of revolution. Whatever the persuasion of a particular terrorist organization, their use of violence leads to repressive measures from governments. Sustained terrorism makes it impossible to govern without extensive searches, massive intelligence gathering, curfews, and other devices for control that affect the entire population.

Terrorism gradually makes liberal methods of government and extensive freedom unworkable. This calls attention to a paradox that in itself is appropriate to be flung in the terrorist's face. Terrorism is a rarity, in societies under totalitarian domination. Any quick look around the world at where terrorism flourishes and where it does not will confirm this. The terrorist can operate only where there is enough personal and political freedom for him to act. Nothing else is so crucial to his even getting a start, or the continuation and enlargement of his operation. Conversely, nothing is so immediately effective in curbing his use of violence as is interdicting his freedom to acquire the weapons and materials he needs and restricting his freedom to move about and use them. These are freedoms he has, however, only because he lives and moves about among a population generally sharing them. He is not singled out for the use of them, nor can he be singled out for the denial of them. Obviously, if he could be so identified he could simply be apprehended and no one else need be involved. Thus, everyone who shared in the freedoms must share in the restriction of them.

The Palestinian terrorists, incidentally, enjoy a peculiar arrangement in this respect. They have freedoms *not* shared with all of the citizens of the countries in which most of them live, and from which most of their attacks are launched. The governments of these countries permit them freedoms they do not generally permit the mass of their inhabitants. Specifically they permit terrorist attacks—outside their own borders. They operate within understandings to this effect. And when they violate these understandings—as some of them occasionally have—they feel repression from the very hands that have made it possible for them to exist and operate.

Some of the initial measures governments take to combat terrorism, such as security checks at airports and selected buildings, are not seriously repressive, and are instituted almost reflexively. They are on the order of steps a householder might take after his house has been broken into a couple of times. Without any great thought as to exactly who he is keeping out, he has a better lock put on his door. Literally millions of people have to go through airport security procedures to keep no more than a few hundred from hijacking airplanes. The imposition is still relatively slight. At least in most places these procedures have been perfected to the point that they are usually considered minor nuisances and the majority of the people who fly often seem to have gotten rather accustomed to them.

However, these little routines only foreshadow the types of repression that continued terrorism can lead to. Under its pressure the searches become more thorough, and are not restricted to airports and a few buildings, but are extended to all forms of transportation, all public buildings, and to key bridges and traffic arteries. Studies are conducted to determine materials critical to terrorist operations—substances normally found in homes, on farms, or in factories and offices, that can be used to make explosives, for example. Roadblocks are established where vehicles are all but disassembled to insure that they contain none of these materials. Personal identification systems are instituted so that people unable to properly account for themselves can be detained for interrogation. The courts become clogged with terrorist and terrorist-related cases, and the jails become filled with people who claim to be political prisoners. The presence of van loads of riot police, special bomb disposal trucks, and units of military forces, become commonplace in the streets. The society assumes much of the tenseness of a war zone.

This, of course, is only a glimpse of the measures terrorism can push governments into taking. And it says nothing of the suspension of mass civil liberties—such as freedom to assemble and freedom of the press. The press is the inevitable object of government attention, even at the approach of terrorism. As the situation becomes worse, even the most benevolent administrations, have to give some thought to abridging this freedom. For, if the freedom to act and move about is the most crucial one for terrorists, the freedom to communicate, to publicize their causes, and to persuade others to join or support them, is next most important one. As with the other freedoms, this one is available to terrorists only because it is generally available. The only way to curb it for them is to take steps that curb it for everyone. And, as we noted in connection with individual freedoms, terrorism is a rarity in countries where the government is totalitarian and thus completely controls the media.

There is no handier index as to the freedom enjoyed by people, or to the degree of true democracy obtaining, in the various countries around the world than in the status of their media of mass communication. In any good political handbook of the world there will be some notation about the press, radio, and television in each country.* By comparing

---

*Political Handbook of The World: 1975, McGraw-Hill Book Company is an example.

these notations, you can easily set up a scale which assesses freedom and democracy in each country. One can almost pinpoint the countries most seriously hit with the modern epidemic of terrorism by studying these notations on the media and nothing else in the handbook. If such a scale were devised one would find it running from countries in which all of the media are simply owned by the government to other countries in which none are owned. In between these two ends of the scale an assortment of arrangements would be found in which some of the media are owned by the government and some by private interests.

The results of these arrangements is quite simple in terms of freedom of expression. To put it mildly, where there is government ownership of the media there is little public criticism of the incumbent regime, and none of the sort of vilification typical of terrorist propaganda. On the other hand, where ownership of the media is completely in the hands of private interests, terrorists can publish and broadcast right along with everyone else. The various mixtures of ownership between these two extremes produce similarly mixed arrangements for the possibility of free expression, including that of terrorist organizations.

And herein lies the condition terrorism leads to that is most finally destructive of true democracy in any society—curtailment of freedom of expression. Governments of countries in which there is no freedom of expression, and thus little opportunity for terrorists to use media to publicize their causes and gain support for them, are not really threatened with terrorism. Governments of countries where there is complete freedom of expression are threatened and realize that printed and broadcast matter make terrorist operations possible. They begin to censor anything that might help the terrorists.

Perhaps there is no better example of this than the Uruguayan government's final prohibition of even the mention of the *name* of the Tupamaros in the public media. The well established media of Argentina as mostly privately owned, but the battlefield terrorists have made of that country has considerably eroded press freedom. Brazil has an extensive, privately-owned media network, but censorship has become an everyday fact of life. Mexico has privately owned media, but they have come increasingly under government regulation during the past few violent years.

The pattern has been similar in country after country. We noted the outlawing of Marighella's book, *Minimanual of the Urban Guerrilla*, in traditionally free-publication societies in Europe. Revolution oriented underground newspapers carrying instructions for making bombs and using weapons have run into conflict with the law in England, France, Germany, and even in the United States. And there have been clashes between the press and the courts in free societies, including the United States, over treatment of information on terrorists. Any country with a serious terrorist problem has experienced some of this.

One of the least publicized aspects of what terrorism leads to is the enormous drain on the pocketbook of the "man in the street" in whose name the liberation struggle of terrorist groups is usually being waged, and whose life and property the government is trying to protect from terrorists. In a rare bit of reporting on some of the hidden costs of terrorism, a story on the seizure of the U.S. consulate in Kuala Lumpur noted that chartering a jet to fly the United Red Army terrorists and their comrades to Libya cost the Japanese government nearly three quarters of a million dollars. There is no question that the whole incident drained off several times that much from the treasuries of the governments involved. Nor is there any question that the threat of such incidents has drained off hundreds of times this amount from the treasuries of countries all over the world in beefing up their security forces—just to combat terrorism.

The customers of airlines are probably aware that the costs of the little security exercises at airports have been added to the price of their tickets. People are probably similarly aware that someone finally has to pay for the general increase in security around public installations. They probably don't realize that we are really talking about multi-billion dollar increases in the costs of expanding law enforcement agencies and providing them with types of equipment they have never before needed. We are talking about additional billions of dollars going into the establishment, expansion, and equipping of privately-operated security forces—guards, detectives, and armed patrols. The simple fact of the matter is that in the past few years commercial and industrial security has become an industry itself, one necessitated almost entirely by the epidemic of terrorism and the imitative crime it has inspired. The cost of all of this must eventually be paid out of tax receipts or fed into computations that finally set the figures rung up on the cash registers as the consumer pays for goods he buys, even the food he eats and the clothes he wears.

And, in turn, the cost of all of these preventive and defensive measures has to be added to the losses in property destruction and the costs of meeting terrorists' demands—amounts we see flitting across the pages of newspapers with little comment from whose pockets they must finally come. For example, no one seems to ask about the inevitable source of the ransoms of one, two, three, or ten or more, millions of dollars paid to terrorists for the return of corporate executives. And almost never is there a comment that although the blowing up of three of four multi-million dollar jetliners certainly provides terrorists with a spectacular piece of publicity, it all must eventually be paid for by the consuming public. Nor does anyone ever draw attention to how far short of the Robin Hood idea the terrorists' gestures to the poor fall. For example, out of all the money the SLA extracted from the Hearst family probably a hundred thousand dollars worth of food went to actually needy people. Much was grabbed by the greedy and many honestly poor people apparently wanted no part of the operation because they regarded the goods as stolen. Published figures on what the SLA's overall antics have cost all American taxpayers, however, are already past the three million mark—and these costs, of course, are still accumulating. Terrorism leads not only to the waste of human lives on both ends of the guns it brings into play, but it causes massive wastes in public resources, much of which is sheer destruction.

Whether the public ever realizes such things as this or not, somewhere along the line there seems always to be a tendency for people in a country to get finally fed up with terrorism. And

168

then we see some of the more drastic reactions we referred to earlier. One of the possibilities at this point is what is often called counter-terrorism, where a government feels it has popular support to crack-down on terrorists in kind. Another possibility is backlash, where groups of private citizens, having come to the belief that the government cannot, or will not, handle the job, take it upon themselves to crack-down on the terrorists.

By its very definition, counter-terrorism seeks to neutralize the fear the terrorists themselves inspire. And by its very nature, it steps beyond whatever normal processes of law and justice might have been traditional in a country. It usually involves not only mounting programs to seek out and destroy terrorists in their lairs, and declaring open season on killing them on sight, but also kidnaping, torture, and assassination. In such an environment the bodies of known terrorists and their key supporters may appear overnight in alleys, or even in public squares. Or certain of these individuals may simply disappear with never any indication as to what happened to them. Numerous reports of this sort of thing have come out of Southeast Asia, at least some of these had to be accurate. There have been spurts of this in Latin America and it has also occurred in Europe, the Middle East, and quite often in Africa.

We hasten to add that Israel's overall policy of retaliation against terrorist attacks is not properly classified as counter-terrorism, although it has generated some incidents that have to be so considered. This was inevitable. Even if the government had done everything possible to prevent them, and to keep the retaliation strictly on the level of overt counterattacks by uniformed armed forces, there would have been some counter-terror by official and quasi-official agencies. Killing and destruction has been so widespread in the Mideast that no one could have insured that the rules of the Marquis of Queensbury were always followed. The open and announced policy of retaliation, however, is another matter. No government could have stood by and merely registered "formal complaints" as terrorists crossed its borders and murdered its citizens, packed bombs into its civilian airliners, or mowed down its foreign visitors in terminals or on the streets.

169

The alternative to government action under the continuous pressure of terrorism is the other possibility we spoke of: backlash—where citizens take the law into their own hands because they feel the government is not doing what they think needs to be done. The instigators of this are usually extremists. They will also usually be of a political persuasion opposite to that of the terrorists whose activities aroused them. And they are usually small in number at the outset. As did the original terrorists, however, they will attempt to draw others to their ranks. They are seldom able to restore order, as they promise, and usually don't even aim to do just that. They more often want to restore some previously superceded political or economic situation, even if the current level of development of the society would make it completely anachronistic. Their chances for success in any of this are generally no better than those of the original terrorists, and the possibility that they will be able to deliver what their propaganda suggests is no better either. What they have most times brought to the scene is another political crap game, to become entangled with the one already in progress. The death and destruction continue. Rival armed groups take up fighting in the streets; additional groups acquire arms and seek coalitions that move toward civil war; and the spreading chaos invites a coup d'etat from within the country or a take-over by some force from the outside. The situation thus produced can be more finally disastrous for the country than any of the others we have mentioned—but this, again, is what terrorism can lead to.

Few terrorists seem to take this into consideration. Many of them gleefully prod at the government thereby to provoke an over-reaction of repression which they believe will cause the people themselves to rise up in arms and overthrow it. The texts they study don't deal very well with this king of Pandora box.

A brief look at Argentina at the end of 1975 will illustrate what we have been discussing. This country has been beset with terrorism dating back to the 1960's, but since the early 1970's as many as six separate guerrilla organizations have carried on campaigns of assaults on police, bank robberies, sabotage of industrial plants and business offices, and the killing or kidnaping of Argentine and foreign political and business figures. The groups were of a variety of far left ideologies, Castroite, Trotskyite, and self-styled independent Marxists, but three of them were operating under names or slogans which gave the impression they were seeking the return of the immensely popular former dictator Juan Peron. It was thus assumed that upon Peron's return to power in 1973, at least these three would give up terrorism and support his efforts to restore order to the country. If anything they increased their attacks. And as if to show where their loyalties really lay, shortly after Peron was elected to return to power by an overwhelming majority, members of one or more of these groups marked the anniversary of Che Guevara's death with a rocket attack on a hotel and the fire-bombing of a bank. Between the time Peron took office in September of 1973, and set out to put a stop to the terrorism, and July 1974 when he died, terrorist organizations staged a series of more than a hundred kidnapings involving Argentine, Swiss, American, and Italian citizens—killing several of their victims and netting a total of more than twenty million dollars in ransoms for their causes. Almost as if to flaunt their lawlessness in his face, some of the bloodiest incidents were by a group calling itself the Peronist Armed Forces. In the middle of this period one of the groups, the Peoples Revolutionary Army, became publicly known as having signed an agreement of revolutionary cooperation with the Tupamaros of Uruguay, the Movement of the Revolutionary Left of Chile, and the National Liberation Army of Bolivia. Incidentally, this last organization is Che Guevara's group, rebuilt from a rural to an urban guerrilla organization.

Neither Peron nor his wife, who as vice president succeeded him when he died in office, were able to put down the terrorists. As the violence from the left increased, in spite of everything the government tried to do, a terrorist tendency emerged from the right. Operating most often under the name Argentina Anti-Communist Alliance, this movement had claimed dozens of murders, kidnapings, and bombings by mid 1975. Its targets appeared to include both leftists and critics of the government and it issued threats against artists, writers, actors, and journalists considered as supporters of the left. Stories circulated that the leadership of the rightist group was within the government itself. And, indeed, one of the President's closest advisors was ousted in July 1975 under charges of secretly being a leader in the right-wing group.

By this time terrorists of both the right and left had killed more than five hundred people in twelve months and the press was keeping track of the dead in such terms as: "190 positively identified leftists; 91 presumed leftists; 38 right-wingers; 54 police officers; 22 soldiers, mainly killed by leftists; 13 businessmen; 4 children; an American diplomat; 20 unclassifiable; and 70 not identified." As suggested by these figures, guerrillas were not only taking on the police, but staging hit and run attacks against elements of the army. At the same time they were putting industrial companies out of business with bombings and internal sabotage, driving remaining foreign businessmen out of the country—along with Argentine businessmen, journalists, and entertainers—taking over whole towns for brief periods of time and forcing political leaders, and even minor officials and ordinary citizens to go about armed or in groups.

In September of 1975 Mrs. Peron was forced into a month's absence to rest, citing nervous strain and intestinal disorders. She was back at her desk in the latter part of October, but there were serious questions as to whether or not her government could survive. The terrorists seemed not to be through yet.

We have described terrorists as usually being rather vague about the alternatives they propose to the institutions and systems they have dedicated themselves to destroying. That is, they don't clearly say what their ultimate goal is. In trying to answer this question for ourselves it is appropriate that we should pursue a bit further what they do have to say, and why they seem not to say more about it. We have noted that one of the prime reasons terrorists don't enter into such dialogues is that they are not in business to negotiate. They seek to accumulate power not trade it away.

Beyond this basically non-negotiating stance characteristic of terrorists, there are two other very enlightening reasons for their being vague about where they are trying to lead. Both are relevant to our deciding for ourselves where terrorism can eventually lead.

First, terrorists probably do not have a fully developed alternative to lay out before anyone. They may not even have a coherent ideology. In their own minds they have concentrated on the negative aspects of what they see before them to the point that any alternative would be more desirable than that which exists. In other words, it would be too much to expect of a small band of saboteurs who are out to wreck a nuclear power plant that they devise a workable alternative means for supplying electric energy. They brought themselves to the point of sabotage in the same way terrorists usually build up to committing such acts—concentrating on the negative. From this sort of negativism terrorists develop a line of propaganda which insists that things are now so intolerably bad that destruction must take priorty over reconstruction. And it must be realized that they are the first victims of their own propaganda. They have to be. Otherwise, they would not be able to rely on anything so drastic and insecure as the future of terrorism. The very discipline required to train and motivate human beings to commit such acts cuts them off from the rest of the world. They talk only to teach others, setting up an intellectual and political incest that totally distracts them from such practicalities as "what comes next," or "will it really work." They have given themselves over to their own strategy and jargon to the point that nothing else matters. They need nothing more than generalities about the future to keep themselves going. In an interview published in the Cuban magazine *Gramma*, and reprinted widely in U.S. underground newspapers, the Tupamaros published two tabloid-size pages explaining their justification for revolution, their tactics, and organizational principles. Just under three column inches were devoted to the alternative social, economic, and political structure they claim their struggle is intended to create:

Q. Let's say the Tupamaros are in power. What do they intend to do with Uruguay?

A. Our program is in no way different from those of other revolutionary movements which are in power—as that of

173

Cuba—or which aspire to power—as the several guerrilla movements in Latin America. The tasks to be tackled are clearly defined: the problem of latifundium, nationalization of the banks, the expulsion of imperialism, the achievement of a higher standard of living, education, health, housing, the restoration of man's full dignity and the eradication of unemployment. These are the tasks that every revolutionary movement keeps in mind, awaiting the time when, once power is attained, the national program that will lead to those objectives can be put into practice. [*Quicksilver Times*, Washington, D.C., December 22, 1971.]

The literature of one of the organizations imitating the Tupamaros in the U.S. explains the concept of what it proposes in even less precise terms:

. . . By "alternative society" we mean a society in which oppressive relationships such as racism, sexism, elitism, and imperialism are *not* institutionalized, in which cooperative relationships and collective actions are encouraged. [Vocations for Social Change, issue # 23, May 1971.]

One of the reasons the terrorists is illusive about the alternatives he proposes is that he is not prepared to be more precise.

The second reason for this illusiveness is the knowledge that if openly stated the alternative he proposes would not be broadly acceptable. A particular terrorist group may not have it all sufficiently worked out in their own heads to be completely straightforward. They know enough about the people they are trying to manipulate to suspect their alternatives would be rejected.

If they adopt an ideology they know will be opposed by the society in which they are operating, the process of obscuring the real alternative will be even more devious. An excellent illustration of this can be taken from an extra edition of the now defunct magazine *Scanlon's* entitled "Guerrilla War in the U.S.A." and published in the U.S. and Canada in late 1969. It contained several interviews with members of the Weathermen. One of these was with a young man—speaking from intricately arranged anonymity—who claimed to have been involved in bombings in the San Francisco area:

> *Question:* *You speak of the revolution in this country coming together under the unbrella of communism. It would seem, at least for now, that communism has a very small following here.*
>
> *Answer:* I think that the following that communism—let's call it the movement for socialism—has in America, is bigger than most people imagine. When people opt for socialism it's not necessarily on the basis of having the book understanding of what socialism means. People move for socialism on the basis of what the f- is empirically necessary.*

In other words, his interpretation of Weathermen stategy is not one of trying to lead people openly to communism—or "socialism" as Lenin always spoke of it—but one of creating the impression that the situation is so bad that they will move toward something they don't even understand—out of "empirical necessity."

At this court trial, the one surviving member of the Japanese terrorist squad that opened fire on the crowd at Lod airport said he and his comrades undertook this mass killing on behalf of the Palestinians as a step toward world revolution. It was preparation to the creation of the world Red Army, and designed to help stir up the Arab world. Then he added:

> I want you to know that the next target may be New York or San Francisco. I would like to warn the entire world that we will slay anyone who stands on the side of the bourgeoisie.

And in his book *Black September* Dobson describes a *Time*

Scanlon's, December 1969, p. 91. *Note;* The circumstances of this interview were in themselves revealing of terrorists and their machinations. The interviewer was said to have been a radio news director in San Francisco who is named and quoted as describing himself as "well-known in the Bay Area for my leftist views." He is said to have received an anonymous phone call offering him the interview with the provisions that he allow himself to be picked up on a downtown street, blindfolded, and driven to a secret hideout. There he was allowed to question an unidentified young man who, in his judgment, was "middle class" and "college educated." He taped the interview, but his contacts transcribed it onto paper and burned the tape before he was again blindfolded and returned to the streets of San Francisco.

175

magazine interview with George Habash, leader of the Popular Front for the Liberation of Palestine, which included the following:

> Time: "Does Israeli retaliation for your raids which often kills innocent Arab civilians bother you?"
>
> Habash: "No. It is exactly what we want, for we are totally against any peaceful solution that leaves behind an Israel. And this is the only possible peaceful solution in prospect."

With respect to Al Fatah, Dobson notes that for diplomatic reasons this group has had to moderate its language, especially in expressing itself to the United Nations, but its ideas about terrorist strategy leading to the destruction of Israel remain as expounded on in 1968 edition of its monthly publication, *The Palestinian Revolution*. In explaining why a conventional war did not suit the Palestinian goal, Yasser Arafat said:

> For the aim of this war is not to impose our will on the enemy but to destroy him in order to take his place . . . In a conventional war there is no need to continue the war if the enemy submits to our will . . . while in a people's war there is no deterrent. . .A conventional war has limited aims which cannot be transcended, for it is necessary to allow the enemy to exist in order to impose our will over him, while in a people's war destruction of the enemy is the first and last duty.

With something of the tone of the New Left, Ulrike Meinhof, the thirty-eight-year-old co-founder of the West German Baader-Meinhof Gang, explained her terrorist actions as follows:

> What we want to do and show is that armed confrontation is feasible—that it is possible to carry out actions where we win, and not the other side. Cops have to be fought as representatives of the system. Cops are pigs, not human beings.

In short, you cannot pin terrorists down as to where they see their activities leading because: a) they don't have fully worked-out directions or destinations they can describe; b) they do know where they are trying to lead, but are afraid that if they spelled it out people would reject them out of hand; and

c) a combination of these two, visible in the words and actions of those terrorists who, whether they realize it or not, may be in the business more for the excitement and adventure than anything else.

The final part of our question about where terrorism can lead, concerns the types and levels of violence. Perhaps the quickest answer to that was given in *Commentary* by contributing-editor Walter Laqueur's ". . .the end is not in sight yet." Many of us probably thought of terrorists originally as typically a small band of wild-eyed fanatics with a few hand guns and a molotov cocktail or maybe a stick or two of dynamite. It should have occurred to us that gangsters in Chicago even in the 1920's whipped submachine guns out of violin cases—much as the Japanese terrorists whipped out their automatic weapons at Lod in 1972. But it would not have occurred to us to think of them using mortars, or rockets as the Argentinians have done. And certainly it was a shock for those of us who read about police in Italy intercepting a group equipped with shoulder-fired anti-aircraft weapons for the purpose of bringing down a civilian airliner. The possibility that this may yet happen is by no means to be ruled out. Such devices weigh no more than twenty-five pounds, cost less than a thousand dollars, and can be operated by a child.

In other words, there is little in the way of weapons typical of modern warfare that terrorists have not at least contemplated using. And, of course, they have long ago set off charges containing as much conventional explosive as moderate sized aerial bombs. One group even stole an air-craft and tried to bomb a military munitions installation with it. The really big question that keeps coming up, is whether they are likely to try for a nuclear explosion of some sort—either with a bomb they might steal from military forces, or one they might fashion themselves. The possibilities for this are so real that they are worth detailed attention.

As early as 1972, Dr. Frank Blackaby, deputy director of the National Institute of Economic and Social Research in London, expressed the fear that such groups could steal a small bomb from military stockpiles of atomic weapons in Europe or America—and hold the world for ransom.

Three years later, the Public Broadcasting System in the U.S. produced an hour-long TV documentary containing highly convincing evidence that terrorists would no longer have to steal an atomic bomb. they can now make their own— and have a blackmail weapon no government could afford to ignore.

This documentary, entitled "The Plutonium Connection," and first broadcast to PBS's 240 member stations on March 9, 1975, was presented with the advice and cooperation of the American Association for the Advancement of Science, with financial backing from The Carnegie Corporation of New York, the Corporation for Public Broadcasting, the National Science Foundation, and the Polaroid Corporation. Its content is supported by impressive research and corroborated by statements from scientists and security experts whose positions or responsibility suggest they know whereof they speak.

The idea behind the program was obviously to present the public with a graphic illustration of how it is now possible for terrorists to produce what might be called a homemade 'A' bomb. The matter was important enough, and complex enough, to warrant documentary attention. In fact, we feel the possibilities for terrorists doing this can hardly be understood without some of the rather specific information this documentary provided. At the same time we would have to argue that this part of the story cannot be fully appreciated without some explanation of how and why terrorists might decide to make use of a nuclear bomb. The two types of information need to be seen together to answer the question of where can terrorism lead in terms of weapons and levels of violence.

The TV documentary makes two basic points. First, it illustrates quite clearly how the information required to build a crude, but workable, bomb is now available to the public at large. Second, it portrays the task of safeguarding fissionable materials as so decentralized in the 1970's that enough plutonium to build this type of bomb could be stolen in any of the twenty-five countries now developing nuclear power.

The previous concern had been that someone would steal a finished military bomb and use it for terrorist purposes.

There had also been murmurings about the possibility of a homemade bomb—a "People's Bomb," which could be used by revolutionaries. Some of these rumors were thought to be little more than scare propaganda. The TV documentary, dispensed with mere rumor and based its contentions on a carefully arranged test. A young student at a large university was simply given the task of seeing if he could produce a bomb design on his own. He did it. Authorities were shocked. Some people wrung their hands that the information the student needed had been publicly available. It probably could never have been kept secret. The first nuclear bomb was put together over thirty years ago. It would be highly unrealistic to expect that information as to how this was done could have been kept secret for so long a time. And, it was not kept secret.

In fact, the TV documentary was inspired by the belief of physicist Theodore Taylor that the scientific data were readily available. Doctor Taylor, whose experience includes working on the atomic bomb design at Los Alamos, was aware of the common concern that a country might go nuclear, and thus increase the possibility of the use of nuclear weapons. But, he asked, why was the concern always only over a country being able to produce a bomb? Could not a small group of people, with some stolen plutonium or highly enriched uranium, make a crude bomb? He thought it could be done.

The TV program begins with the reenactment of the experiment in which a 20-year-old chemistry major, working without prearranged assistance of any kind, took only five weeks to dig out the necessary information and design a bomb that nuclear scientists agreed would go off. An actor played this part in the telecast to protect the student's identity lest he be kidnaped and forced to participate in actual bomb making.

The student said he was surprised at how easy it was to design a bomb similar to the one that was first tested at Alamagorda in 1945. He said that during his work he kept thinking "there's got to be more to it than this, but actually there isn't . . ." His design called for a central core of plutonium about the size of an orange, surrounded by an iron tamper, in turn, surrounded by a shell of TNT. This type of information is all but common knowledge. The precise data he needed was how big the plutonium core should be and how much TNT would have to be placed in the shell around the iron tamper. This he took from Los Alamos reference books and other publications he checked out from a public library. With this information he discovered the rest was simple: you devise a means for detonating the TNT, it squeezes the tamper and the core together until the plutonium becomes super critical, it stays together long enough for a chain reaction, and "boom, you've got a bomb."

The less than fifty page report he wrote was studied by nuclear weapons experts to see if the design had a chance of producing a nuclear explosion and, if so, what size. They described the chances of such a bomb going off as about even. According to the experts it would have produced a rather small explosion: probably equivalent to less than that of a thousand tons of TNT and maybe even less than a hundred tons of TNT.

Looking around for an historical explosion that might have been of comparable size someone hit upon one that occurred more than twenty-five years ago in Texas City, Texas. There, in 1947, a ship, loaded with a fertilizing material that also happens to be highly explosive, caught fire and blew up at the dock. It touched off a series of other explosions as it did so. The number of casualities was relatively low for the size of the blast, but it created havoc. Hitting the docks, warehouses, and a refinery, full force, it hurled debris for miles and cut off roadways and communications lines to an extent that made rescue operations initially all but impossible. This ship was said to have exploded with a force equal to about the maximum the student's bomb design was estimated to be able to produce.

From the standpoint of what could happen in a busy city, an explosion one-tenth this size, which Doctor Taylor felt was pretty well guaranteed for a crude bomb, would be enough to kill perhaps fifty or a hundred thousand people in a crowded urban area. With such a bomb in the hands of terrorists, no one negotiating with them could depend on the chance that it might not go off.

As should be expected from the title, "Plutonium Connection," the TV documentary then turned its attention to the possibilities of terrorist obtaining a fissionable component for a bomb—plutonium. They would most probably settle on plutonium because the uranium that they could most easily steal is not sufficiently enriched for the job. Plutonium is more readily available because it is a by-product of commercially used uranium at nuclear power plants scattered around the world. In other words, as uranium fuel rods are spent in the process of producing industrial energy some of the uranium is converted into plutonium, and some into pure waste. Every few months, at each nuclear plant, spent rods are removed from the reactor and transferred to reprocessing centers, where the plutonium is extracted prior to dispostion of the purely useless waste. The plutonium thus extracted is then distributed to various manufacturing sites for conversion to military purposes or to further industrial use. This presently occurs worldwide. From the moment plutonium is extracted,—as it is packaged, stored, transported to other installations, stored again, reshaped for final usage, and actually consumed—it is vulnerable to both pilferage and bulk theft. It could be spirited out, by an insider, in amounts too small to be missed, until enough is collected to make a bomb. It could be taken at gunpoint from a truck during one of the transfer operations, or it could be taken in a determined, armed attack against a processing, storage, or manufacturing installation.

As attested to in the TV program, security officials are aware of these possibilities. Indeed, certain security precautions are required by law wherever these materials are being handled. In many instances imaginative and energetic security officers have instituted measures beyond those required by law. Undoubtedly all of them would like better security. Security, however, can hardly be expected to be the first concern of the operators of nuclear installations—safety is. An inordinately vocal clamor has arisen which seems to be designed to condition all of us to the idea that nuclear power plants are hazardous beyond all imagination. Law suits and demonstrations running somewhere almost all of the time have invoked concern over these hazards, and not only slowed the development of an energy source that may be crucial to us. but have forced its developers into a safety not a security posture.

Nuclear materials are dangerous. It would be foolish to

argue otherwise. The simple truth of the matter is that the public has had little opportunity to find out how dangerous, or how safe, their industrial use really is. If we listen to the one-sided views usually offered on the matter we might easily conclude that there is nothing else posing an even comparable threat to us. Yet, the sound of these voices, and the flood of anti-nuclear literature notwithstanding, actual experience in no way supports the idea that accidents with nuclear materials pose a fraction of the threat to public safety and well-being that incidents of terrorism do, even without "A" bombs.

The clamor is too loud for this sort of discussion. We are experiencing the overlapping circles of radical manipulation and valid public issues. The majority of the people whose voices make up this clamor are undoubtedly citizens with honest concerns about hazards they believe to be unacceptable. There is ample evidence also that a number of those voices belong to radicals and revolutionaries who see this issue only as another way to get at the system they seek to destroy. For, we find some of them following patterns of terrorist strategy in sabotaging nuclear facilities and turning the attention they get by doing so into propaganda exercises. We also find some of these same people active in purely revolutionary activities.

Strangely enough, there is another cry in these protests against the nuclear industry that frequently injects the argument into the general discussion that the use of nuclear energy for industrial purposes will produce terrorism with atomic weapons. This is something like arguing that the use of gasoline in trucks and automobiles produces arson—or that the existence of rifles in the sports club from which the Tupamaros first stole weapons was responsible for the initiation of terrorism in Uruguay.

The emotional tone of the protests against the use of nuclear energy combined with the generalized fear terrorism is intended to create, has all but prevented any rational discussion of such matters. And by no means the least result of this combination has been the general circulation of what is undoubtedly an unrealistic view of the safety requirements for the nuclear industry. The lack of emphasis on security as opposed to safety could increase the possibility of terrorists deciding to use an "A" bomb. Even the best security can do only so much. Security officials are quite realistic about this.

The TV documentary points out that one reprocessing plant is capable of extracting enough plutonium oxide from nuclear wastes in a year to fit out a couple of thousand crude bombs. The material is dustlike before it is formed into pellets no bigger than a child's marble. It is packed in containers about the size of a large coffee can. As we noted from the student's description of his design, it takes relatively little of this material to make a bomb. Security officials certainly have checks and detection methods they are obviously not willing to disclose.

However, none of those interviewed on the TV program— either in government or in the private sector—claim they can reduce the possibilities for pilfering to absolute zero, or guarantee that there will be no chance for theft by determined armed attack.

Of course, the use of an insider slowly draining off small amounts of dust or pellets would be the most subtle way by which terrorists could accumulate the plutonium for a bomb. And some speakers in the TV documentary commented on the degree of internal security required to prevent this. Several, including consumerist Ralph Nader, claimed that the personnel investigations and evaluations required to do so would produce a garrison state. However overdrawn such statements might or might not be—public sentiment at the moment is not supportive of internal security measures anywhere nearly sufficient to give assurance that terrorists will not be able to use an insider to obtain the ingredients for a bomb.

As to the possibility of the hijacking of a truck transporting nuclear materials, or the success of an organized attack against an installation where they are stored, security officials make no pretense as to where they stand. Armored transporters offer some security, but not enough for any real guarantee. Fixed installation security is sufficient to resist little more than an ordinary armed robbery attempt—two or three well armed individuals. In no case was it said to be sufficient to hold off a sudden, but carefully planned and coordinated, assault by ten or twelve trained and determined terrorists. Reinforcements sufficient to withstand an assault of this sort are certainly available—from state police, national guard, or other military units—but not in time to prevent the terrorists from penetrating a given installation and removing the materials they would be after.

Such grim pronouncements as those above are not born of either inefficiency or complacency, although charges of both have been leveled at the security and law enforcement officials involved. These statements are born out of experience in dealing with terrorists. If you were discussing security against ordinary, non-politically motivated criminals, not terrorists, you would have a different picture.

For example, law enforcement officials would tell you that the show of force—the visible appearance at the SLA hideout of an overwhelming display of manpower and weaponry—would have caused conventional criminals to respond to police loudspeaker demands for surrender by throwing their weapons through the windows and walking out with their hands raised. Even the old big-timers would have reasoned they could not win against such force and would rather take their chances with "beating the rap" in court, or escaping from prison later. The SLA members responded to the surrender order with a barrage of machine gun fire.

Convert this fanatic attitude and behavior in a situation where the terrorists were surprised, and clearly outnumbered and outgunned, to one wherein they suddenly swoop down on a nuclear plant—where the advantage of surprise and superior firepower is in their favor—and you begin to have some feel for why security, in any ordinary sense, is simply not enough. What the officials responsible for it are saying is that each nuclear plant would have to be comparable to a military installation, constantly on full combat alert, to guarantee its defense against an attack force of this sort.

There is little need to ask whether a group such as those we have been discussing could hit a nuclear plant with enough force to take the plutonium they sought, nor is there a need to wonder if they would have anyone among them with the mental equipment on a par with the twenty-year-old chemistry student who came up with a bomb design on his own. On both counts events of the past few years speak for themselves. These same events also testify to the fact that the spread of terrorism does not depend on whether or not there is industrial use of nuclear energy. Indeed, the primary reason for its spread is probably a general lack of understanding of how it works—a tendency more toward actions that play into the terrorists' hands than rational attention to how to cope with them.

To cope with the above problem we should first answer the question: "Under what conditions are terrorists likely to use an 'A' bomb?" There is a strong tendency for people to throw up their hands at this question and say: "Who knows?" That is true only in that it has not happened yet, and we cannot see an answer from actual experience. Otherwise it equates to the frequent use of the term senseless in connection with the violence we see terrorists using. Both of these reactions are purely emotional. They suggest there are no patterns of terrorist activity and thinking for us to go on.

Hopefully, we have illustrated enough about how a terrorist organization operates, and how it gets itself in the position to do so, that we can look together into the possibilities of one of these groups using a nuclear weapon without having to wait for them to try it. We believe their ways of thinking and operation are sufficiently similar that we can say that they have only three basic considerations in deciding to use an "A" bomb:

a) Their ability to obtain the required materials and make them into a bomb.

b) Their willingness to take upon themselves the decision to employ this level of violence.

c) Their conviction that by doing so they will advance their cause.

All of the available evidence suggests that consideration "a" must be checked off immediately. From what we can read in open literature, about both nuclear weapons and terrorism, it would be folly to do otherwise. Consideration "b" has to be checked off in similar fashion. Nothing in the world's recent experience, or in the history of terrorism itself, suggests we can count on any final squeamishness from groups of people who have already decided to be judge, juror, and executioner at lesser levels of violence.

185

The only consideration of any import is whether or not some terrorist group will become convinced that the use of an "A" bomb would advance its cause. This is, indeed, the heart of the matter. Yet, it is not as simple as our emotions might at first lead us to believe. If we put such emotions aside and think strictly in the strategical terms the terrorists must think, as they plot their courses, we can see some ways for lessening the likelihood that they will choose this particular course.

To think along these lines we must discard any ideas we may have that terrorists indiscriminately adopt any kind of violence. They do not do this. They orchestrate violence. We have seen them do it. They use violence to edge themselves forward politically. On the one hand, they use it to gain a platform from which to propagandize the people they hope to win over to their side. On the other, they use it to weaken the institution or system they are attacking—and to intimidate those who are trying to defend it. They could do nothing worse from their standpoint than to get those wires crossed by using unprogrammed violence that intimidated those they seek to propagandize and at the same time by giving those they seek to intimidate the advantage of a reverse kind of propaganda.

Thus, the use of an "A" bomb poses some real tactical adjustments for terrorists. Such a weapon is not suitable to use in the midst of the very people from which they must recruit and take their support. Thus, before using it, not only would they have to identify a target sufficiently hated to justify the level of destruction the bomb would deliver, they would have to pick a target so physically isolated from any part of the general population that its destruction would not have the crossed wires effect we just described. For, as pointed out in the "Plutonium Connection," even a small atomic explosion in an urban area would probably kill tens of thousands of people. There are few circumstances under which an atomic attack would advance the terrorists' cause if they were held responsible.

There are many circumstances, however, under which they could use an atomic explosion to advance their cause if that explosion were seen as coming from some other source. For, whereas they could do no worse than to be responsible for killing tens of thousands of innocent people, they could do no better than to engineer an incident of this sort for which the system or regime they have under attack would be blamed.

We can therefore come up with several conditions under which some group of terrorists might decide to avail themselves of the possibilities of a homemade "A" bomb. As examples, they might do so if they thought they could do any of the following:

1) Provoke some type of drastic reaction from the government by creating the belief that they have an "A" bomb and will use it.

2) Actually set off an atomic explosion with a homemade device, but do so in such a manner as to put the blame elsewhere.

3) Or, set off an atomic explosion because they were able to find a target, isolated from sizeable elements of the general population, for which there appeared to be enough hate to justify its destruction.

Any one of these courses of action a terrorist group might take could have disastrous consequences. Even their setting up a hoax whereby they claimed to have a bomb set to go, when they actually did not, could get thousands of people hurt in the ensuing panic. All of these courses, are made more likely by those who join in the emotionalism and smother rational discussion of both nuclear materials specifically and terrorism in general. Of course, the three conditions cited above do not comprise an exhaustive list. They are adequate for considering the possibilities with terrorist groups in the middle stage of their development—where they have acquired enough following and strength to be able to acquire the materials and make a bomb. There are some additional ones to be considered, however, in looking at groups in more advanced stages of development. For instance, when their movement has made really great progress, they might be looking for that one last surge of violence needed to topple a government. Or, on the other hand, a group might be in an advanced stage, but suddenly suffers serious reverses, and is looking for some way to forestall the further loss of gains which after years of patient work are about to be snatched away by a powerful reaction finally mounted against them. There are certainly these possibilities of some advanced terrorist group using an "A" bomb".

4) They have gained sufficient control over the situation that they feel they no longer have to concern themselves over killing a large number of people.

5) Their long-fought-for cause is already in such jeopardy that they are desperate and will try anything.

It should take little imagination to see how some of the possibilities in any of these courses could result in panic, death, and destruction of gigantic proportions. At best, the words of the narrator on the TV documentary come ringing back: "The student's bomb, if it was built, would inevitably be the most terrifying blackmail weapon ever built."

In designing our responses to the situation, we need to be very realistic in making a distinction between what is a potential but unthinking, tool for this level of blackmail—or actual violence—and the already practicing, and quite calculating organizations for using it. There is too little practical consideration of what terrorism is all about, and too much romanticism about what it might lead to.

J. Bowyer Bell's book *The Myth of the Guerrilla* says something on both scores. In it he writes that repeated failure had taught Che Guevara only that the war he was fighting, wherever he went, would be long and cruel but it was the only hope for victory in the revolution. He quotes Guevara as saying:

. . .rivers of blood will have to flow. The blood of the people is our most sacred treasure, but it must be spilled in order to save more blood in the future. What we affirm is that we must follow the road to liberation, even if it costs millions of atomic victims.

Of course, back there in the middle 1960's, Che was probably not even dreaming of guerrillas making or using a nuclear bomb, he was pre-ordaining the martyrdom of millions that he believed the "imperialist powers" would finally use atomic weapons against. The chances are, however, that with his rivers of blood he never came close to telling his adoring disciples what terrorism itself can lead to—even if all of the atomic weapons in the world were to be consigned to some uninhabited desert in outer space.

188

6.   What Can Be Done About It?

The First, the greatest and most decisive act of the judgment
which a statesman and commander performs is that of
correctly recognizing the kind of war he is undertaking, of
not taking it for, or wishing to make it, something which by
nature of the circumstances it cannot be.

[Karl von Clausewitz, *On War*]

As we have seen, most of the terrorist groups in the world
today consider themselves to be waging war—revolution, they
generally call it. The reality of that should not be missed, even if
it seems an implausibility for a particular group at the moment
they proclaim it. It should not be taken, however, as an
indication that the proper response to their militaristic
posturing would be the wholesale mobilization of armed forces
to do battle with them. The theorists among them would like
that. Marighella, for one, actively sought this type of
confrontation and believed it would create such alienation
among the population as to lead in the direction of civil war.

Marighella was sometimes wrong. He was not wrong,
however, in suggesting that when terrorism is allowed to go so
far that only military forces can handle it, things are truly out
of hand. Yet, the terribly painful paradox of it all is that unless
the military nature of what the terrorists are doing is taken
seriously, and studied, from the outset, things generally do get
out of hand. For, whether it is their political propaganda or
their pseudo commando valiancy that is uppermost at any

particular moment, they are always using tactics woven into discernible strategy, in the military sense of both terms. They are, indeed, waging a form of warfare.

And although the lines we chose from Clausewitz's all-time classic on war were written a century before Black September, the Tupamaros, the Weathermen, or any of the others set out to wage it, there is no other situation of human conflict to which these lines have more application. The first, and unquestionably the most decisive, step in even considering what can be done about terrorism is, indeed, to recognize it for what it is, and, even more importantly, not to try to make it something it cannot be—in order to respond to it in ways we happen already to understand.

The temptation to do the latter often seems to be overwhelming. Five or six years ago the media were noting that the outbreak of political violence seemed to be epidemic because all of the terrorists were using the same tactics. Yet, few writers outside the technical journals and books on such matters attempted to pursue this notion, to expound on those tactics, or to try to put them together in any pattern of explanation. Instead, people at one end of the political spectrum congregated around cross-national spontaneity as an explanation for it all, and people at the other end headed toward international conspiracy as their explanation—neither doing more than trying to make the terrorist epidemic into something they were accustomed to thinking about.

These opposing views of the situation naturally prompt equally opposing answers to it. The one assumes that socio-economic conditions are the totality of the cause of the terrorism, and thus fundamental changes in those conditions will end it. The other assumes that some unseen network is directing it all, and thus the relentless rooting out of that network will end it.

Although one can dig up evidence in this case, or that one, or on one group or another, to support either end of this argument, none of it holds up when you look at case after case and group after group around the world. The greatest commonality you find in such an examination is in strategy. Whether it is a large group or a small one, whether it claims to be seeking some relatively limited objective, or proclaims all-out revolution, the basic strategy being followed is usually the same. And it is the undoing of this strategy that must be recognized as the task to be undertaken in combatting terrorism. It is self-defeating to try to make that task into something else.

This strategy is not drawn up into a blueprint that you will find all terrorists carrying around in their hip pockets. In fact, many of them would not agree with the way we have drawn it up. It is however, the sum and substance of the undergirding theory of the texts and manuals on guerrilla or "people's" warfare you find most of them reading from. More generally still, it is the sum and substance of what you will find all of them doing—whether they have actually read the books or not. It is something that works and the gist of it gets passed around.

Brian Crozier, director of the Institute for the Study of Conflict in London refers to it as a continuum of processes that undermine and alienate a society, of which the actual violence is only "the sharp cutting edge." It is what we were referring to back in chapter 2 when we used the analogy of an iceberg to illustrate that the violence which catches our attention, and the issues over which the terrorists claim the violence was done, are only the visible parts of what really goes on. There are propaganda and organizing activities which exploit the selected issues and systematically build up to the violence. All four together, and in proper order, are the strategy.

If we pull that iceberg we talked about then completely out of the water, the distinctiveness, yet sequential relaitonship, of these four parts of the strategy can be more easily visualized. The numbers in the drawing below are the same as those in the iceberg illustration, and indicate the sequence in which the activities represented are conducted.

But to provide a better foundation for discussing a counter-strategy we need to consider a bit further what the terrorists do in each of these activities:

Illustration No. 6

1. At this point in the drawing we have tried to represent the people and institutions of the society in the midst of which a group forms over real or imagined injustices—the issues which they will eventually claim justify their violence. In chapter 2 we noted that with the Tupamaros in Uruguay these were such things as high prices, taxes, low living standards, police brutality, and poor working conditons.

2. Here the underground newspaper vender, the soapbox speaker, and the figure passing the hat represent the propaganda, recruiting, and resource gathering part of the strategy. The issues seized upon in the preceding part are used as the basis of an effort to draw recruits, funds, and supporters from within the population. During the period 1967-1970 the underground press in the United States did enough of this type of work to move forward dozens of groups with potential for terrorism.

3. Here they organize and train themselves, and whatever support they have been able to gather, in accordance with the issues they have developed and the propaganda line they have formulated. Both the Weathermen and SLA tried to shortcut this phase. One blew up a bomb factory. The other got trapped in a fatal shootout. Black September was more thorough here, and the Tupamaros were perhaps even more so.

4. This is the "cutting edge" of Crozier's continuum. The attacks at this point may be physical, psychological, or both, but they will be direct products of the agitation, propaganda, organization, and training that preceded them. The level of militancy achieved by this time almost guarantees at least some violence. When a group at this stage is not in agreement that the time is ripe for using violence it is not uncommon for some faction to splinter off and do so on its own. We saw some of this with the Palestinians, and in the Venceremos faction pulling out of the Revolutionary Union in the U.S. and setting off a spree of violence of its own.

All of the tactics for persuasion and coercion that we have discussed earlier are woven into each of these activities.

Again, these are the basic elements of the strategy one

finds terrorist groups following. And this is the sequence in which they move through the strategy. The progress is not as smooth, nor are the parts as completely separate, as a drawing almost unavoidably suggests. As the Weathermen wrote in *Prairie Fire,* the capability for armed attacks:

> . . . matures unevenly, with setbacks and at great post. It will not spring fullblown at the magical moment of insurrection.

Thus, you may find a group backtracking momentarily, or occupied with more than one part of the strategy at any given time. The effects are cumulative, however, because the whole operation is a cyclic affair. This, indeed, is the most significant thing about the numbers we have assigned to the parts of the strategy. They outline the cycle through which a new group goes before it gets up enough steam to commit its first act of violence, and through which it will repeatedly move subsequently. The groups are never organizationally still, but continuously moving within the strategy. Even if they are keeping a low profile, they are re-assessing the situation of the issues they are dealing with, gathering information with which to exploit the issues, redoing or elaborating on their propaganda, tightening up their organization, retraining, and planning future ventures. And everytime they make an attack, or have any other public encounter—even a court trial, for example—they pick up whatever propaganda advantage they were able to generate with the incident and take it back around the cycle toward a buildup for the next occasion.

The incidents themselves, which come so violently to public attention, and create pressures which threaten whole governments, are in reality the end points of rotations along this cycle through which the groups committing them are persistently moving all of the time. The violent actions, by design, compel attention and provoke some type of reaction. This is the genius of the strategy. By the time a group has come around the cycle to point 4 a scenario for attack has been produced in which everyone—the individual victim, target institution or government, and media—has been assigned a role: a reaction role upon which the attackers count for the advancement of themselves toward their own goals. And each rotation of the cycle sets up an action-reaction sequence in which the size and type of reaction needed to accomplish a particular objective was determined first, then an action was designed to draw this particular reaction. As one simple example, if police brutality is one of the issues seized upon at point 1, by the time the incident comes off at point 4 the group will have designed it to all but guarantee what will appear as an overreaction by the police. And they will be already prepared to use anything the police do that complies with this role as material for propaganda and the gathering of further support for themselves. This is the primary reason for the widespread use of the scheme. It runs on the energy of reaction rather than that of action, and thus provides a means by which a group beginning with little or no power can cause things to happen that require great power.

Further, the cycle has additional self-refueling features from the fact that the groups are emboldened by the feel of unaccumstomed power when they have any degree of success, and heartened by the attention and the amount of public sympathy that almost always flows to the underdog when they are beaten down. In the Munich affair, for exmaple, Black September committed to action a number of men no greater than that of the smallest unit of any army in the world, yet they had the personal attention of the heads of several governments and forced a confrontation among them that continues to have repercussions four years later. And, with an estimated world-wide media audience of 500,000,000, if they had the sympathy of only one out of ten of the people watching them take on the odds they did, they came away with a public opinion prize probably unmatched in history.

This was the sort of thing that was troubling the FBI official we quoted earlier, as he was looking back on the shootout with the members of the SLA. These violent incidents automatically require some reaction from law enforcement, usually involving some amount of force. He was apparently noting that there is always the chance that this force will be, or can be made to seem, excessive. As he undoubtedly knew, the problem was more intricate than his comments made it sound, because the situation had been set up to have boomerang possibilities long before law enforcement was, or could have been, involved in it. The SLA had begun at 1 scarcely a year before, but had swung completely through the cycle at least three times—the Foster murder, the Hearst kidnaping, and a bank robbery—before it came around to 4 again in the shootout. After that, the cycle picked up various shades of criticism of the police for excessive force and continued on its own momentum for a while, then was nudged further along by surviving members of the SLA through their messages to the press.

In other words, in its advanced stages a prevalence of terrorism in a society can pull a substantial part of the population into this cycle. Then the situation begins to teeter on the brink of some of the possibilities we discussed in chapter 5—what it can lead to.

Most authorities who have studied the problem agree that the perpetrators of terrorism must be shown to lose if a society is to avoid the dire consequences it can eventually bring on. In his book *Protest and the Urban Guerrilla* Dr. Richard Clutterbuck says the only way to prevent these consequences at the extreme levels of violence is "to establish an unmistakable pattern of failure and retribution" for those who run the scheme at lesser levels. As hopefully our discussion of the cyclic strategy which the terorrists follow has suggested, this requires more than the application of sheer force. The task is, indeed, beyond the capability of the agencies whose business is the use of force.

Crozier says quite simply that "when it goes beyond isolated kamikaze gestures" terrorism "is not merely a problem for the police or the army, but for the society as a whole." Clutterbuck indicates it will require a lot of good work on the part of law enforcement, even "a good deal of loyal and determined international cooperation," but he says:

> The most effective control, however, lies in the minds of the public. The dilemma will be to break the few dozens of guerrillas without eroding the liberties of the millions of

innocent people, and to prevent or punish violence without stifling legitimate protest. This can be done only if the bulk of ordinary people are aware of the nature of the threat and are willing to take personal risks to defeat it.

And here lies the real challenge. There is really little question but what this paragraph is an accurate statement of what must be done, but getting it done under the conditions of confusion and division of a nation deep into period of active terrorism is something like getting a consensus statement at the foot of the Tower of Babel.

There is, again, a pressing urgency for recognition of the nature of the task at hand—and at the earliest possible moment. The advantage of studying the problem of terrorism from a diagram such as we have drawn is that it can immediately bring some order to visualizing the main thrust of a counter-strategy, and it can do so at the earliest possible moment: in the very beginning. For, whatever else the counter-strategy does it must break the cycle we have been discussing. And this cycle can be identified whether a country is faced with one terrorist group or a dozen, with a score of incidents or hundreds. Indeed, a diagram of this sort can be drawn up for any country beset with terrorists, with supporting data elaborating on the activities at points 1 through 4—specific issues, propaganda themes, organizations involved, and incidents occurring. In other words, the cycle can be fleshed out to show rather precisely what is to be broken.

That is one of the sub-tasks to be undertaken and we want to come back to it. But, of more immediate concern is where the attempt to break the cycle should be made. If we think of the task in these terms, it becomes obvious that what Clutterbuck was saying is that the cycle should be broken at the point we have labeled 1. This is where it touches the bulk of ordinary people—where they are first being tapped for recruits and support on the basis of the type of corrosive criticism of the society that finally allows no alternative but violent destruction of whatever is being criticized. Robert Moss, whose book *The War for the Cities* we quoted earlier, is pointing to this same spot when he singles out "the rhetoric of vilification" as being the polarizer, the activity which sets in motion forces within the society that make violence inevitable. It is, indeed, the beginning of the cycle and the critical point at which a break will cause the remainder of it to wither and die. The mechanics of making this break are, as Clutterbuck says, making the bulk of the ordinary people aware of the nature of the threat terrorism poses to their liberties and well-being and enlisting their efforts in defeating it.

We need to be coldly realistic, however, about the conditions under which this must usually be attempted. In the beginning, a population has a tendency to regard terrorist incidents as little more than rather frightening nuisances, to be dealt with by law enforcement. Indeed, as we have illustrated, some elements of the population will be supporting the terrorists although they would not engage in political violence themselves. Some other elements will take at least a verbal anti-terrorist stand, but will have little hard information to support their point of view or any well defined direction in which to focus their concern. The great majority of the population, however, will take little serious and consistent interest in the matter and thus not consciously take either side. Where there is a relatively large governmental structure, the branches of which have some capability for independent expression, the division among them will be similar. As we noted in the case of Uruguay, this type of division can be manifested *within* branches of government. Only in line law enforcement agencies will there be much real unity in the perception of the problem. There the focus is likely to be sharper not only because these agencies will be under pressure to stop the violence, but because their members are at the front in the battle and losing their lives by being there.

When the violence becomes really pervasive, this same population will tend to surge toward law and order, either condoning the government's assumption of extraordinary powers to put down the violence, or lending support to citizens' groups simply taking the law into their own hands to do what they think the government should be doing but is not.

Between the time scattered incidents of terrorism begin to appear and the time the situation gets completely out of hand, the strategy keeps the attention of the society as a whole on points 4 or 1—4 when there is violence, and 1 as issues are exploited. Pressures mount for law enforcement to control the situation with the application of force at 4. Law enforcement acquires additional capabilities for violence, and terrorists do likewise. At the same time massive resources are expended at 1 on issues exploited by terrorists, at the expense of attention and resources for more rational and longer-range problem solving.

Thus, although the terrorists will never be really defeated without breaking the cycle at point 1, i.e., having the bulk of ordinary people consciously repudiate the extremist manipulations which promote and sustain terrorism, this can seldom be the sole point of attention. Something has to be done about the violence itself. No institute or society can put all of its attention on long-range corrective measures, even though they may be more effective finally, while the terrorists are killing people and destroying property. At least initially, a multi-pronged counter-strategy must be mounted. One of these prongs must be at least reasonable protection of life and property against the attacks. Otherwise, the government will eventually lose the loyalty and support of even the most steadfast of citizens. Simultaneously, however, another prong must be aimed just as vigorously at the addressing of real grievances among the issues being raised. If this is not done, the cycle cannot ever be broken here. The initiative will remain with the terrorists. They will select the issues which remain in the public consciousness and exploit them to feed their own movement. And they will thus divert valuable human and material resources from the type of real problem solving that would undercut them. Still simultaneously, the propaganda operation at 2 must be exposed for what it is, and thoroughly discredited as having any final purpose but to mislead the population into supporting the turmoil in which people are trying to live and work. Depending upon the sincerity, precision, and diligence with which these three efforts are mounted the activity at 3 can be expected to dry up for lack of support and outlet.

Before we look further at some of the specifics of these

three efforts, we need to give attention to who is to mount them. If there is general agreement on any particular aspect of combatting terrorism it is that it is something in which the largest possible portion of a society should be involved. We just cited Crozier, who said it is a "problem for the society as a whole," and we found Clutterbuck saying the most effective approach would be one in which the bulk of the ordinary people would be aware of the threat and "willing to take personal risks to defeat it."

The question then becomes one of who is to control this broad participation in a counter-effort. From the stand point of insuring maximum coordination, this should be a single authority, responsible directly to the head of the national government. And, if the level of volence in a society is allowed to reach military proportions there is little choice but to have this type of centralized control. Short of this, however, it is extremely important that the government not be cast in the role of being the authoritative reactor to the terrorists' strategy. As we have noted, one of the frequent objectives of terrorist attacks is to make the government appear oppressive. And whereas a government may actually have to curtail some individual liberties, at least temporarily, in order to curb the violence, it can easily be led into wholesale abridgement of civil liberties if it attempts to do all that must be done without participation from the private sector. For instance, it usually becomes obvious that propaganda has a great deal to do with the terrorists' success. If the government tries to run a counter propaganda campaign on its own, it invariably runs into opposition from the press. Then, the situation becomes one in which the government feels it must curb press freedom in order to curb terrorism.

Experiences of the media in countries with extensive terorist problems offer obvious examples. As we have already seen, governments trying to win in the propaganda part of the struggle have restricted media from even mentioning the terrorists' organizational names. In aggravated cases editors have gone to jail, or papers have been closed.

Business is usually one of the most important institutions

to be brought into participation in the management of the counter-effort. Especially in the highly industrialized societies of the world privately-owned business organizations are involved in such a mass of communications and transactions with all elements of the population that they already have far more influence on the situation than their governments. If that influence is not exerted from a thorough understanding of what must be done to combat terrorism, at least some of that influence will invariably be exerted in ways that promote it. This will eventually result in the government intervening in how private organizations use their influence and conduct their affairs.

As examples, advertising and marketing practices that glamorize the terrorists or give further publicity to catchwords in their propaganda provide them psychological support. The paying of multi-million dollar ransoms for kidnap victims provide them material support. Even in the United States there have been some clashes with the media over the handling of information and publicity on terrorists and related groups. And there have been some murmurs by legislators in the direction of making the payment of ransom in political kidnapings illegal.

Of course, it is not just the business community that is likely to do things which turn out to be at cross purposes with a government's programs to eliminate a terrorist threat. Educational and religious institutions the world over have consciously or non-consciously done so—some have even harbored their own members as they trafficked in information and supplies, even weapons and explosives, with terrorists. Their leaders have collided with governments and been jailed, and had the activities of their institutions restricted or simply closed down.

Many of these things are really products of arrangements wherein the government is trying to run the counter-effort alone and leaders of other institutions in the society do not fully understand the threat the terrorists actually pose. In truth, there are times when some of the non-governmental organizations in a country become involved in activities that undercut the government's counter-effort literally for the lack of something better to do. They have resources, and are being pressured to do something about some of the issues being noised about, so they set out to do what seems most appropriate to them. Of course, they are being set up to fight with the government by the strategy the terrorists are following.

Conversely, pulling non-governmental institutions into sharing the control of the counter effort actually assists in the breaking of the terrorists' cycle of operation. Indeed, the primary reason for anyone saying the society as a whole should be involved in the effort is the necessity for getting everyone to do the kind of soul searching that will cause them to see where and how they might be supporting the terrorists, and to stop doing it. There is no surer way to accomplish this than getting everyone to become a part of the counter effort themselves. If this is to be done, if individual citizens are to incorporate the the nature of the threat and the requirements of the counter effort into their thinking, so must the institutions to which they belong and in which they work. And there is no surer way to have the institutions thinking in this fashion than by getting them to assume some of the responsibility for the conduct of the counter effort.

The concept of sharing the management of the counter-terror effort must begin with complete candor as to the nature of the problem the society has with terrorists. This is not an easy beginning. Not many political leaders want to admit that things are slipping in terms of the government's ability to maintain law and order. And until the situation has already slipped rather badly, not many aspirants to political office are willing to take the risks of running a campaign based on putting down what may have some of the trappings of being a populist movement.

Again, candor is needed. The truth of the matter is that no government can use the force required to prevent attacks by well established terrorists without turning itself into a police state. A small body of trained and disciplined guerrillas can attack when and where they choose, and ordinary law enforcement methods will not stop them. The terrorists know this. Law enforcement and industrial security specialists know it. There is nothing to be lost by business and professional leaders knowing it, and being brought into a coordinated effort to combat the problem from their own positions of influence, using resources they already have available to them. For the political leader, encumbent or aspirant, there is no shortage of statistics to show the costs of terrorism, nor any lack of evidence that the movements of which they are part are usually not genuinely popular ones. There is every reason to make terrorism a political and civic issue, and virtually none for not doing so.

The specific organizational arrangement for bringing this type of coordinated effort about is not so important to our considerations here. The philosophy on which it is to be based is. The keystone of that is simplicity and sincerity. The effort should not be the occasion for creating some massive new organization or ministry of government. This is not only a waste of personnel and resources, but an invitation to failure. In a highly complex society there will have to be some national council, or committee, to exchange information and maintain liaison between political leadership and that of the private sector. This should be kept to the bare minimum, however, because for the concept to work it must have the attention of the leaders in the political, business, and professional communities, not supernumeraries who will not really be in the mainstream of the regular affairs of the organizations and institutions in those communities. The counter-terrorist effort must be completely integrated into normal executive and staff functions. Specialists may be used to help with research and planning, but not to have exclusive responsibility for execution of the effort. That must be grafted into every department of the organization, be it government or private. Grafted is the proper word, because the general understanding of how to counter the terrorism must become such a living part of planning and operations that specific ideas as to what should and should not be done are generated within the context of the everyday work of each organization.

Law enforcement and security operations are a good place to begin looking at the nature of some of the specifics that should be worked out. They are perhaps more easily seen in those operations, and immediate actions of some type have to taken in the face of the physical attacks by the terrorists if the system is to survive.

Law enforcement agencies are obviously up against problems in coping with terrorism different from those they are accustomed to encountering in dealing with traditional crime. In combatting terrorism they are frequently confronted with people using military-type weapons and military tactics. Thus, police forces usually have to organize and train special units that are more paramilitary than normally required. These units, and many police officers outside them, will have to be provided with sophisticated weapons and communications equipment. No one should expect it to be possible, however, to simply hand over the larger mission of police operations against terrorism to special units or newly created divisions within police departments. For one thing, there are never enough officers available for such special assignments to do more than cope with the actual incidents of violence. More than that, though, the entire law enforcement mission needs to be carried out in such a manner as to put the terrorists out of business. The top officials in police and security organizations have to make themselves experts in countering terrorism, so that they can insist that all of the operations under their control will be designed to undo the terrorists' strategy.

As we have discussed several times, one of the inevitable issues the terrorists will try to exploit is police brutality—or at least the use of excessive force by law enforcement officers. It goes without saying that no society should be asked to tolerate brutal or corrupt lawmen. Wherever they exist, they should be removed and prosecuted. That is not really what we are getting at here. Police officers do not have to be brutal or corrupt to be so labeled in terrorist propaganda. Nor can the police do anything to change such themes within that propaganda. Any sort of debate with the terrorists and their supporters, for example, can only hope to give additional publicity to the charges and deepen the issue. The problem must be addressed in a more positive manner. And, it must be addressed, or it will eventually destroy the best of law enforcement agencies.

Addressing the problem does not mean being lenient with the terrorists. Another of their objectives is to show that law enforcement is weak and inefficient. The requirement is for the conduct of all law enforcement activities in accordance with the highest standards of professionalism, coupled with a concerted effort to have this quality of performance recognized by the public at large. Neither will be sufficient alone.

Again, the police are not usually called into action against the terrorists until they are at point 4 on the strategy cycle. At this point the terrorists have already gotten some elements of the general population behind them, and they and their supporters have been hard at work trying to condition all elements of the society to join them at least in spirit. Thus, just, effective, and humane law enforcement must be demonstrated in all contacts with all elements of the public. This is more difficult than it would normally be because the activities of the terrorists force the police to subject more members of the public to investigate procedures than do those of ordinary criminals.

The fact is that the requirements for intelligence in fighting terrorism are enormous, and since the terrorists are operating within the population this intelligence must be gathered from within the population. The terrorists and their supporters will invariably try to make an issue of this. Obviously, they do not want their organizations penetrated, their leaders identified, nor their sources of assistance, supplies, and weapons revealed. This is exactly the type of informaiton needed to defeat them. Law enforcement agencies must accumulate as much detail as possible on the people and organizations behind the violence. They must chart the command structures and communications and alliance networks of these organizations. Points 3 and 4 on the strategy diagram must be fleshed out with as much information as possible on the means the terrorists have developed for being able to commit the violence and disappear. The more information of this type the agencies fighting them have the more precise they can be in going after the real perpetrators of the violence and the less danger to the lives and property of innocent citizens.

The public must be told this, repeatedly, in detail, and in every way possible. It must be true. Every care must be taken to insure that innocent citizens are not unduly harassed by the police, and their civil liberties not unnecessarily curtailed by the government, and they must be told and shown that this is the case. Indeed, the counter-terrorist campaign should inspire a continuous review on *all* law enforcement regulations of public behavior, not just those instituted to fight terrorism, to eliminate those which are not really necessary. To cite what may appear to be the extremely trivial, if there is a single no parking sign in a city that is not actually required in the public interest, it should be removed. Law enforcement must be seen to be designed to serve the public, not simply to regulate it. On the other hand, the terrorists must be seen as a common threat to life, property, and the public peace, not the servants of the people they claim to be. In short, the public must be kept informed that it is the terrorists, not the government or the police, who inject danger into otherwise safe pursuits, and cause the interruptions of their lives and the invasions of privacy.

This has not been widely done. For example efforts to deal with aircraft hijackings and the security procedures instituted to stop the hijackings were negligent in this respect. There was no general attempt to make the public aware of the enormity of the danger, to everyone aboard and to others on the ground, when a huge airliner is taken over by force and ordered about the world. And, indeed, signs were posted in air terminals suggesting that the security measures designed to prevent hijacking were carried out only because the government required them—not because the hijackers necessitated them, and not because of the safety of innocent passengers demanded them.

In similar fashion, some of the elaborate security precautions planned for the 1976 Olympics were portrayed as if they were simply the contrivances of law enforcement authorities. For the most part, the athletes and the public were not reminded that these precautions, which did invade the privacy and freedom of the participants, were injected into the situation by the attack of Black September on the 1972 games at Munich—and the constant threat of terrorism throughout the world since then.

Of course, non-governmnetal institutions do not want to accept the blame for inconveniencing or endangering the public. There is no reason they should. They must be shown, however, that it is equally to their disadvantage to shift the blame to the government. One has only to read the terrorists' propaganda to realize that having anyone but the terrorists themselves blamed works to the disadvantage of all of the institutions that can be said to make up the societal system. As we saw in the reactions of various revolutionary groups in the U.S. to the SLA attacks on an educator, the media, banks, and the police, a blow against any one institution is a blow against the system. A psychological success, achieved by setting these institutions to blaming each other for whatever happens, is also a blow against the whole system. Revolutionaries in the U.S. are fond of quoting Benjamin Franklin's famous remark: "We must all hang together, or assuredly we shall hang separately." That is exactly the situation of the various social, economic, religious, educational and political institutions within any system under attack by them or their like-minded comrades around the world.

The revolutionary texts they are following have schooled them in the necessity for eroding the cultural structure of a society as a means of getting at its political structure. Mao's little red book told them:

> Revolutionary culture is a powerful revolutionary weapon for the broad masses of the people. It prepares the ground ideologically before the revolution comes and is an important, indeed essential fighting front in the general revolutionary front during the revolution.

This little passage has been expanded into volumes of argumentation and instruction over how this is to be done. Of course, all any of this amounts to is a recognition of the fact that political and economic arrangements within a society are related to the values advocated by its cultural institutions. Even in a state under totalitarian control these values are factors to be reckoned with. Hence a dictatorship will seek to manage them either through propagandistic manipulation or police control. In a free society, where people govern their personal actions more according to customs stemming from these basic values, rather than according to formal laws, cultural integrity is crucial to the continuation of the society in a democratic tradition. The revolutionary theory simply fastens onto the idea of programming the future form of a society through manipulation of its value system.

The attempt at this manipulation begins at point 1 in our diagram when the operators of the strategy seize upon some matter over which to violate the accepted code of the system, be it a law or a seriously held value not spelled out in the law. To the extent that they are able to gain acceptance for this they are successful in manipulating some part of the value system. Were they able to transform the entire culture in this fashion they could forget about the political angle of the triumvirate of factors which control a society of people and concentrate on whipping the economic factors into line. That is, if a people can be led into adopting the value system of a police state they will through their own devices align their laws and political structures accordingly. The only thing left to be done is to use the altered political authority, and the force it carries with it, to re-arrange economic matters. Mao is correct, cultural change "prepares the ground ideologically before the revolution comes . . ."

This sort of change is not easily accomplished, however. Values are deeply held within a society. Slight or temporary departures from them may be fairly easily tolerated, but drastic or permanent ones are instinctively resisted by major elements of a society. This is suggestive of where the common line of defense against this strategy lies. All of the institutions in the society can take up stands on the society's basic values and contribute to the counter-effort by clarifying and encouraging adherence to them within their own spheres of expertise and influence. People can be rallied around these values to exert themselves against the terrorists because they are already inclined toward them basically. This does not mean holding to the status quo. It does not mean taking a stand against social, political, and economic change. It means refusing to be manipulated into going against values vital to the integrity of the social system because of the way issues are presented.

For example, no institution should have any trouble taking a stand against terrorism as a political tool. The sanctity of one's own life and belongings is a universal inclination in human cultures. No society can approve murder, vandalism, or looting—for any reason, social, political, or economic—and maintain its integrity. Certainly these cannot be acceptable avenues of political expression as long as any legal means are available. And as long as a society has non-governmental institutions capable of either approving or disapproving of terrorism there are some legal means left. Thus, all institutions can take a stand against terrorism and conduct themselves in such a manner as not to support it.

What we are saying about the course of action of non-governmental institution is really no different from what we said about the government and its law enforcement agencies. The first order of business is the straightening out of their own houses. The police cannot successfully uphold the basic value of abiding by the law unless they do so themselves. And they cannot hope to convince people that they are not brutal in their enforcement of the law without demonstrating it—going about their business with true professionalism. Where institutions are not themselves acting according to the basic values it is their position in society to uphold, they should do so with all haste. And where they are not going about their business—be it education, religion, or business itself—with professionalism, they should bring themselves up to this level and demonstrate their efforts to do so.

As we have previously indicated, the U.S. experience with the SLA offers us a view of terrorism as a tactic of revolution, in microcosm. It does exactly the same thing in the type of cultural manipulation we are discussing now. And, again, though tiny, and rather bumbling, this group took its cues, and its propaganda themes, from the self-same texts that organizations with similar goals around the world use, and they ran the strategy out for us to see. Of course, all of the people who made up the SLA ranks, and all of the money, supplies, and weapons they used, came from the very institutions they were later to attack. At most, the issues they came together around were prison conditions, racial equality, and poverty. And they became involved in these not because they were particularly suited to do so, or had any answers waiting to be put into practice, but because they themselves were living in the midst of constant vilification of the entire existing social, economic, and political system. Their ties to all that they had formerly believed in thus eroded, they seized upon a body of revolutionary dogma and propaganda and set off on a path of destruction.

It is worthy of note here to observe the process of shedding basic values commonly followed by terrorists widely separated in time and ideology. Part of the preparation the ancient Arab religious teacher put the original "assassins" through was the destruction of whatever values they had previously held. His creed was: "Nothing is true, and all is permitted." Vincent Bugliosi writes that Charles Manson conditioned his followers toward murder by teaching them a completely amoral philosophy which insisted that "everything is right, then nothing can be wrong" and "nothing is real, and all of life is a game, then there need be no regret." The SLA, of course, came out of the new left where the philosophy was that there are no basic values: "All truth is relative."

And when the SLA actually came to do battle, the original concerns over which they had come together had been almost totally eclipsed by a broadened attack which took in essentially the whole system and every institution in it. With physical violence they hit: education, in the killing of an educator; wealth, in the kidnaping of a wealthy man's daughter; law enforcement, in taking up arms against police; and the press, in using the kidnap victim as a hostage to force publication of their propaganda without editorial comment. But within their propaganda, they also made psychological attacks on such values and institutions as: individuality, the family, marriage, religion, ownership of property, and representative government.

The more impact these attacks on basic values has as the

issues are raised the more susceptible the people in the society are to the next point in the strategy cycle—propaganda and recruiting. The non-governmental institutions in the society not only have an opportunity to share in the conduct of the counter-effort by holding the line on basic values here, they have an obligation to do so as a matter of helping individual citizens defend themselves against propaganda—against the sort of brainwashing that the terrorists lack of hold on a basic belief system allowed them to succumb to.

As we have contended previously, this brainwashing is most successfully accomplished when the propaganda can be fed as the sole diet to a single individual, isolated in a small cell. This is obviously not possible with mass audience targets. Trying to fill the public media with a single point of view has some of the same effects, but not all. As long as an individual has trusted loved ones, even a single boon companion, or a deeply revered Diety, with whom to talk and compare notes, the required isolation is not complete. Deep religious faith has allowed people to resist persuasion and even coercion throughout history. Men held as military prisoners of war have relied on their religious faith, or when it was perhaps not strong enough, on a buddy to take them through truly forceful propaganda attempts. The wife or husband in an open society can be the same hindrance to the propagandist's attempts. The devoted family can be the same. The much maligned nuclear family, with well-defined sex roles for its members, father, mother, and children is the most solid basic building block against propaganda a soceity can be composed of. As a complete unit dedicated to its own common survival and welfare it has the built-in comparison of male and female and older and younger viewpoints of what it reads and hears. All of these are real obstacles for the revolutionary propagandist and he will seek to destroy their viability if possible. The non-governmental institutions in the society can make no greater contribution to the defeat of his strategy than the constant and studious upholding of the basic values by which these forms of human companionship exist.

At the same time, these institutions can make another

great contribution by dealing quite openly with the subject of propaganda itself. It is quite common for people to be manipulated by the propagandist whether they believe what he says or not. The aspect of his operation that needs to be spread far and wide is that he is really operating somewhere between the truth and the lie that many people expect when they knowingly encounter propaganda. In a sense he is operating at two levels of thought and communication as he speaks or writes. Missing this point puts the average citizen in double jeopardy.

For, to assume that a speaker or writer is passing out only false information because he is identifiable as a propagandist is to assume that he has undertaken an extremely complex task with no preparation. This is seldom the case. The trained or experienced practitioner of this art will have labored long and hard to produce good data upon which to base his statements. The chances are that he knows more about certain conditions in a community than most of the people who live there do. These are the points around which he will weave his argument. A part of his success is measured on whether or not he can trap some member of his opposition on one or more of these points and publicly make that opposition appear either incompetent of dishonest.

On the other hand, to assume that because the issues he cites appear to be real and thus the solutions he offers will be valid is, again, to assume that he is not prepared for the task he has undertaken. This is still not likely. If he is so committed to a political idea that he will use violence to advance it, or even advocate this, he will be embued with goals and a body of tactics for which he will sacrifice his very life. Thus, he may be quite clever at keeping these goals and tactics in the background, but whatever truth he deals in will be used toward them, not toward solving the problems he talks about.

The media and the educational institutions of a society, in particular, should help to prepare people to devise their own strategies against the trained propagandist. A simple one, and one that most propagandists like least to encounter is focus switching. That is, when he is citing hard data, don't argue about that, question him about himself and his goals—who he is, why he is interested in your area, and what, precisely, he proposes to do about the problems he cites. At other times when he is describing his action program, the focus should be switched to hard data—questions as to how much time and money will be required to do what he is proposing, who will get the benefit of it, how will it be administered, etc. This requires some homework on the part of anyone who challenges him thusly, but it offers better chances for success, even with minimum preparation, than allowing oneself to be trapped into playing his game, on his terms.

The importance of people being able to detect propaganda and resist it is generally understated. There is apparently a widely held notion that propaganda is put out simply to give further circulation to the ideas it contains. Putting out any sizeable body of convincing propaganda is time consuming and expensive. It is seldom done for any less purpose than to get people to take some action, or to join others in doing so. Another mistaken impression is that propaganda has little effect. The number of radical and revolutionary organizations that exist today, and the number of them well enough indoctrinated to commit the violence we have discussed, is testimony to the contrary. The propaganda operation at point 2 on our strategy diagram is designed to organize people into groups to make these kinds of attacks or to support those who do make them.

This propaganda was tailored for the job, and organizing techniques were developed to hook right into it. Perhaps the primary reason the left has been so much more successful in fielding groups capable of political action and violence than has the right is the left's attention to organizing as follow-on to propaganda. Any public library will have several recognized works on propaganda. Scholars have written on the subject for years. Not so with organizational techniques. There has been considerable writing on guerrilla and terrorist tactics, but relatively little on organizational methods. The left has filled this gap with its own writings on the subject.

One of the most commonly available of these writings is a

366-page paperback entitled simply *The Organizer's Manual,* produced by the O.M. Collective in Boston, and published in 1971 by Bantam. It covers organizing small or large political groups, raising funds, organizing high schools and universities, organizing in the military, in labor unions, and setting up alternate community services, legal and medical self-defense groups, and conducting mass education and communications.

More directly to the point of how to organize people and move them progressively toward actually committing violence is less widely circulated literature printed by such organizations as the Revolutionary Union. The effectiveness of their methods is evidenced by the spread of local branches of the organization into all parts of the U.S. since its founding in 1969. The Revolutionary Union is not on our list of terrorist groups because it has never been found committing violence itself. However, it openly declares a dedication to destroying the present system in the U.S. by revolution, and it has spawned some terrorist offshoots.

The primary device within the organizing techniques prescribed by organizations such as this is, not surprisingly, manipulating people around values. As we noted earlier it attempts to get people to give up the values that hold them in the existing societal system and to accept others that will orient their allegiance toward revolution.

The process may take a few weeks, months, or a year or so, depending on the nature of the organization being developed and the type of people to be organized. It is begun with a rather detailed study of these people and how they are already organized—in families, clubs, churches, unions, etc. It also seeks to identify the people's long-range goals—the value reasons for their being where they are, such as religion, devotion to family, country, etc. And it seeks to pinpoint some of their short-range goals—more mundane things, such as family or self needs, neighborhood improvements, work conditions, personal recognition, etc.

The organizer on the ground then tries to pull the least committed people from the loosest organizations by offering to help them attain short-range goals of his own selection. He will have chosen only those he knows he can show as not being met by the organizations to which these people already belong—church, civic, social, labor, etc. These may even be matters beyond the purview of these organizations. The organizer, however, encourages his potential recruits to believe these are legitimate needs that should be met, and can be if they will get together with him.

Once he has gotten them to divert some of their time, energy, and interest into the short-range project he has proposed he will look for an opportunity to convert the goal involved to a long-range one. The point is that if he can raise the goal level to something out in the future, an ideal, a new life—a different value—he can get a deeper commitment. The opportunity to do this can be either success or failure in the effort toward the short-range goal. If the goal is reached, in whole or part, he can use the success to spur his recruits on to greater achievement. If it is not reached, he can blame it on their level of commitment and insist they push harder in another try, or he can blame the lack of success on the oppression of what he can picture as an insensitive system, and raise the level of militancy of the group. Either way, he can make a play for greater effort and deeper commitment, moving the people further from the immediate concerns over which they were recruited on toward broader participation in the "movement for a new society"—feeding specifics into their consciousness only to the extent required to keep them going and never fully articulating what this new society is to be like.

The best large scale example of this has to be the sort of mass manipulation we saw earlier when organizers who had been successful at pulling large numbers of people behind them in actions against the Vietnam war asked themselves the question: "What do we do when the war is over?" If this is only an anti-war movement, their article in the *Great Speckled Bird* went, then it will die. But that was not the case, they reasoned, it was a movement against imperialism, and they immediately chose the new name, Anti-Imperialist Alliance. And they set about producing propaganda against the economic system and organizing anti-business projects.

Of course, the Peoples Bicentennial Commission came into being in similar fashion. It came out of a nest of anti-war organizers whose specialties had been such things as trying to get signatures on a Peoples Peace Treaty, which some of their number had written under the tutelage of the North Vietnamese in Hanoi, and running War Crimes Commissions, mock or kangaroo court trials of the U.S. military for atrocities alleged by the Viet Cong. The people in this nest had a problem with the war ending too. They switched to a variety of issues—taxation, industrial health and safety, prisons, child care, housing, anti-corporate agitation, and the bicentennial.

The group which formed the nucleus of the Peoples Bicentennial Commission produced a bag of propaganda material more easily measured by weight than page count, and aimed for mass organizing on a nationwide basis. Their scheme avoided the necessity for having to send one or two of their own people into each community to do the job. They took a leaf out of the books of the corporations they pledged themselves to abolish and developed a franchise technique. They held regional sales meetings, to which they enticed prospective local representatives for a weekend of orientation and indoctrination. With these people they insisted that three documents "essential to a proper understanding of the revolution of 200 years ago, and the tasks it left incomplete," are: the Declaration of Independence; the Bill of Rights in the Constitution; and the Bible.

Accordingly, one of the franchise possibilities they offered to those of the weekend listeners who stayed around long enough for the handing out of the prime territories was the church. And the pitch went something like this:

> Religious bodies offer a great network of communication into half of the population of this country. It is a network that can be used by PBC. Religious people are already sensitized to the idea of concerning themselves with other people, they only need to be provided some political content to these concerns. PBC can provide that.

> There are several liberal denominations that are already tuned in to social action projects, and they can be reached to do more. In fact, many of the activities of the civil rights movements in Mississippi a few years ago were funded under programs of the churches.

But there are several more conservative branches of Christiniaty—the fundamentalists. They have not been so ready to step into the type of activities PBC advocates, but if they can be reached they can really be the most powerful influence possible, because of the high level of dedication they have. They *believe* in the Bible, and if you can show them how the Bible backs up the idea of revolution, their dedication and evangelistic spirit can literally work miracles.

When this argument was being made at a PBC meeting in Ann Arbor, Michigan in May of 1975, a young woman interrupted the speaker to ask if "socialism and communism" would not turn off deeply religious people. The speaker replied essentially as follows:

I don't think we are talking about socialism or communism. PBC contends the rhetoric has to be re-examined. Some of the labels we are accustomed to using have to be reconsidered. PBC has done this and found that we don't have to talk about socialism or communism. We can talk about returning to the basic principles on which this nation was founded. We can talk about "economic democracy," that is what PBC stands for.*

Somehow in all of this manipulation of goals and people one hears an echo of the words of the young Weatherman bomber we quoted in chapter 5. You may remember that he was discussing his assurance that a revolution in the U.S. was "coming together under the umbrella of communism." But, he said, "—let's call it the movement for socialism" and:

When people opt for socialism it's not necessarily on the basis of having the book understanding of what socialism means. People move for socialism on the basis of what the f--- is empirically necessary.

Thus, the manipulation is designed to give the propagandists and organizers control of what the people see as being "empirically necessary."

This is illustrative of what goes on at point 3 in the strategy

*These are not verbatim quotes as our others have been. They are quite accurate reconstructions of what was said, however, and are based on detailed notes the author took at the meeting and transcribed two days later.

cycle. At this point, some of the people who have become deeply convinced of the worthiness of the cause which has led them thus far see the move to point 4 as empirically necessary for them. These are the ones who make up the strike units that deliver the actual blows to the targets—whether these blows be psychological or physical. Some of their fellows remain poised at point 3 for some future time—whole organizations can be seen in this stance. Others will probably never move beyond point 3. They provide the close in support to those who actually carry out the attacks. They only watch as the cycle rotates through point 4, but they pick up the gains and see that they are properly used.

The strategy cannot be defeated at point 4, only suppressed for the moment. Fighting the violence with mere force helps run the cycle. If the society chooses to escalate the violence to the level required to eliminate the practicing terrorists without doing anything about the rest of the cycle it will probably destroy its own democratic traditions and only postpone the threat.

The cycle can hardly be broken at point 3, because the people who have been pulled into it are at that point too committed, too far along in their indoctrination, to give in to persuasion. And the police have difficulty touching them because they seldom actually break laws. When they do, the circumstances are such that legal measures against them do little more than clutter up the courts. There is a need for extensive intelligence on the organizations fermenting at this point because they support the terrorists the police have to search for, and many people in the population are led into unwittingly supporting them when they probably would not if they understood their manipulative methods and goals. Law enforcement runs into difficulties gathering this intelligence, however, because it tangles with charges of invading the privacy of innocent citizens. The media can and should do it, through investigative journalism, because segments of the population are victims of the strategy's duplicity by not knowing the truth. To the extent that the media does not do this it is sacrificing freedom of the press and turning over its columns and airwaves to propagandists.

218

The cycle can be attacked some at point 2, but not by the government without risking the erosion of mass civil liberties, especially press freedom. The media, educational institutions, the church, and business can throw light on this propaganda operation, however. This is a part of the counter-effort they should shoulder.

As we said in the beginning, however, point 1 is where the main effort must be made. It is here, where the cycle begins, that all of the institutions in the society, government and non-government, must re-examine themselves, clarify the values upon which the system actually rests, and see that they are living up to them. It must be an honest and thorough effort. It must not try to gloss over actual injustices, corruption, or stagnation, but it must not disregard the reality of the inherent frailty of human institutions. Indeed, it must expose the totalitarian direction which all utopian schemes must eventually take. It must create a broad realization that true freedom always makes it possible for people to err, even to sin—man cannot be free unless he has this choice, and having this choice, he will sometimes avail himself of it. To eliminate the possibility of human error, or misuse of freedom, entirely, a system would have to take away this right to choose—for everyone. Values, again, must be brought to the surface, and not be sacrificed over spectacular issues of the moment.

This is the nature of the task of defeating terrorism. It requires some force, inevitably. But it should be used with the highest degree of professionalism, and it should be explained to the public as it is used. The more important part of the task, however, is massive information and education. And, if this is to be done without sacrificing the basic freedoms of the society, including the right to honest dissent, it must be done by a combination of government and private institutions, not government alone.

No one should think the task is an easy one. It is not. And the worst thing anyone can do is to try to make the job into something it cannot by its nature be—in order to make it appear easy.

Appendix

Significant Incidents—1968-1975

The following chronology is by no means complete. For example there were some thirty aircraft hijackings in 1968 and 1969 that could probably be classified as terrorist incidents. And there were hundreds of bombings in the U.S. alone that we have not listed. If we looked back into the three or four years prior to 1968 we could add hundreds more. The chronology was begun with 1968 because that is generally regarded as the beginning of the current epidemic of deliberate and systematic terrorism. Much of that which went before was not so easily identified as such, and some of it was vandalism and mob action as these are more traditionally understood. The chronology is not complete for another reason: sheer manageability. Only incidents regarded as having some significance in the illustration of the types of incidents, demands, and responses, and the trend in terms of time and geography were included. A listing as complete as any good researcher could make it would fill a book in itself.

1968

Jan 16   GUATEMALA: Kidnaping of two U.S. military officers by FAR.* No ransom demands. Both men shot to death.

Feb 18   FRANCE: Bomb explosion in residence of Yugoslav ambassador. 1 killed; 14 injured.

Aug 28   GUATEMALA: Assassination of U.S. Ambassador

*A key to the organizational names represented by those and other initials within the chronology is incorporated in the list of terrorist organizations e list of incidents.

John Mein by FAR. First U.S. ambassador ever assassinated.
Oct 12   BRAZIL: Assassination of U.S. Army captain by members of VPR claiming he was a Vietnamese war criminal sent to organize right-wing terrorists.
Nov 22   ISRAEL: Bomb explosion in open-air market. 12 killed; 52 wounded.

1969

Feb 18   SWITZERLAND: Machine-gun attack on El Al Israel Airliner by 4 PFLP terrorists. 1 terrorist killed; 4 Israeli crew members and 3 passengers injured. Terrorists captured, tried and sentenced.
Feb 21   ISRAEL: Bomb attack on supermarket. 2 killed; 8 injured.
Mar   GERMANY: Bomb damage at airport to Ethiopian Airlines jet by ELF. Several cleaning women injured.
Jun 20   URUGUAY: Attack on U.S. company facility by 2 Tupamaros in police uniforms. Damage estimated at $1,000,000.
Aug 9-10 U.S.: Tate-La Bianca murders by the Manson Family.
Aug 19   SYRIA: Hijacking of TWA plane by PFLP. Plane destroyed as a strike at imperialist interests. Passengers removed and released except for 2 Israelis held for 3 months.
Sep 4   BRAZIL: Kidnaping of U.S. Ambassador Charles B. Elbrick. ALN and MR-8 believed responsible. Demands met for release of 15 prisoners. Elbrick freed Sept. 7.
Sep 6   ECUADOR: Hijacking of Ecuadoran Air Force plane by 12 men and 1 woman. Co-pilot killed; 1 crew member wounded.
Sep 9   ETHOPIA: Kidnaping of American diplomat and British businessman by ELF. Released several hours later after attesting to instruction in ELF's objectives.
Oct 6   COLOMBIA: Kidnaping of Swiss diplomat and son of Swiss consul. Undisclosed amount of ransom reported paid by families and both released Oct. 23.
Nov 27   GREECE: Hand-grenade attack on El Al Airlines Office. 1 child killed; 13 persons injured. 2 Jordanian terrorists arrested but released on demands of hijackers several months later.
Dec 12   SPAIN: Two ELF members, armed with pistols and explosives, killed by security guards as they attempted to hijack an Ethiopian Airlines shortly after take-off from Madrid.

1970

Jan 11   ETHIOPIA: Murder of U.S. soldier by unidentified gunman, suspected member of ELF.
Feb   U.S.: Bank of America branch at Isla Vista, Cal.

destroyed by fire by mob chanting revolutionary slogans.

Feb 10   WEST GERMANY: Grenade attack on bus at Munich airport by 3 members of PFLP. Israeli killed and 11 other Israelis injured. Terrorists arrested but later set free on demand after three Sept. 6 hijackings.

Feb 21   SWITZERLAND: Explosion in Swiss plane en route from Zurich to Tel Aviv. PFLP presumably responsible. 47 passengers and crew killed.

Feb 23   JORDAN: Attack on tourist bus by guerrillas. 1 U.S. woman killed.

Mar   ETHIOPIA: 5 members of U.S. film crew taken hostage by ELF. No ransom demands. Group released unharmed after 17 days.

Mar 6   U.S.: Weatherman bomb factory explosion demolished a Manhattan townhouse. 3 Weathermen killed.

Mar 6   GUATEMALA: Kidnaping of U.S. diplomat by FAR. Demand met for release of 4 prisoners. Victim released Mar. 8.

Mar 11   BRAZIL: Kidnaping of Japanese diplomat by VPR. Demands met for release of 5 prisoners. Diplomat released unharmed Mar. 14.

Mar 24   DOMINICAN REPUBLIC: Kidnaping of U.S. military attache by Dominican Peoples Movement, United Anti-Reelection Command. Demands met for release of 22 prisoners. Officer released Mar. 26.

Mar 24   ARGENTINA: Kidnaping of Paraguayan diplomat by FAL. Demands rejected for release of 2 prisoners. Diplomat released unharmed Mar. 28.

Mar 24   ARGENTINA: Attempted kidnaping of Soviet diplomat by MANO. Diplomat escaped.

Mar 31   GUATEMALA: Kidnaping of West German Ambassador Count Karl von Spreti by FAR. Demands refused for release of 25 prisoners and $700,000. Victim shot to death Apr 4.

Apr 5   BRAZIL: Attempted kidnaping of U.S. diplomat, presumably by VPR. Wounded by gunfire but escaped.

Apr 13   U.S.: Explosion toppled tower carrying power to Lawrence Radiation Laboratory in California.

Apr 16   U.S.: new Bank of America branch set afire in Isla Vista, Cal.

Apr 21   ETHIOPIA: Kidnaping of U.S. Peace Corps volunteer, and wife from train by ELF. No ransom demands. Released unharmed Apr. 26.

Apr 26   U.S.: Louisiana State capitol dynamited. Political message sent to press.

May 4   PARAGUAY: Shooting death in Israeli Embassy of wife

222

of a diplomat and wounding of an employee, allegedly by Al Fatah.

May 22   ISRAEL: Bazooka attack on school bus by Palestinian guerrillas. 8 children killed; 22 injured.

May 29   ARGENTINA: Kidnaping of former President Aramburu by Montoneros. No ransom demands. Shot to death, July 16.

Jun   JORDAN: Attack on homes by Palestinian guerrillas. Looting, and raping of 2 wives of U.S. officials.

Jun 7   JORDAN: Kidnaping of U.S. diplomat by PFLP. Demands refused for release of prisoners. Diplomat released unharmed next day.

Jun 10   JORDAN: Shooting death of U.S. military attache in his home by guerrillas.

Jun 11   BRAZIL: Kidnaping of West German Ambassador Ehrenfried von Hollenben by ALN and VPR. Demands met for release of 40 prisoners. Diplomat released June 16. 1 guard killed.

Jul 21   BOLIVIA: 2 West German technicians taken hostage and hidden in jungle by ELN. Demands met for release of 10 prisoners. Victims released unharmed July 23.

Jul 31   URUGUAY: Kidnaping of U.S. advisor Daniel A. Mitrione and Brazilian diplomat, and attempted kidnaping of another U.S. diplomat by Tupamaros. Demands refused for release of approximately 150 prisoners. Mitrione found dead 10 days later. Brazilian diplomat released Feb. 21, 1971 after reported payment by family of undisclosed ransom.

Jul 31   URUGUAY: Tupamaro guerrillas attempted to kidnap second secretary to the U.S. Embassy in Montevideo.

Aug 7   URUGUAY: Kidnaping of U.S. agricultural advisor by Tupamaros. Demands refused for release of approximately 150 prisoners. Released on Mar. 2, 1971 after suffering heart attack.

Aug 24   U. S.: Bombing of Army math lab on University of Wisconsin campus by New Year's Gang. 1 graduate student killed.

Sep   JORDAN: Hijacking of 4 airliners (2 American, 1 Swiss, 1 British) by PFLP. 1 blown up in Cairo, other in Jordan.

Sep 5   JORDAN: Kidnaping of U.S. soldier by Palestinians. No ransom demands. Interrogated and released Sep. 13.

Sep 11   JORDAN: Kidnaping of U.S. diplomat by PLA. No ransom demands. Released unharmed next day after interrogation.

Sep 12   ENGLAND: Kidnaping of 3 employees of Egyptian Embassy by JDE. Demanded release of airline passengers held in Jordan following multiple hijacking by PFLP.

Oct 5   CANADA: Kidnaping of British trade commissioner James Cross by FLQ. Demands rejected for release of 13 prisoners and $500,000. Cross released Dec. 3 in return for kidnapers' safe passage to Canada.

Oct 10   CANADA: Kidnaping of Labor Minister Pierre LaPorte by FLQ, repeating demands of Cross' kidnaping. Demands rejected. LaPorte found strangled on Oct 18. Kidnapers arrested in December, tried and sentenced.

Oct 15   SOVIET UNION: Hijacking of Soviet plane by 2 Lithuanians. Stewardess killed; pilot and navigator injured.

Nov   IRAN: Attempted kidnaping of U.S. Ambassador Douglas MacArthur by urban guerrillas. Escaped without injury.

Nov 6   ISRAEL: Explosion in bus station. 2 killed, 24 injured.

Dec 1   SPAIN: Kidnaping of West German diplomat by ETA. Demanded release of 16 prisoners. Diplomat released Dec. 24.

Dec 7   BRAZIL: Kidnaping of Swiss Ambassador Giovanni Bucher by ALN and VPR. Demands met, 70 prisoners freed. Victim released.

1971

Jan 8   URUGUAY: Kidnaping of British ambassador Geoffrey M.S. Jackson by Tupamaros. Demands rejected for release of prisoners, but 105 escaped. Diplomat released Sept. 9.

Feb 15   TURKEY: Kidnaping of U.S. Air Force security policeman at Ankara Air Station by TPLA. No ransom demands. Released 17 hours later.

Mar 1   U.S.: Bombing of U.S. capitol by Weathermen.

Mar 4   TURKEY: Kidnaping of 4 U.S. airmen by TPLA. Demands refused for 400,000 Turkish lira. Released unharmed Mar. 8. Terrorists arrested, tried and convicted; 3 hanged, 1 imprisoned, 1 killed in gunfight.

Apr 1   WEST GERMANY: Assassination of the Bolivian consul in Hamburg, by member of the ELN of Bolivia.

Apr 7   SWEDEN: Assassination of Yugoslav ambassador by Croatian terrorists. 2 Yugoslav diplomats injured.

May 17   TURKEY: Kidnaping of Israeli diplomat by TPLA. Demands refused for all guerrilla prisoners to be freed. Victim found dead May 23. 2 kidnapers later killed by police in gunfight.

May 23   ARGENTINA: Kidnaping of British diplomat by ERP. Demands for $62,500 met in food, clothing and supplies to the poor. Released unharmed May 30.

May 29   SPAIN: Attempted kidnaping of French diplomat by ETA. Victim escaped.

Aug 24   JORDAN: Black September attempted assassination of Jordanian Queen Mother by bomb explosion in her plane after it landed in Madrid.

Sep   CAMBODIA: Explosive devices thrown on softball field by terrorists. 2 U.S. Embassy employees killed; 10 wounded.

Sep 16   ISRAEL: Hand grenade attack on American tourists. 1 child killed, 5 persons injured.

Nov 28   EGYPT: Black September assassination of Jordanian Prime Minister Wasfi Tell.

Dec 15   ENGLAND: Attempted assassination of Jordanian ambassador by Black September.

1972

Jan 16   ISRAEL: Killing of American nurse, and wounding of several other persons, by terrorist attack on Israeli-occupied Gaza.

Jan 26   SWEDEN: Bombing of airliner by Croatian emigres. 26 killed.

Feb 5   BRAZIL: Slaying of British sailor by 4 extremists whose leaflet claimed this an expression of solidarity with the combatants of Ireland and of all the world.

Feb 6   WEST GERMANY: Murder of 5 Jordanian workers, presumably by Black September on claims they were spies.

Feb 22   ENGLAND: Bombing attack on British army barracks by IRA. 7 killed and 19 injured in first IRA bombing in Britain since World War II. 2 died later.

Mar 22   ARGENTINA: Kidnaping of director of Italian auto plant by ERP. Ransom demand for $1,000,000 agreed to by company, but government rejected demand for release of 50 prisoners. Victim executed just before capture of kidnapers on Apr. 10.

Mar 27   TURKEY: Kidnaping of 3 NATO radar technicians by TPLA. Demands refused for release of 3 prisoners. Police trapped terrorists, who killed the hostages and were themselves killed in the gun battle.

Apr 4   CANADA: Bomb explosion in Cuban Trade Office. 1 killed; several injured.

May   JAPAN: Japanese authorities discovered more than a dozen bodies, slain in an organizational purge by URA comrades.

May 4   MEXICO: Kidnaping of British diplomat and Mexican businessman by 23rd of September Communist League. Demands refused for release of 51 prisoners and payment of 2.5 million pesos ($200,500 U.S.) Briton released unharmed on Oct. 14; body of Mexican businessman found Oct. 21.

May 8   ISRAEL: Hijacking of Belgian airliner by 2 men and 2 women of Black September. Demanded release of 317 prisoners or passengers and plane would be blown up. Israeli paratroops stormed airliner, killed the men and wounded 1 woman. Both women tried and sentenced. 5 passengers injured, 1 later died.

May 11   WEST GERMANY: Bomb explosions in U.S. Army

headquarters by Baader-Meinhof Gang in retaliation for U.S. action against North Korea. 1 U.S. officer killed; 13 persons injured.

May 19 U.S. Bombing of Pentagon by Weathermen.

May 24 WEST GERMANY: Car bombings at U.S. Army European headquarters, allegedly by Baader-Meinhof Gang. 1 killed; 2 wounded.

May 30 ISRAEL: Attack at Lod Airport by Japanese URA supporting PFLP. 25 killed and more than 70 wounded; 1 terrorist killed, 1 killed himself, and 1 tried and given a life sentence.

May 30 IRAN: Bombing of U.S. Information Service offices by Iranian terrorists. 1 killed; 2 injured.

Jun 20 YUGOSLAVIA: Attack on town by 19 Croatian guerrillas. 13 local security officers killed; guerrillas defeated.

Jun 30 ARGENTINA: Kidnaping of bank president by 4 terrorists. $200,000 paid. Victim released unharmed.

Jul 17 COLOMBIA: Assassination of Swedish diplomat by unidentified gunmen.

Jul 22 NORTHERN IRELAND: Bombing attacks by IRA killed 11 and injured 130.

Jul 28 URUGUAY: Kidnaping of manager of U.S. news service. Released unharmed next day.

Aug DOMINICAN REPUBLIC: Killing of police officer by 3 leaders of Dominican Revolutionary Party. Terrorists arrested.

Sep 5 GERMANY: Black September attack on Israeli athletes during Olympic Games. Killed in attack and subsequent German police ambush were 11 Israelis, 5 terrorists, 1 policeman. 3 surviving terrorists jailed, but freed two weeks later when comrades hijacked a Lufthansa jet.

Sep 5 ARGENTINA: Kidnaping of Dutch business executive by Montoneros. $500,000 ransom paid. Victim released.

Sep 19 NETHERLANDS: Mailing of letter bombs to Jordanian and Israeli officials. Israeli diplomat killed in London. Black September claimed responsibility.

Nov 2 SPAIN: Bombing of French consulate by 3 youths. Fatal injuries to 1 diplomat; lesser injuries to 2 others.

Nov 7 ARGENTINA: Kidnaping of Italian industrialist. $500, 000 ransom paid. Victim released unharmed Nov. 10.

Dec 6 ARGENTINA: Kidnaping of Spanish industrialist. $100,000 ransom paid. Victim released unharmed Dec. 8.

Dec 8 AUSTRALIA: Car bombing killed vacationing U.S. businessman.

Dec 8 FRANCE: Explosion in apartment. Local head of PLO and Al Fatah killed.

Dec 10 ARGENTINA: Kidnaing of British executive by ERP.

Ransom of $1,000,000 reportedly paid. Victim released Dec. 19.

Dec 17   ARGENTINA: Kidnaping of Italian executive by Montoneros. Released Dec. 30 after payment of ransom.

Dec 28   THAILAND: Attack on Israeli Embassy by Black September. Demanded release of Arab guerrillas imprisoned in Israel, but settled for safe conduct to Egypt.

1973

Jan   IRELAND: Steel erector, member of local defense regiment, shot to death in home by IRA.

Jan 11   WEST GERMANY: Attack on restaurant by suspected Arab terrorists. 1 tourist killed; several persons injured.

Jan 23   ETHIOPIA: Kidnaping of 2 Italian businessmen by ELF. Victims released Feb. 4, probably after payment of ransom.

Jan 23   HAITI: Kidnaping of U.S. Ambassador Clinton E. Knox and another U.S. diplomat by Coalition of National Liberation Brigades. Demanded more, but settled for $70,000 and release of 12 prisoners. Both men released next day.

Jan 15   CYPRUS: Assassination by bomb in hotel room of Al Fatah representative. Palestinians claim Israeli agents were responsible.

Jan 16   SPAIN: Assassination of Israeli tourist by Black September on grounds he was an intelligence officer.

Feb 3   ARGENTINA: Kidnaping of U.S. business executive. Because of continuing kidnapings and extortions numerous companies began to move executives and families out of Argentina.

Feb 20   ENGLAND: Attack on Indian High Commission by alleged Black December group of 3 Pakistanis to get release of Pakistani prisoners. Staff members held hostage, and some injured. Police shot 2 terrorists and arrested third.

Mar 1   SUDAN (Khartoum): U.S. Ambassador Cleo A. Noel, Jr., an assistant, and a Belgian diplomat killed by Black September members when demands were not met for release of Sirhan B. Sirhan from U.S. prison and 17 comrades from Jordan and West Germany jails. Terrorists surrendered 2 days later, were later convicted by the Sudanese then turned over to PLO.

Mar 8   ENGLAND: 2 bomb explosions, presumably by IRA. 1 killed, 200 injured.

Mar 12   CYPRUS: Assassination of Israeli businessman by Black September. Reportedly a Zionist intelligence officer.

Mar 28   ARGENTINA: Kidnaping of Argentine banker allegedly by ERP. Between $500,000 and $1,000,000 reported paid by bank. Victim released on April 4.

Apr 2   ARGENTINA: Kidnaping of U.S. businessman by 6

terrorists, allegedly FAL. Demands met for $1,500,000 and victim released unharmed on Apr. 7. (First U.S. citizen kidnaped in Argentina.)

Apr 2   ARGENTINA: Kidnaping of retired Argentine admiral by 3 ERP terrorists. Reprisal for killing of 16 guerrilla terrorists in escape attempt from navy's prison in August 1972. Released June 8 after being forced to sign propaganda statements, and following signing of general amnesty for prisoners, including terrorists, by Argentine president.

Apr 4   ARGENTINA: Murder of Argentinian Army chief of intelligence by 2 terrorists.

Apr 8   ARGENTINA: Kidnaping of British businessman. $1,800,000 ransom paid. Victim released.

Apr 10   LEBANON: Raid by Israeli commandos. 17 killed, including 3 Palestinian guerrilla leaders; several wounded.

Apr 12   GREECE: Bomb explosion in hotel room, killing an Arab carrying a Jordanian passport. Bomb was probably in his suitcase.

Apr 14   LEBANON: Burning of Caltex-Mobil oil tanks by Lebanese Revolutionary Guard.

Apr 16   U.S.: Shots fired at New Zealand diplomat's home in suspected attempt to kill Jordanian. Black September apparently responsible.

Apr 16   BURMA: Kidnaping of 2 Soviet doctors by Shan insurgents. Demanded release of imprisoned Shan leader. Soviet Union and, reportedly, U.S. intelligence officials reached secret settlement with rebels. 1 doctor released Feb. 2, the other June 19, 1974.

Apr 27   ITALY: Murder of Italian employee of El Al Airlines by Lebanese claiming membership in Black September, and alleging victim was Israeli spy responsible for killing Al Fatah leader.

May 1   ARGENTINA: Kidnaping of son of Swiss businessman by terrorists. Demands met for $1,500,000. Youth released May 4.

May 1   ARGENTINA: Murder of retired Argentine admiral and former chief of staff of armed forces by 2 terrorists. Apparently second reprisal for killing of 16 guerrillas in escape attempt from navy's prison August 1972.

May 4   MEXICO: Kidnaping of U.S. diplomat by FRAP. Demands met for release of 30 prisoners and $80,000. Victim released.

May 22   ARGENTINA: Attempted kidnaping of 2 executives of U.S. company by ERP. 1 died a month later of injuries.

May 22   ARGENTINA: Kidnaping of manager of U.S. plant. Terrorists paid ransom of $100,000. Victim released Jun 2.

228

May 23   ARGENTINA: Bombing forestalled at offices of U.S. company by agreement to meet ERP demands for $1,000,000 in ambulances and donations to hospitals.
May 23   ARGENTINA: Kidnaping of Argentine business executive. Demanded $1,000,000. Victim released June 3.
May 30   ARGENTINA: Extortion demanded of U.S. company by alleged ERP member for $500,000 and 100% raise for all employees. 13 foreign employees subsequently left the country.
May 30   COLOMBIA: Hijacking of Columbian jet and bomb threat by 2 ELN terrorists. Demanded $200,000 and release of 140 prisoners; received $50,000. 1 terrorist later captured.
Jun 2   IRAN: Assassination of U.S. army advisor by terrorists.
Jun 6   Argentina: Kidnaping of British businessman by several terrorists, probably ERP. Demanded $7,500,000; later negotiated for $2,000,000. Victim released July 30.
Jun 7   ARGENTINA: Death and kidnap threats to officials of U.S. company by ERP, unless company rehired 1,000 workers. Demands rejected.
Jun 18   GUATEMALA: Kidnaping of manager of U.S. firm by FAR. Demands met for $50,000. Victim released.
Jun 18   ARGENTINA: Kidnaping of U.S. businessman by ERP Demands met for $3,000,000. Victim released July 6.
Jun 19   ARGENTINA: Kidnaping of West German businessman by terrorists, demands met for reported $100,000 ransom. Victim released July 1.
Jun 25   ARGENTINA: Kidnaping of vice president of Italian bank, presumably by ERP. Demanded $2,000,000. Victim released July 5 after payment of undisclosed amount.
Jun 28   FRANCE: Bomb explosion in automobile killing Algerian supporter of terrorists and suspected Black September member.
Jul 1   U. S.: Assassination of Israeli military attache, presumably by Arab terrorists.
Jul 2   ARGENTINA: Kidnaping of bank executive. Demanded $1,000,000. Victim released July 13 after payment of undisclosed amount.
Jul 19   GREECE: Attempted attack of El Al airline offices by lone Palestinian guerrilla who fled and cornered 17 hostages in a hotel. Claimed to be member of Organization of Victims of Occupied Territories. Negotiations by ambassadors of Egypt, Libya and Iraq ended with terrorist being flown to Kuwait where he vanished. Hostages released unharmed.
Jul 20   NETHERLANDS: Hijacking of Japan Airlines jet from Amsterdam by PFLP squad calling itself Organization of Sons of

229

Occupied Territory, cooperating with Japanese URA. 1 woman terrorist accidentally killed himself. Plane blown up on the ground in Libya. Passengers and crew released.

Jul 21   NORWAY: Murder of Moroccan writer, allegedly either by members of Wrath of God, militant wing of JDL, or by Israeli counter-terrorist agents, believing he was involved in Black September operation.

Aug 2   FRANCE: Bomb explosion in hotel room killing U.S. citizen, member of militant anti-Castro Cuban Revolutionary Directorate.

Aug 4   YUGOSLAVIA: Bombing of railroad station by terrorists. 1 killed; 7 injured.

Aug 5   GREECE: Attack on airport by terrorists claiming to be Black September. PLO spokesman denied connection. Later, group calling itself Seventh Suicide Squad claimed responsibility. 5 killed; 55 injured.

Aug 12   ARGENTINA: Extortion threat to a U.S. company by ERP. Demands rejected for $1,000,000; all 25 U.S. executives and families ordered by company to leave Argentina.

Aug 26   ARGENTINA: Kidnaping of former judge of special subversives court by 5 ERP terrorists. [Apparently third] reprisal for killing of 16 prisoners in escape attempt from navy's prison in August, 1972.

Aug 27   PARAGUAY: Kidnaping of British businessman. Ransom note signed by ERP, but authorities suspected MoPoCo, dissident faction of ruling Colorado Party. Victim rescued Sept. 6 by police. 2 kidnapers killed; several arrested.

Sep 5   FRANCE: Attack on Saudi Arabian Embassy and 13 hostages taken by Palestinian guerrillas claiming to be members of "Punishment." Demand rejected for release of Al Fatah leader from Jordanian prison. 9 hostages released next day; last 4 released Sept. 8; guerrillas surrendered.

Sep 7   ARGENTINA: Attack on military supply center to obtain weapons by 11 ERP terrorists. Surrendered after 5 hour gun battle.

Sep 9   ARGENTINA: Kidnaping of newspaper executive by ERP. Demands met for publishing ERP propaganda. Offices later attacked by 50 terrorists who sprayed gunfire, wounded 2, manhandled employees and started a major fire.

Sep 11   ZAMBIA: Parcel bomb explosion killing British employee of Zambian Ministry and his wife, injuring their son.

Sep 23   ARGENTINA: Kidnaping of British businessman. $300,000 ransom paid by family. Victim released Oct. 20.

Sep 28   AUSTRIA: Kidnaping of 3 Soviet Jews and an Austrian customs official by Black September group calling itself Eagles of the Palestinian Revolution. Demands met by Austrian officials for closing facilities to Soviet Jews emigrating to Israel. Hostages released; terrorists were flown to Libya.

Sep 28   DOMINICAN REPUBLIC: Kidnaping of young son of Mexican ambassador. Demand granted for kidnaper's safe passage to Spain. Victim released unharmed.

Oct 4   COLOMBIA: Kidnaping of 2 U.S. employees of gold mine by 50 ELN guerrillas. Demanded $10,000,000. Victims rescued Mar. 8, 1974 by troops surrounding terrorist hideout.

Oct 8   ARGENTINA: Attacks on American hotel and bank commemorating death of Che Guevarra. Considerable damage to bank.

Oct 10   MEXICO: Kidnaping of British diplomat by 23rd of September Communist League. Demands refused for release of 51 prisoners. Not known if $200,000 ransom met. Victim released Oct. 14.

Oct 18   LEBANON: Raid and seizure of hostages at office of an American bank by 5 guerrilla members of Lebanese Socialist Revolutionary Organization. Demanded $10,000,000, release of prisoners and safe passage to Algeria or South Yemen. After 25 hours police and army stormed bank. 1 U.S. citizen hostage had already been killed; 1 policeman and 2 guerrillas killed and 16 persons injured in final gunfight.

Oct 22   ARGENTINA: Kidnaping of Swiss executive by terrorists, allegedly ERP. Demands met for ransom estimated at more than $4,000,000. Victim released Nov. 29.

Oct 23   ARGENTINA: Kidnaping of U.S. executive of oil company. Demand reported to be $1,000,000 to $3,500,000. Company paid unspecified amount. Victim released Nov. 11.

Nov   ARGENTINA: Kidnaping of employee of British bank. Demands met for estimated $1,145,000. Victim released in 3 months.

Nov 6   U.S.: Killing of school superintendent Dr. Marcus Foster and serious wounding of his deputy, by SLA.

Nov 12   ARGENTINA: Kidnaping of Argentine Army officer by ERP claiming he had taken U.S. Army course "to make his repression of the Argentina people more effective."

Nov 13   ARGENTINA: Take-over of milk production plant and hijacking of 10 trucks of milk by 30 heavily armed men and women. Guerrillas distributed milk and disappeared.

Nov 20   VENEZUELA: Kidnaping of West German diplomat, probably by Bandera Roja. Victim released Nov. 22.

Nov 22   ARGENTINA: Assassination of U.S. executive and 2

231

bodyguards. 15 members of FAP claimed credit.

Nov 28   ARGENTINA: Threats on lives of all executives of U.S. company, claiming they had pillaged the country by exploitation of workers. In 3 days, 25 company executives and their families left Argentina.

Dec 6   ARGENTINA: Kidnaping of U.S. oil executive by ERP. Demands met for payment of $14,200,000, reported by ERP to have been used for rural guerrilla movements. Victim released April 1974.

Dec 17   ITALY: Five Arabs, caught with weapons in their baggage, opened fire inside Rome air terminal, then ran outside, attacked a Pan American airliner with grenades killing 29 persons, hijacked a Lufthansa plane to Athens, following seizure of 12 hostages. 1 hostage killed, others released.

Dec 20   SPAIN: Assassination of Premier Luis Carrero Blanco, reportedly by ETA. 2 others killed in same auto explosion.

Dec 20   ARGENTINA: Kidnaping of U.S. engineer by ERP. Demands met for $1,500,000. Victim released mid-January, 1974.

Dec 29   ARGENTINA: Kidnaping of French businessman, attributed to FAP who denied responsibility. Demanded $4,000,000; amount paid was not revealed. Victim released March, 1974.

Dec 30   ENGLAND: Assassination of prominent Jew by PFLP, forcing their way into his home.

1974

Jan 2   ARGENTINA: Kidnaping of Italian businessman allegedly by ERP.

Jan 3   ARGENTINA: Kidnaping of U.S. executive, allegedly by ERP. Demands met. Kidnapers arrested and victim freed Feb. 2.

Jan 19   MEXICO: Kidnaping and murder of uncle of state governor allegedly by 23rd of September Communist League.

Jan 31   MALAYSIA: Attack on Singapore oil refinery and hijacking of harbor ferry by 2 members of URA and 2 Arabs, probably PFLP. Demands met for flight to Kuwait and subsequent release.

Feb 1   BOTSWANA: Killing of official of South African Students' Organization by parcel bomb explosion. Parcel reportedly stamped by International Unviersity Exchange Fund in Geneva, Switzerland. Identity and motive of perpetrator unknown.

Feb 4   ENGLAND: Time-bomb explosion in bus filled with British servicemen and families. 11 killed; 14 wounded.

Feb 4   U.S.: Kidnaping of Patricia Hearst, by SLA. Demands met for give-away food program. Miss Hearst and 2 SLA members captured Sept. 18, 1975.

Feb 8   KUWAIT: Seizure of Japanese Embassy by 5 PFLP and URA members, to force release of terrorists held for a previous incident. Demands met. Terrorists flown to Yemen and released.

Feb 22   U.S.: Tower at Massachusetts nuclear plant site destroyed. Act claimed to be protest against dangers of nuclear power industry. Perpetrator tried and acquitted.

Feb 23   GREECE: Bomb explosion in U.S.-owned chemical plant, probably by protestors of U.S. support of government. 2 demolition experts killed attempting to defuse bomb.

Mar 14   ARGENTINA: Kidnaping and murder of retired non-commissioned Argentine navy officer, presumably in further retribution for killing of 16 prisoners in escape attempt at navy prison.

Mar 21   MEXICO: Planned kidnaping of U.S. Nobel Peace Prize winner ended with arrest of 5 members of 23rd of September Communist League.

Mar 22   MEXICO: Kidnaping of U.S. diplomat. Ransom note signed Mexican People's Liberation Army (a previously unknown group) demanded $500,000. Diplomat's wife attempted payoff of $250,000, but never made contact. Mexican police claimed kidnaping was work of American criminals. Victim found dead 3 months later.

Mar 26   ETHIOPIA: Capture of helicopter pilot and 4 passengers (3 oil company employees and UN official) by ELF. Demands discussed for release of 75 political prisoners, publication of ELF story, suspension of oil exploration, and hostages to stay out of Ethiopia. Pilot released June 26 and hostages Sept. 10.

May 27   ETHIOPIA: Capture of another helicopter pilot and kidnaping of American and Dutch missionary nurses by ELF (further action in above incident). Murder of Dutch nurse same day; American nurse and pilot released unharmed June 23.

Apr   CHAD: Kidnaping of French woman archaeologist by rebels. Her husband also kidnaped in October when negotiations stalled for ransom of arms and $2,000,000. Both still captive in 1975.

Apr 4   ARGENTINA: Assassination of executive of Italian company. FAP claimed responsibility.

Apr 11   ISRAEL: Attack on village by PFLP-GC. 18 Israelis killed, including 16 civilians. Terrorists died in gun battle. Israelis retaliated with raid in Lebanon.

Apr 12   ARGENTINA: Kidnaping of U.S. Information Service employee by ERP. Victim survived being shot, beaten, interrogated for some 15 hours and abandoned in dry river bed.

Apr 15   U.S.: SLA robbery of $10,690 from Hibernia Bank. Cameras identified Patricia Hearst as present during the robbery.

Apr 18   EGYPT: Attack on Technical Military Academy by organization led by Iraqi national and having connections with Libya. Palestinian ringleader confessed his "Islamic Liberation Organization" aimed to overthrow existing regimes in Arab countries. 11 killed, 27 injured.

May 13   LEBANON: Abduction of U.S. Foreign Service Officer by persons identifying themselves as Palestinians. No demands. Victim interrogated, roughed up but not seriously injured, and released 14 hours later.

May 15   ISRAEL: Attack on village of Maalot by 3 alleged members of PDFLP. Some 25 Israelis killed and 70 wounded, mostly school children.

May 16   U.S.: SLA firing on sporting goods store in connection with shoplifting incident. Few hours later 3 SLA members from that scene kidnap youth in his van, and are identified as Patricia Hearst and Emily and William Harris.

May 17   U.S.: 6 SLA members cornered in house in ghetto area respond to police demands for surrender with burst of gunfire and are killed in subsequent shootout.

May 18   IRELAND: Car-bombing in Dublin, allegedly by Protestant extremists from Northern Ireland. At least 28 killed.

June 3   COLOMBIA: Killing of 20 ELN members between March and June ordered by ELN leader for "acts of indiscipline: including negligence, disobedience and alcoholism."

June 13   ISRAEL: Terrorist attack on kibbutz by 4 members of PFLP-GC. Reported purpose was to denounce Egypt President's reception of President Nixon. 3 women killed, 3 men wounded, all of the terrorists slain.

June 17   ENGLAND: Bombing of Westminster Hall, oldest and most historic part of Houses of Parliament, allegedly by Provisional IRA. 11 injured.

June 18   LEBANON: Air attacks by Israeli planes in retaliation for Palestinian terrorist attack on Israeli kibbutz June 13. Approximately 100 killed, 200 wounded.

Jul 17   ENGLAND: Bomb explosion in Tower of London, allegedly by IRA. 1 killed, at least 41 injured.

Jul 18   ARGENTINA: Kidnaping of newspaper executive by unidentified guerrilla group. Victim later was shot to death.

Jul 21   LEBANON: Shooting of Chilean Ambassador Alfredo Canales Marquis by 4 assailants, allegedly of the Lebanese Revolutionary Socialist Organization. Ambassador critically wounded; assailants escaped.

Jul 24   COLOMBIA: Hijacking of Columbian airliner. Hijacker, believed to have previously hijacked a plane to Cuba, killed by police.

Jul 30   LEBANON: Clash between members of PLO and right-wing Falange Party. 4 PLO members and a bystander reported killed.

Aug 3   FRANCE: Car bombings outside offices of 2 right-wing publications and a Jewish welfare organization. PFLP claimed responsibility. 2 injured.

Aug 4   ITALY: Train bombing. Ordine Nero (the Black Order) claimed responsibility. 12 killed, 48 injured. 3 arrests made.

Aug 8   GREECE: TWA jet from Tel Aviv to New York exploded and crashed just after take-off from Athens. ANYO claimed responsibility for bomb being put aboard. All 88 persons aboard killed.

Aug 14   SYRIA: Bomb explosion near U.S. Pavilion at Damascus International Fair. "The Arab Communist Organization," a newly surfaced group, allegedly claimed responsibility. Serious damaged to exhibit and injuries to 2 persons.

Aug 15   SOUTH KOREA: Fatal wounding of wife of President Chung Hee Park during assassination attempt on President. Would-be assassin, reportedly recruited by North Korean agents, was former member of Korean Youth League, anti-Park organization of Korean residents of Japan.

Aug 19   CYPRUS: Shooting death of U.S. Ambassador Roger Davies by Greek Cypriots demonstrating against U.S. alleged pro-Turkish policy.

Aug 27   ARGENTINA: Assassination of executive of French Company. FAP claimed credit.

Sep 2   GREECE: Bomb explosion in parking lot of U.S. Chancery in Athens, killing 2 terrorists carrying it, causing extensive damage.

Sep 8   ARGENTINA: Bomb explosion in terrorist car during police chase following bomb attack on USIS Center, allegedly by Montoneros. 3 terrorists died in car explosion; no injuries in attack on USIS Center.

Sep 13   NETHERLANDS: Kidnaping of French Ambassador Jacques Senard and 10 other hostages from the Embassy by 4 URA. Demands met for release of URA prisoner and part of $1,000,000 ransom. Hostages released Sept. 17. Guerrillas later surrendered and $300,000 ransom was recovered.

Sep 15   FRANCE: Grenade explosion in crowded cafe. "Group for the Defense of Europe," right-wing extremists, claimed responsibility. 2 killed, 34 injured, attacker escaped.

Sep 19   ARGENTINA: Kidnaping of 2 Argentine executives by Montoneros. Demands met by company for reported $60,000,000 in cash and supplies. 1 victim released several months later, the other on June 20, 1975. 2 other persons killed during kidnaping attack.

Sep 27   DOMINICAN REPUBLIC: Kidnaping of woman director of U.S. Information Service and 6 other hostages, reportedly by 7 members of 12th of January Movement of the Popular Mexican Movement. Demands rejected for $1,000,000 and release of 37 prisoners. Hostages released on Oct. 10 and terrorists given safe passage to Panama.

Sep 29   ARGENTINA: Bombing deaths of Chilean Army general and his wife, supposedly by Argentine Anti-Communist Alliance, or by Chileans.

Sep 30   ARGENTINA: Kidnaping of Argentine business executive by ERP.

Oct 5   ENGLAND: Bombing of 2 pubs, reportedly by IRA. 5 killed, 54 injured, 13 arrested.

Oct 6   ITALY: Arson and bombing of warehouse and offices by 4 terrorists, claiming revenge for U.S. corporation's role in Chile. Approximately $9,000,000 damage to warehouse, $15,000 to offices.

Oct 7   ARGENTINA: Assassination of Argentine Army major, fourth by ERP in revenge for army's alleged shooting of 16 guerrillas. Victim's son killed 2, wounded 1 of terrorists.

Nov 6   ENGLAND: Killing of 4 British soldiers by Provisional IRA. Reprisal for death of Maze prisoner.

Nov 7   ENGLAND: Bomb explosion in tavern. "Red Flag 74," a new left-wing group, claimed responsibility. 1 killed, 19 injured.

Nov 9   UNITED STATES: Bombing of UN information center, termed "thank you note from the PLO to the UN." Caller used slogan of JDL. Approximately $5,000 damage to building plus loss of nearly $15,000 worth of UNICEF Christmas cards and UN calendars.

Nov 9   UNITED STATES: Bombing of Pan American Union, headquarters of Organization of American States, supposedly by Cuban Movement C-4, an anti-Castro group. Damage estimated at $100,000.

Nov 12   UNITED STATES: Jewish Defense League publicly vowed to assassinate Yassir Arafat, leader of PLO delegation to U.N.

Nov 14   MEXICO: Kidnaping of wife of U.S. real estate dealer, reportedly by United Popular Liberation Army of America. Demanded nearly a million dollars in food and land for the poor.

236

Nov 19   ISRAEL: Attack and gun battle in apartment in attempt to seize hostages. PDFLP claimed responsibility; intended to trade hostages for release of 20 terrorist prisoners in Israel. 4 civilians killed, 23 injured, 3 terrorists killed by Israeli troops.

Nov 21   ENGLAND: Bomb explosions in pubs. Red Flag 74 claimed responsibility. 19 killed, 202 injured.

Nov 21   DUBAI: Hijacking of British airliner by Palestinian terrorists. Demands partially met for release of prisoners in Egypt and Netherlands, 1 hostage killed, 1 stewardess wounded, other hostages released within few days. Terrorists surrendered in Tunisia.

Dec 6   ISRAEL: Raid on Rosh Hanikra kibbutz. PLO claimed responsibility. 1 terrorist killed, 2 Israelis injured.

Dec 11   ISRAEL: Hand grenade attack on movie theater. PFLO claimed responsibility. 2 killed, including terrorist, 54 injured.

Dec 16   ENGLAND: Three bombings attributed to IRA. 1 killed, 8 injured.

Dec 18   FRANCE: Shooting death of Uruguayan military attache. "Raul Sendic International Brigade," a Tupamaro-affiliated group, claimed responsibility.

Dec 30   NICARAGUA: Assault on diplomatic party and seizure of 25 hostages by 9 FSLN. Demanded $5,000,000, release of 14 prisoners, broadcast of anti-government statement and safe passage to Cuba. Accepted $1,000,000 and release of prisoners. Hostages release 61 hours later; guerrillas flown to Cuba.

1975

Jan 20   FRANCE: Attempted attack on Israeli airliner with rocket launcher by 3 Arab terrorists. 8 wounded, 10 hostages released after 18 hours; terrorists flown to Iraq.

Jan 24   U.S.: Fraunces Tavern in New York bombed reportedly by Puerto Rican FALN. 4 killed, 44 injured.

Feb 1   COLOMBIA: Kidnaping of Netherlands diplomat by 30 members of FARC. Demanded release of FARC prisoner. As of August 1975 diplomat had not been releasd.

Feb 26   ARGENTINA: Kidnaping of U.S. diplomat John P. Egan by Montoneros. Demands not met for proof of well being of 4 missing guerrillas. Kidnap victim shot to death Feb. 29.

Feb 27   WEST BERLIN: Kidnaping of Christian Democratic Union Party candidate for mayor by 2 men and 1 woman. Woman identified with Baader-Meinhof urban guerrillas. June 2nd Movement claimed responsibility. Demands met for release of 8 prisoners and a hostage. Prisoners given $50,000. Victim released Mar. 4.

Mar 4   BURMA: Kidnaping of West German geologist by Kachin Independence Army. Demanded $390,000 U.S. West German government agreed to pay, but Burmese government refused. Not known if ransom demands were met. Victim released unharmed May 7.

Mar 5   ISRAEL: Gun battle at hotel between Palestinian terrorists, allegedly Al Fatah, and Israeli soldiers. Demands rejected for release of 10 prisoners and Greek Catholic Archbishop of Jerusalem. At least 18 persons died including European and African tourists taken hostage, terrorists and soldiers.

Mar 10   ARGENTINA: Blasting of new cars at American-owned auto plant by leftist guerrillas in protest of forthcoming visit by U.S. Assistant Secretary of State.

Apr 16   LEBANON: Seizure of U.S. official by Palestinians at refugee camp. Released unharmed after 2 days of interrogation.

Apr 25   SWEDEN: Seige of West German Embassy by 7 Baader-Meinhoff terrorists. Demands rejected for release of 16 prisoners and $500,000. 3 killed, including 2 hostages.

May 3   FRANCE: Bomb explosions in nuclear power plant under construction by self-proclaimed Meinhof-Puig Antich Group. No injuries and slight damage, but caused repercussions on reactor safety in both France and Germany.

May 19   TANZANIA: Kidnaping of 3 Stanford University students and Dutch administrative assistant by PRP. Demands rejected by Tanzania for $450,000, release of prisoners and aid in arming rebel movement in Zaire. University and parents paid cash ransom of about $40,000 and all hostages were released unharmed.

May 21   IRAN: Slaying of 2 U.S. Air Force colonels by 2 Iranian terrorists who had allegedly killed an Iranian general and his chauffeur in March. Attackers said to be carrying documents outlining further assassination plans when they were arrested July 28.

Jun 14   ISRAEL: Seizure of hostages by 4 ALF. Demanded release of 12 Arab prisoners. Killed by Israeli troops.

Jun 29   LEBANON: Kidnaping of U.S. Army officer, allegedly by Organization of Revolutionary Socialist Action (splinter of PFLP). Demands rejected by U.S. for food, clothing and supplies. Anonymous donor made partial contribution to impoverished neighborhood. Victim released unharmed July 12.

Jul 4   ISRAEL: Bomb explosion during morning rush hour in central market. Lebanese guerrilla command claimed responsibility for "Farih Bobali Squad." At least 14 killed, 32 wounded.

Jul 7   LEBANON: Air and sea attacks on Palestinian terrorist bases by Israeli troops. Retaliation for terrorist bombing in

Jerusalem market July 4. Military attacks left 13 dead.

Jul 14   ETHIOPIA: Kidnaping of 2 U.S. civilians and 4 Ethiopians at U.S. communications center, presumably by members of ELF.

Aug 4   MALAYSIA: Seizure of U.S. consulate and 50 hostages by 5 URA. Demands met for release of 5 comrades imprisoned in Japan. Prisoners released and they and terrorist attackers were flown on Japanese plane to Libya.

Aug 5   COLOMBIA: Kidnaping of U.S. business executive by 5 gunmen and a woman.

Sep 5   U.S.: Manson-family Lynette Fromme made attempt on life of President Ford.

Sep 13   ETHIOPIA: Kidnaping of 3 American military men and 6 Ethiopians from U.S. communications facility, adding these hostages to others kidnaped by ELF on July 14. Demanded stop to U.S. arms supplies to Ethiopia.

Sep 15   SPAIN: Seizure of Egyptian Embassy and 3 hostages, including the ambassador, by 4 Palestinian guerrillas. Demands rejected that Egypt scrap Sinai agreement with Israel. Hostages released; guerrillas flown to Algiers and turned over to representative of PLO.

Sep 22   U.S.: Sara Jane Moore made attempt on life of President Ford.

Oct 3   IRELAND: Kidnaping of Dutch business executive, by IRA. Demands rejected for release of 3 IRA prisoners. Victim freed on Oct. 3 and abductors taken into custody.

Oct 8   ARGENTINA: Seizure of 13 hostages at office of U.N. High Commissioner for Refugees by 10 to 15 Chilean refugees, protesting poor living conditions for Latin American refugees. Demands met for safe passage to Algeria.

Oct 9   LEBANON: Attempted plane hijack by 4 Arab terrorists protesting Egyptian-Israeli Sinai accord. 3 killed, including 1 terrorist; 14 wounded including 1 terrorist; another terrorist captured; another later seized by PLO and turned over to Lebanese authorities.

Oct 22   LEBANON: Kidnaping of 2 U.S. embassy employees.

Oct 22   AUSTRIA: Assassination of Turkish ambassador by killers reported to be English-speaking Greeks.

Oct 23   ETHIOPIA: Kidnaping of British diplomat by 2 gunmen presumed to be members of secessionist movements.

Oct   ITALY: Assassination of Turkish ambassador.

Oct 24   FRANCE: Assassination of Turkish ambassador, believed to be linked to that of Turkish ambassador to Italy earlier.

Oct 25   LEBANON: Kidnaping of 2 Scandinavian diplomats and

French diplomat; Later released unharmed after intervention by PLO.

Oct 26   UNITED STATES: Simultaneous bombings at State Dept. in Washington, 4 banks and the U.S. Mission to U.N. in New York, 3 buildings in Chicago.

Oct 26   PHILIPPINES: Assassination of Presidential assistant near the Presidential palace.

Nov 12   ISRAEL: Bomb explosion near scene of last July 4th's bombing in central downtown area. PLO claimed responsibility. 7 killed, 32 injured.

Dec   ENGLAND: Middle-aged couple captured and held hostage in their apartment nearly a week by 4 IRA. Terrorists surrendered and couple freed.

Dec 2   NETHERLANDS: Train hijacking and seizure of hostages by 5 calling themselves Free South Moluccan Youths. Demanded release of South Moluccans in Dutch prisons and recognition of what they called their government in exile. 2 killed in initial attack; 1 hostage killed Dec. 4; 64 hostages taken; terrorists surrendered Dec. 14.

Dec 4   NETHERLANDS: Seizure of Indonesian consulate and hostages by approximately 7 South Moluccan terrorists. Demands refused for safe passage out of the country. Initially took an estimated 30 hostages, 16 of them children. 1 died in escape attempt. Last of the hostages freed and terrorists surrendered on Dec. 20.

Dec. 21   ETHIOPIA: Kidnaping of American civilian from U.S. communications facility by ELF. 5 Americans kidnaped in 5 months by ELF, reportedly also holding 1 Italian businessman, 2 Hong Kong factory owners and the British consul.

Dec 21   AUSTRIA: Attack on OPEC meeting by 5 men and a woman. 3 killed. Terrorists fled by plane to Algiers taking 35 hostages, including oil ministers of 11 nations. Last of hostages released unharmed and terrorists surrendered Dec. 23 in Algiers.

Dec 23   GREECE: Assassination of senior member of U.S. diplomatic mission after his name was published on alleged list of CIA agents.

Organizations Practicing Terrorism

As with the incidents, no complete list is really practical. These 97 are the ones we identified. All of the initials appearing in the incident list are included herein, as well as the name each set of initials stands for. Thus, some organizations are listed twice so that you can find them by either initials or name. Most

240

of the names have been translated into English. Therefore initials and names sometimes appear mismatched. For example, the *FAR* in Guatemala is the *Fuerzas Armadas Rebeldes* in the Spanish native to the country, but translates into Rebel Armed Forces in English. We have listed the full name only in the interest of simplicy and brevity in compiling the list. A few names, such as the Ordine Nero [Black Order] in Italy, we list only in the native language, because that seems to be the most common reference to them. Also in the interest of brevity, we have recorded only the organization and, if not obvious from the name, its country or regional area of operations. More detailed information on all of these groups requires more space than we can give it here. No single publication was found that does contain details on them all. The collection of materials we have referenced within the text covers most of them. And, although it is by no means oriented toward a treatment of terrorism, the McGraw-Hill *Political Handbook of the World* carries information on a number of them, within its description of the political situation in each country.

Afro-American Liberation Army—U.S.

ALF (Arab Liberation Front) — Israel.

ALN (National Liberation Action) —Brazil.

Americans for Justice—U.S.

Angry Brigade —United Kingdom

ANYO (Arab Nationalist Youth Organization) —Libya.

Arab Communist Organization —Syria.

Argentine Anti-Communist Alliance.

Argentine Nationalist Organization Movement (MANO).

Armed Forces of National Liberation —Venezuela.

Armed Liberation Forces —Argentina

Baader-Meinhof Gang—West Germany

Bandera Roja —Venezuela

Black December— Pakistan/U.K.

Black Guerrilla Family—U.S. prisons.

Black Liberation Army—U.S.

Black September—Mideast.

BSO (Black September Organization same as above.)

Catalan Liberation Front— Spain.

Coalition of National Liberation Brigades—Haiti.

COREMO (Revolutionary Committee of Mozambique).

Croations—Yugoslavia and Western Europe.

Cuban Movement C-4—U.S. anti-Castro.

Dominican People's Movement —Dominican Republic.

Dominican Revolutionary Party —Dominican Republic.

Eagles of the Palestinian Revolutionary Movement.

ELF (Eritrean Liberation Front) —Ethiopia and Mediterranean Area.

ELN (National Liberation Army)—Bolivia.

ELN (National Liberation Army)—Colombia.

Eritrean Liberation Front—Ethiopia.

ERP (People's Revolutionary Army)—Argentina.

ETA (Freedom for Basque Homeland)—Spain.

Escuadrao Da Morte (Death Squad) —Brazil.

FAL (Armed Liberation Forces) —Argentina

Falange Party —Lebanon.

FALN (Armed Forces of National Liberation)—Puerto Rico.

FAP (Peronist Armed Forces) —Argentina.

FAR (Rebel Armed Forces)— Guatemala.

FARC (Revolutionary Armed Forces of Colombia).

Fatah—Mideast.

FLQ (Liberation Front of Quebec).

FRAP (People's Revolutionary Armed Forces) —Mexico.

Free South Moluccan Youth — Netherlands.

Front for the Liberation of Brittany —France.

FSLN (Sandinista National Liberation Front)— Nicaragua.

Group for the Defense of Europe —France.

Irish Republican Army ("Official" and "Provisional" wings) —Ireland/U.K.

Islamic Liberation Organization —Egypt.

JDL (Jewish Defense League) — U.S./Europe.

Kachin Independence Army — Burma.

Lebanese Revolutionary Guard.

Lebanese Socialist Revolutionary Movement.

Liberation Front of Mozambique.

Liberation Front of Quebec.

Malayan National Liberation Army —West Malaysia.

MANO (Argentine Nationalist Organization Movement).

Manson Family —U.S.

Meinhof-Puig Antich Group — France/West Germany.

Mexican People's Liberation Army.

MIR (Movement of the Revolutionary Left) —Bolivia.

MIR (same name as above) — Chile.

MIR (same name) —Venezuela.

Montoneros —Argentina.

Movement of the Revolutionary Left —Bolivia.

Movement of . . . —Chile.

Movement of . . . —Venezuela.

Movement of National Liberation (Tupamaros) —Uruguay.

MR-8 (Revolutionary Movement of October 8) —Brazil.

National Liberation Action— Brazil.

National Liberation Army— Brazil.

National Liberation Army—
Colombia.
National Liberation Movement
—Iran.
National Youth for the Liberation of Palestine —Libya.
New People's Army—Philippines.
New World Liberation Front —
U.S.
New Year's Gang —U.S.
Ordine Nero —Italy.
Organization of Revolutionary
Socialist Action —Lebanon.
Organization of Victims of Occupied Territories/Sons of . . .
—Mideast.
PDFLP (Popular Democratic
Front for the Liberation of
Palestine).
People's Revolutionary Armed
Forces (FRAP) —Mexico.
People's Liberaton Army—
Colombia.
People's Liberation Front—
Turkey.
People's Liberation Front —Sri
Lanka.
People's Revolutionary Army
(ERP) —Argentina.
Peronist Armed Forces (FAP)
—Argentina.
PFLP (Popular Front for the
Liberation of Palestine).
PFLP-GC (Popular Front for
the Liberation of Palestine—
General Command).
PLA (Palestine Liberation
Army).
PLO (Palestine Liberation Organization).
Popular Revolutionary
Vanguard (VPR) —Brazil.
Poor People's Party —Mexico.
PRP (People's Revolutionary

Party) —Tanzania.
Punishment (Palestinian faction).
Raul Sendic International Brigade (after name of founder of
Tupamaros)—France.
Rebel Armed Forces (FAR) —
Guatemala.
Red Flag 74 —United Kingdom.
Red Guerrilla Family —U.S.
Revolutionary Organization of
the Tudeh Party —Iran.
Revolutionary Youth Movement —Turkey.
Sandinista National Liberation
Front (FSLN)—Nicaragua.
Shan Insurgents—Burma.
Siakhal—Iran.
Symbionese Liberation Army —
U.S.
TPLA (Turkish People's Liberation Army).
Tupamaros (Movement of National Liberation)—Uruguay.
12 of January Movement—
Dominican Republic.
23rd of September Communist
League —Mexico.
United Popular Liberation
Army of America —Mexico.
United Red Army (URA)—
Japan.
Union of the People —Mexico.
VPR (Popular Revolutionary
Vanguard) —Brazil.
Weatherman —U.S.
White Flags —Burma.
Wrath of God —Israel.
Zapata Urban Front —Mexico.

Index

246

247